# HOMES
## and gardens
# Cook Book

**MICHAEL SMITH**

**Photographs by Michael Boys**

**Allen Lane**

For Jenny Greene

ALLEN LANE
Penguin Books Ltd
536 King's Road
London SW10 0UH

First published 1983

ISBN 0 7139 1605 2

Designed by Paul Bowden

Set in Linotron 202 Sabon
Printed in Italy by New Interlitho, Milan

# Contents

# Introduction

If you'd asked me four years ago whether, after a lifetime of cooking, I'd be doing it for a woman's magazine I'd probably have laughed. Until then my career had been fundamentally connected with television in 'Pebble Mill', 'Upstairs, Downstairs' and 'The Duchess of Duke Street', and restaurants – I'd already launched Walton's and the English House and cooked in some of the greatest hotels in Europe and America. On the writing side I'd published five books.

Suddenly I found myself, in the spring of 1980, without an anchor. Everything coasting along nicely but no particular thing into which I could sink my creative drive. Out of the blue came an offer to contribute to the 'Bon Appétit' section of *Homes and Gardens*.

Here was a fascinating assignment. The possible sublimation of artistic passion, cookery, design and presentation all rolled into one. And the opportunity to make friends – the 2,000,000 odd people who read the magazine each month regard it as their special property and coming on, as it were, as the new guest contributor was a bit like being asked into someone's elegant home for the first time.

I soon found out what the readers of this glossy up-market magazine expected – and liked. They were prepared to discuss endlessly the correct version of Denmark's *Rød Grød med Fløde* and write me letters saying why on earth was I so fussy about using unsalted butter in everything when the next month they'd find me using a stock cube in a recipe. Some wrote to say their marriages had been saved by my marble cake (well, almost), others that they'd panicked when the *boeuf en daube* recipe said *four* hours and cooked it for only *two* with strange results. Then there was the controversy of the tangerine soufflé. Should it be stiff and look like sculpture or was it permissible to have it falling over if it tasted better that way? You'll begin to see what I mean about getting involved.

The other area of involvement was my work with the photographer Michael Boys and props girl Helen Payne. When, in that first flush of enthusiasm, I had said yes to working for *Homes and Gardens* I had no idea that one day I'd nearly drown, another I'd catch pneumonia and another the National Trust would threaten to hold us hostage in a stately pad until some minor financial problem was cleared.

I had reckoned, you understand, without the ingenuity of Michael Boys and the awesome determination of the Editor. When she and Michael decided my fish on silver plate was to be served with a boat club house in the background no one told me I'd be spooning mousseline sauce on this dish mid-stream up to my waist in water. Then there was the ploughed field episode, another idea we all had for a good picture, where the hot food had to be dashed to the squelchy furrows every time the rain stopped. Should I tell you the story, I wonder, of the game pie the photographer forgot to photograph and found in his car covered in mould a few weeks later? Perhaps, on reflection, I shouldn't.

I assure you, I sometimes wondered whether I'd *found* an anchor or *needed* one. It wasn't like this in the Palace in Copenhagen.

But one thing is certain. Contrary to popular belief, none of the food is faked. I myself have cooked and presented it all – sometimes several versions in order to get the best photograph. The Editor was not well pleased the day the butcher's bill arrived for *five* complete beef fillets, for example . . .

Above all, what happens when you write for a magazine is that you do have an enormous amount of pleasure. It's like the difference between cooking for a dinner party or for yourself. The former is stimulating, the latter a bore. Doing recipes for readers is great fun because you are in touch. And because one can suggest easy ways to achieve a glamorous effect.

This book is all about that: glamorous food in glamorous surroundings. Some recipes are complicated, others deceptively simple. It is a recipe book for the discriminating. The recipes are grouped into first courses, main dishes and puddings to help you plan your dinner party.

Any recipe you cook and enjoy and your friends enjoy will have served its purpose. It will please me that I've pleased you.

Happy cooking and Bon Appétit.

*Michael Smith*

# First Course

If lunch or dinner is to get off to a good start, the first course must be something special. Not so special as to turn the cook into a nervous wreck but something which says this is no ordinary meal.

Smoked salmon is succulent and luxurious but it's not cheap. As it demands no effort whatsoever some of you may feel this looks like taking the easy way out. A soufflé couldn't be more different. The fear of total collapse, for both soufflé and cook, is the main deterrent – and it does leave so many bowls, pans, spatulas and spoons to wash up.

Soup very rarely lets a cook down. At one time soups were always hot and robust. They were served on chilly winter days and had a comforting aura about them. But tastes have changed and soups now appear in many guises, not least of which is the chilled soup. I don't think soups should be restricted to any particular season or state of the weather and a chilled soup should no more be dismissed from a winter menu than a chilled pudding would be.

Starting with a salad makes a refreshing change. No matter how simple or how elaborate the ingredients, it's the dressing that counts. Whenever I am tempted to try and get away with a basic French dressing my hand soon reaches for the herbs on the window-sill – and I notice that two or three different oils have appeared in my cupboard. Alongside the mild arachide and rich olive oils I now have small bottles of walnut oil, sesame and grape seed oil. Properly dressed, there's no stopping a salad. If you don't want to serve it as a first course just bring out the French bread and butter and you've got a main-course lunch or supper dish. A salad sits just as happily on a side plate, often being the perfect accompaniment to a substantial main course, and is an essential ingredient in a buffet meal.

This flexibility, of course, applies equally to terrines, pâtés and savoury mousses. They are also extremely obliging in that once made they can be left to their own devices and need no last-minute attention apart from the addition of a garnish.

Garnishes are all important – and I don't necessarily mean the edible variety. Just as it takes time to choose the ingredients of a menu so it takes time to decide on its presentation. I like to serve the first course on a small plate resting on a base plate with a folded napkin between the two. Even egg mayonnaise becomes a colourful delicacy when given this special treatment. Little touches like this are always a winner – it's the element of surprise that gains the points.

*Pecorino, cucumber, tomato and orange salad*
*with anchovies*

# Soups

## GOOD RICH CHICKEN STOCK

It is well worth making a fresh chicken stock and using it in home-made soups. The chicken can be used for dishes served 'en mayonnaise' or as a filling for sandwiches.

---

*2 × 2½–3 lb chickens (fresh is best)*
*4 leeks, cleaned and cut into pieces*
*2 large carrots, peeled and cut into pieces*
*2 medium-sized onions, peeled and quartered*
*½ head of celery, cleaned and cut into pieces*
*1 bay leaf*
*1 sprig thyme*
*12 peppercorns*
*1 teaspoon salt*
*½ bottle dry white wine*
*juice of ½ lemon*

---

**1.** Select a deepish pan that will just contain the chickens with the vegetables, herbs and seasoning packed round them. Just cover with *cold* water (2 pints or more).

**2.** Add the wine and the lemon juice. Bring to the boil slowly so that the juices will come out into the stock. Simmer until the chickens are tender. Remove these on to a dish and deal with them at will.

**3.** Continue cooking the stock until the vegetables are soft. Strain, cool and refrigerate ready for use.

## CHILLED CREAM TOMATO SOUP WITH TURMERIC, ORANGE AND SHRIMPS

While I think this soup is at its best when served well chilled and in smallish portions as it is very rich, it can also be served hot.

---

*14 fl oz tomato juice*
*1 level teaspoon turmeric*
*1 level teaspoon mild curry powder*
*1 clove garlic, crushed*
*1 teaspoon caster sugar*
*juice of ½ lemon*
*1 heaped teaspoon of finely grated orange rind*
*½ pint double cream*

GARNISH:
*2 navel oranges, segmented*
*2 tomatoes, skinned, seeded and cut into dice*
*4 oz peeled shrimps (fresh or frozen)*

---

**1.** Put all the ingredients except the cream into a heavy-bottomed pan, bring to the boil and simmer for 10 minutes. Add the cream and simmer for a further 10 minutes.

**2.** Leave to cool. Strain into a bowl, cover with clingfilm and chill well, preferably overnight.

**3.** Ladle into chilled soup cups, and garnish. Serves 4–5.

*Chilled cream tomato soup with turmeric, orange and shrimps*

# CHILLED ALMOND AND FENNEL SOUP WITH SOURED CREAM

This soup, which should be prepared two or three days in advance, can be made equally well with celery.

---

*1 large head fennel (or 1 head celery)*
*1½ pints chicken stock (use stock cube)*
*4 oz whole, blanched Valencia almonds*
*½ pint single cream*
*salt and pepper*

GARNISH:
*¼ pint soured cream*
*1 oz flaked almonds*
*1 tablespoon fennel fronds, chopped*

---

1. Wash the fennel and cut into pieces. Cook in the chicken stock with the whole almonds, until tender. Make a fine purée in a food processor or blender. Cool, then chill.

2. On the day of serving, stir in the single cream and check the seasoning. Chill again.

3. To serve: ladle into chilled soup cups. Put a blob of soured cream on top. Sprinkle with a few flaked almonds, lightly toasted, and fennel fronds. Serves 6.

# CHILLED FENNEL SOUP

This soup freezes successfully, and is enough for 4 people.

---

*2 heads fennel (about 1 lb)*
*1½ pints chicken stock*
*1 teaspoon fennel seeds tied in muslin*
*salt and milled white pepper*
*1 pint double cream*

---

1. Clean and quarter the fennel (reserving the fronds in cold water).

2. Cover with chicken stock, add the seeds, and simmer until tender. Season carefully. Discard the seeds.

3. Blend the fennel to a fine but thick purée with a little of the stock. Cool and reserve the rest of the stock. For a really fine soup, laboriously press the purée through a hair sieve.

4. Add enough cream to give a delicate consistency. Chill well.

5. Before serving, thin down the soup with some of the chilled reserved stock if necessary.

6. Garnish with some of the fennel fronds, chopped.

7. If freezing the soup for storing, add the chopped fennel fronds when the soup is cold, but before freezing.

# CHILLED RED PIMENTO AND GINGER SOUP

See photograph on page 25.

---

*4 oz butter*
*4 large red peppers, seeded and roughly chopped*
*2 large leeks (mostly white part only) roughly chopped*
*2 level teaspoons ground ginger*
*2 heaped teaspoons sweet paprika*
*1 tablespoon caster sugar*
*1 level teaspoon sea salt*
*1 teaspoon freshly milled white pepper*
*zest and juice of 1 large orange*
*1 pint strong chicken stock (or stock cube)*
*1 pint buttermilk (or natural yoghurt which will be similar)*

---

1. Melt the butter without browning. Soften the leeks and peppers with a lid on and stirring from time to time.

2. Add all the seasonings and stock. Simmer for 30 minutes. Cool, blend to a fine purée (pass through a hair sieve for a truly refined soup). Chill.

3. Stir in the buttermilk. Chill again. Serve in chilled soup cups with a dish of buttered almonds. Serves 4–6.

*Chilled almond and fennel soup with soured cream*

# RICH GAME SOUP

A good game soup cannot be made without good ingredients (nor can anything for that matter), so assuming that you have decided to make the soup, the quantity I give is for upwards of 8 servings. It is rich and gamy, and worth every ounce of effort you put into it.

---

*2 large carrots*
*1 large onion*
*2 stalks celery*
*½ lb field mushrooms*
*½ hare, fresh or frozen*
*1 old grouse or pheasant, fresh or frozen*
*½ lb lean ham*
*½ lb stewing steak, weighed* without fat
*3 oz flour*
*salt and freshly ground pepper*
*2 oz butter*
*4 tablespoons olive oil*
*3 tablespoons tomato purée*
*1 pint red wine*
*8 cloves*
*3 bay leaves*
*1 teaspoon thyme*
*brown colouring (optional)*
*1 × 4 oz glass tawny port*

---

**1.** Clean, peel and cube the carrots, onion and celery. Slice the mushrooms.

**2.** Strip the raw meat off the hare and the grouse or pheasant. Cover all the bones with cold water (4 pints), bring to the boil, skim well and simmer for 2 hours, adding an extra ½ pint water after the first hour. Do not season. Strain, and reserve the stock.

**3.** Cut all the meat, except the grouse or pheasant breasts and liver, into cubes. Take a large plastic bag, put in the flour, salt and pepper and shake the cubes of meat in this until they are thoroughly coated.

**4.** Melt the butter and oil together in a large pan. Add the vegetables (except the mushrooms) gradually and fry them over a good heat, taking care to brown them without burning. Stir them constantly.

**5.** Remove the browned vegetables to a platter and, in the remaining fat, brown all the meat cubes. Add the uncut breasts and the vegetables to the pan and shake over them any remaining flour.

**6.** Add the tomato purée and the mushrooms. Lower the heat and, stirring all the while, let all this acquire a good brown colour. Pour over 3 pints strained stock and the red wine. Add all the seasonings.

**7.** The breasts of the grouse or pheasant will be cooked in 15 minutes. Remove and skin these. Allow them to cool before cutting them into ¼ inch dice. Set aside for the garnish.

**8.** Cook the rest of the soup very slowly for 2½–3 hours, occasionally stirring well to ensure that nothing is sticking to the bottom. Strain the soup and check the seasoning. Bring the quantity up to 4 or 5 pints, depending how thick you like it, using the remaining stock. Skim off any fat that has risen to the surface.

**9.** If great care has been taken with the frying at all the different stages, the soup should be rich, brown and glossy. If not, add a little brown colouring (not gravy powder), for the soup must look bold and strong, and adjusting colour is as important as adjusting thickening and seasoning.

**10.** Quickly fry the game liver in a knob of butter and cut into dice. Reheat the soup, and just before serving add the diced breasts, liver and the port. Serves at least 8.

# CAULIFLOWER SOUP

---

*1 poached egg per serving*
*1 small tight-flowered cauliflower*
*2 pints chicken stock*
*¼ pint double cream*
*1 teaspoon lime mustard (or other*
*mild French mustard)*
*¼ teaspoon nutmeg*
*salt and pepper*
*beurre manié (2 oz softened butter,*
*1 oz flour made into a soft paste)*

---

**1.** First poach the eggs. Do this in advance and store in a dish of cold water. Select a shallow pan or frying pan. Lightly oil the bottom. Pour in 1 inch water and add ½ teaspoon salt.

**2.** As soon as the water is simmering, but not boiling, break each egg into a cup, one at

*Cauliflower soup*

a time. Make a whirlpool in the water with a teaspoon, slide the egg into this and collect the white around the yolk with a slotted spoon. Leave to poach until cooked (about 3–4 minutes. Lift out carefully with a slotted spoon, and lower gently into the dish of cold water. When cold, trim off any bits of egg white straggling out of shape.

3. To make the soup: break the cauliflower into tiny florets. Bring the stock to the boil with the cauliflower *stalk* cut into pieces. Strain these out when cooked; discard.

4. Put in the cauliflower florets and simmer until just cooked: they should still be crisp. Remove and set aside.

5. Add the cream to the stock and bring to the boil. Whisk in the mustard and sprinkle in the nutmeg. Bring to the boil again and taste for seasoning.

6. Whisk in little bits of the *beurre manié*, allowing the soup to return to the boil between each addition. The finished soup should be the consistency of single cream. Lower the heat and simmer for 5 minutes.

7. Return the cauliflower florets to the pan to heat through. Place a poached egg in the bottom of each soup cup, and carefully ladle over the steaming soup. Serves 5–6.

# CREAMY CHICKEN SOUP WITH SMOKED SALMON

*2 oz French or Dutch unsalted butter*
*1 oz plain white flour*
*1½ pints chicken stock*
*⅓ pint double cream*
*1 egg yolk*
*1 sherry glass of whisky*
*salt and freshly milled pepper if*
*necessary*

GARNISH:
*1 chicken breast cut into striplets*
*2 oz smoked salmon, cut into strips or*
*rolled and cut into rings*

*Creamy chicken soup with smoked salmon*

1. Melt the butter slowly in a heavy-bottomed pan. Do not allow it to get too hot or it will add a nutty flavour to the soup, which is not desirable in this case.

2. Stir in the flour and add the stock, whisking as you go along.

3. Allow the soup to simmer for 10 minutes to ensure the flour is 'cooked out' and has done its thickening job. Add the cream.

4. Just before serving, put equal amounts of the garnish into warm soup cups. Whisk the egg yolk with the whisky in a large bowl: bring the soup to the boil and *strain* into the bowl, whisking to incorporate the whisky and yolk mixture. (Once the yolk has been added the soup cannot be allowed to boil again or the yolk will curdle.) Check for seasoning and ladle immediately into the soup cups. The marriage of whisky and smoked foods is excellent, and makes this a very unusual soup. Serves 4–6.

# GREEN LENTIL AND ITALIAN SAUSAGE SOUP

I have devised this wholesome soup to retain the full texture of the lentils, which, while called green, are in fact more of a muddy grey colour. Any lentils can be substituted.

*1½ pints chicken stock*
*2 onions*
*4 large sticks celery*
*1 clove garlic, crushed*
*½ lb green lentils covered in boiling water*
*and soaked overnight*
*6 oz piece Italian smoked sausage (or other*
*Continental sausage of your liking)*
*4 oz piece of boiling bacon or hock*
*1 bay leaf and 1 sprig thyme or 1 bouquet*
*garni sachet*
*salt and pepper if necessary (this will*
*depend on the saltiness of the sausage and*
*bacon)*

1. Using ½ pint of the stock, in a blender or food processor make a purée of the onions, celery and garlic.

2. Drain the lentils and rinse them well under cold running water. Put them with the purée, sausage, bacon, herbs and the remain-

ing stock into a heavy-bottomed pan. Bring to the boil and simmer for 1½ hours or until the lentils are tender but not a total mush. Skim off any scum which rises to the surface early in the cooking process. Taste for seasoning.

3. Remove the sausage and bacon, and discard the herbs or bouquet garni. Cut the sausage into discs or pieces and shred the bacon. Put a little sausage and bacon into a soup bowl and ladle over the boiling soup. Serves 4.

# SWEETCORN CHOWDER

A chowder is often made with clams, oysters or other shellfish. Corn chowder is a cheaper but not-to-be-scorned type of dish, filling and warming on a winter's day.

---

*4 large waxy potatoes*
*3 pints chicken stock*
*3 oz butter*
*4 rashers bacon, cut into small dice*
*2 onions, finely chopped*
*½ head celery, cleaned and chopped into small dice*
*1 × 12 oz tin sweetcorn, drained and rinsed under cold water*
*4 dashes tabasco sauce*
*1 tablespoon Worcestershire sauce*
*juice of ½ lemon*
*3 egg yolks*
*½ pint single cream*

GARNISH:
*4 slices of white bread*
*butter for frying*
*8 oz piece salt pork*

---

1. Cut the potato into ¼ inch dice if you can manage to get the dice that small. Cook the potatoes in some of the chicken stock until just tender. Strain the potatoes, retaining the liquid.

2. Melt the butter in a large heavy-bottomed pan, and fry the bacon in this until crisp.

3. Remove the bacon with a draining spoon, and put to one side while you fry the onions and celery over a low heat until transparent and tender.

4. Add the sweetcorn and the stock and potato liquid. Bring to the boil and simmer for 30 minutes.

5. To make the garnish: cut slices of bread into ½ inch cubes and fry these in butter until they are crisp and golden brown. Do this slowly so that they brown evenly and don't burn. Cut the salt pork into ¼ inch dice and fry slowly until crisp right through, an essential factor.

6. Add the tabasco, Worcestershire sauce and lemon juice to the soup, and return the potatoes and bacon to the pan to get hot right through.

7. Just before serving, line up your warm soup bowls on a tray.

8. Whisk the egg yolks with the cream and pour directly into the boiling hot chowder, stirring well as you do so.

9. Ladle into the bowls and top with garnish. Serves 6, with second helpings.

# DUCK AND MUSHROOM SOUP

---

*1 oz butter*
*1 onion*
*8 oz field mushrooms*
*¾ oz flour*
*1 pint duck stock*
*½ pint red wine*
*1 large sprig or 1 teaspoon dried sage*
*1 clove garlic, crushed*
*1 × 3 inch piece of orange peel*
*salt and pepper*

---

1. Melt the butter, add the onion, and brown well over a low heat. Add the mushrooms and fry for a minute or so, stirring from time to time.

2. Add the flour. Stir in well. Add the stock, wine, herbs, garlic, orange peel, salt and pepper. Simmer for 30 minutes.

3. Strain the liquid into a clean pan. Remove the sprig of sage if used. Blend the mushrooms to a fine purée. Combine the purée and the liquid.

4. Reheat and serve with croûtons. Serves 4.

# MINESTRONE

There are as many 'right' ways of making this soup as there are for making fruit cake; it is the type of soup that cannot really go wrong, though I prefer to control just when certain items go into the pot in an attempt to retain a bit of their character. I cook the pasta separately, for example, and I don't add the green vegetables until just before everything is cooked in order to retain their pretty green colour; but it doesn't matter a hoot really. I think it has to be made for a lot of people or for a large family, and it keeps and reheats well.

My recipe is fulsome, perhaps too fulsome for some, in which case just add a little more stock or water.

The only essential ingredient, almost, is the freshly grated Parmesan cheese, but this may be difficult to obtain in your particular area, so bottled or tinned will have to do.

---

*6 oz pasta 'bows' or spaghetti*
*broken into 2 inch pieces*
*3 tablespoons olive oil*
*4 rashers plain bacon, cut into strips*
*1 large onion, chopped*
*½ head celery, chopped*
*2 cloves garlic, crushed*
*2 tablespoons tomato purée*
*4 pints chicken stock*
*4 carrots, cut into discs*
*1 small cauliflower broken into tiny florets*
*1 × 8 oz tin flageolet beans, drained and*
*rinsed (or haricot beans soaked*
*overnight in boiling water)*
*4 oz salami, cut into strips*
*salt and freshly milled pepper*
*1 small packet petits pois*
*1 small packet cut French beans*
*4 tomatoes, seeded and chopped*
*2 tablespoons freshly chopped parsley*
*(some basil, too, if you have it, adds a*
*lovely flavour)*

GARNISH:
*freshly grated Parmesan cheese*

---

**1.** Cook the pasta separately in boiling lightly salted water for 15 minutes. Drain and reserve.

**2.** Heat the oil in a large (8–10 pint) heavy-bottomed pan. Fry the bacon until golden brown. Add the onion and celery and fry for 10 minutes over a low heat until transparent and golden.

**3.** Add the garlic and tomato purée and continue frying for a further 5 minutes, stirring to ensure that nothing burns.

**4.** Pour in the stock and bring to the boil. Add the carrots and, after 10 minutes, add the cauliflower florets, flageolets and salami. Simmer for a further 15–20 minutes. Season lightly with salt and milled pepper.

**5.** Add the cooked pasta, peas, French beans and chopped tomatoes and cook at a steady roll for a further 15 minutes or so. If you prefer your Minestrone less thick than it appears, add ½ pint or more of water or stock just after adding the pasta.

**6.** Sprinkle in the chopped parsley just before ladling the soup into warm earthenware bowls.

**7.** Pass grated Parmesan cheese for people to help themselves and chunks of plain or garlic bread for dunking. Serves 8 good family helpings.

# ARTICHOKE, TOMATO AND RICE BROTH

The success of this broth, which is aimed at the slimmer and those not having my penchant for rich soups, rests entirely on the quality of the chicken stock.

---

*2 pints fresh chicken stock (see page 10)*
*large glass of dry sherry (optional)*
*4 artichoke hearts, quartered*
*4 small tomatoes, skinned, seeded*
*and cut into eighths*
*2 oz boiled rice*
*1 tablespoon snipped fresh chives*
*1 tablespoon freshly plucked basil*
*or tarragon*

---

**1.** Bring the stock to boiling point together with the sherry if used.

**2.** Just before serving, put in the vegetables and let them heat through. Put a spoonful of rice into each warm soup cup and ladle over the hot soup. Sprinkle liberally with the fresh herbs. Tarragon and basil go black if chopped in advance so I suggest chopping the herbs just before you need them. Serves 5–6.

# CHILLED GINGERED CARROT AND ORANGE SOUP WITH SOURED CREAM

This soup is equally good served hot and is quite delicious and unusual.

---

*1½ lb carrots, peeled*
*1 pint strong chicken stock*
*grated rind of 1 orange*
*1 teaspoon ground ginger*
*½ teaspoon ground mace*
*1 pint orange juice*
*½ pint single cream*
*salt and freshly milled pepper*
*⅓ pint soured cream*

---

**1.** Cut the carrots into even-sized pieces. Simmer until tender in the chicken stock together with the orange rind, ginger and mace. Cool.

**2.** Blend to a fine purée. Stir in the orange juice and single cream. Check seasoning.

**3.** Chill well, overnight. Serve with a teaspoon of soured cream in each serving. Serves 8.

# CHILLED PEA, MINT AND LEMON SOUP WITH SOURED CREAM

*1 lb packet frozen petit pois*
*2 teaspoons sugar*
*1 clove garlic, crushed*
*10–12 mint sprigs*
*juice of 1 lemon*
*½ pint single cream*
*1 pint cold chicken stock*

GARNISH:
*1 small carton soured cream*
*snipped chives*

---

**1.** Toss the peas for 3–4 minutes with the sugar and crushed garlic and mint in a pan over a low heat, using *no* liquid.

**2.** When the juices are fully drawn and the peas tender, leave them to cool. Add the lemon juice.

**3.** Put the peas through a food mill (a blender makes the soup too smooth, though this is a fine detail).

**4.** Stir in the cream, then add enough chicken stock to make a soup of the consistency of single cream. Chill well, preferably overnight.

**5.** Serve each portion with a spoonful of soured cream for guests to stir in and a sprinkling of finely chopped chives. Serves 5–6.

# Terrines and Pâtés

## PÂTÉ OF TURBOT WITH SCALLOPS

This pâté can be served hot or cold. It is essentially French in concept but there are similar fish and chicken creams on Victorian and Edwardian menus.

If you want to serve individual portions hot, layer a half scallop cut equator-wise between two layers of fish mousse and cut the cooking time down to 25–30 minutes. See photograph on page 22.

*1 lb turbot fillet, skinned*
*¼ teaspoon mace*
*salt*
*freshly milled* white *pepper*
*lemon juice*
*3 large egg whites*
*1 pint double cream*
*6 scallops cut in thinnish slices*
*parsley-aspic jelly (optional)*

1. Cut the turbot into smallish pieces. Put them into a china bowl with the mace, 1 level teaspoon salt, 1 level teaspoon freshly milled white pepper and 1 tablespoon lemon juice. Stir, and put to chill in the refrigerator. In a separate bowl, chill the egg whites which should be broken up loosely with a fork until they are 'pourable'. Chill the cream as well.

2. Put the fish through a blender or food processor using the egg whites as the slackening agent, and using the metal blade. Change to the plastic blade and add the cream, pouring quite steadily at one speed. Stop the machine as soon as the cream is incorporated. Test for seasoning, adding a little more salt if you like. When served cold this type of pâté will require a slightly more generous amount of seasoning.

3. Butter a terrine or seamless loaf tin well. Spoon in half the mixture: give the mould a sharp bang on the table top to settle the mixture right into the corners. Smooth over the top of this layer, arrange the sliced scallops over, seasoning lightly with salt, milled pepper and a modest squeeze or two of lemon juice. Spoon over the remaining fish mixture, give the dish another good bang and level the top.

4. Cover with a lid or foil. Stand the dish or terrine in another shallower one containing hot water and bake at Gas Mark 7 (220°C, 425°F) for 45–50 minutes. Leave to cool before covering with a piece of board covered with foil and a weight to press things down. Put in the refrigerator overnight.

5. The pâté can be served direct from the dish, using a sharp stainless steel knife (carbon steel taints) to cut ½ inch slices.

6. The alternative at party time, but I think hardly worth the effort and agony, is to turn out the terrine, wash the dish, then rinse well with clean water. Dry it and pour in the bottom a good ¼ inch layer of double-strength commercial aspic to which you have added an abundance of freshly chopped parsley. Put this to set.

When set, carefully replace the fish pâté on top and pour over and around enough aspic jelly to fill up the mould or tin. Put to set again.

The amount of jelly you'll need depends on the surface area of your tin. Make up at least 1 pint because you don't want to start making more when you are halfway through the operation. You will also need a large bunch of parsley, preferably picked fresh from the garden.

If you think you will not work fast enough, stand the bowl of liquid aspic inside a bowl of tepid water to stop it setting. If it starts to thicken, add a little hot water to the outer bowl – not to the aspic!

Do not whisk it if it does set; this action only beats bubbles into it. Just wait for it to melt again in the warm water.

7. To turn out: run a hot palette knife round the sides and ends of the mould, stand the bottom of the mould in boiling water for a few seconds, and invert on to a serving dish. Mop up any wayward melted jelly, and decorate as liked. Serve the pâté with Cranberry Purée (see page 163). Serves 6–8.

## CHICKEN AND SWEETBREAD TERRINE

---

*3 lb farm-fresh chicken*
*2 large calves' sweetbreads (about 1 lb) or*
*1 lb frozen lambs' sweetbreads, defrosted*
*salt and milled pepper*
*1 level teaspoon ground mace*
*1 clove garlic*
*6 fl oz dry white wine*
*4 fl oz brandy*
*3 small eggs*
*⅓ pint double cream*

---

1. Skin the chicken.

2. Butter a 10 × 4 inch terrine or seamless loaf tin and line with the chicken skin. Cut off the chicken breasts and the meat from the legs. Remove any sinews. (Keep the carcass for soup.)

3. Bring the sweetbreads to the boil in

water, simmer for 1 minute, discard the water and cool the sweetbreads under cold running water. Carefully remove all skin and tissue from the sweetbreads and put half of them into a basin with a little salt, pepper and the mace. Leave for 2 hours.

4. Cube one chicken breast. Put the rest of the chicken meat and the remaining sweetbreads to marinate, with the garlic, in the white wine and brandy for 2 hours. Put this mixture, including the liquid, through a food processor or blender, adding the eggs as you go along.

5. Cut the whole sweetbreads into even-sized cubes. Beat the cream into the minced mixture. Season well. Mix in the cubes of chicken breast and the sweetbreads. Spoon the mixture into the terrine. Cover with foil or a lid.

6. Stand the terrine in a roasting tin half filled with hot water. Bake at Gas Mark 5 (190°C, 375°F) for an hour. Cool.

7. Press with a weighted piece of board wrapped in foil. Refrigerate for 1 day to allow the subtle flavours to meld.

8. Serve cut into ¼ inch thick slices with a savoury jelly such as apple and sage. Serves 8–10.

## TERRINE DE LAPIN AU RHUM

---

*1 rabbit*
*5–6 chicken livers*
*3 tablespoons Jamaica rum*
*2 lb loin or leg of pork*
*8 fl oz rosé or dry white wine*
*1 clove garlic*
*1 lb extra pork fat*
*1 teaspoon ground ginger*
*4 oz pistachio nuts, split*
*1 beaten egg*
*salt and freshly ground pepper*
*¾ lb streaky bacon to line dish*

---

1. Bone the rabbit, keeping the two back fillets whole. Cut the back fillets into ½ inch cubes and put to marinate with the trimmed chicken livers, also cut into cubes, in the rum.

2. Put the pork meat and rabbit leg meat to

*Pâté of turbot with scallops*

marinate overnight in the wine with the garlic clove. Next day, mince the pork and leg meat with the pork fat using the fine blade of a mincer. Mix in the wine from the marinade, the ginger, drained fillet and chicken livers, and the pistachio nuts.

3. Crush the clove of garlic and mix this in, adding the rum, juices and beaten egg. Season well with salt and pepper. Line a terrine or seamless loaf tin with the bacon and pack in the mixture. Cover.

4. Stand this in a second container of hot water (a bain marie) and bake at Gas Mark 4 (180°C, 350°F) for 1½–1¾ hours.

5. Remove the foil half an hour before the end of the cooking time. A terrine or pâté is cooked when the juices look quite clear. Cool before pressing it with a board and 3–4 lb scale weights or an equivalent load, and refrigerate.

6. Serve cut into elegant slices with a watercress salad and fingers of lemon-buttered brown toast.

# TWO MUSHROOM PÂTÉ

### FIRST PÂTÉ:
*8 oz field (dark) mushrooms*
*2 oz butter for frying*
*4 oz onion, finely chopped*
*¼ teaspoon ground mace*
*2½ fl oz madeira (medium dry)*
*2 oz extra butter, softened*
*3 oz full fat cream cheese*

### SECOND PÂTÉ:
*8 oz white button mushrooms, finely chopped*
*2 oz butter for frying*
*1 clove garlic, crushed*
*1 teaspoon grated lemon zest*
*juice of ½ large lemon*
*2 oz extra butter, softened*
*salt and milled white pepper*

### ASPIC JELLY:
*2 teaspoons commercial aspic crystals*
*2 teaspoons gelatine crystals*
*¼ pint dry white wine*
*pinch of salt*

1. To make aspic jelly: pour ½ pint boiling water over the two crystals and stir until completely dissolved. Add the white wine and salt. Leave to cool but do not let the jelly set.

2. To make pâté 1: wipe the mushrooms and trim the stalks. Melt the butter in a heavy-bottomed skillet or frying pan. Soften the onion, letting it fry to a golden colour. Remove with a draining spoon. Turn up the heat and, in the residue butter, fry the mushrooms until cooked. Sprinkle with the mace, pour over the madeira, return the onions to the pan and simmer for 2–3 minutes.

3. Leave the mixture to cool but, before it becomes quite cold, blend to a fine purée in a food processor. Squeeze in the softened butter (if the mushroom purée is too warm the butter will melt and will be grainy when set). Gradually blend in the cheese.

4. To make pâté 2: melt the butter in a heavy-bottomed skillet or pan, add the mushrooms and, over a low heat, sweat these until they are cooked without taking on any colour. Add the crushed garlic and lemon zest and juice. Season carefully but adequately. Leave to cool before proceeding as the recipe for pâté 1.

5. Fill the pâtés into two separate moulds. Smooth over the tops using a palette knife dipped into boiling water. Put the moulds to cool.

6. Gently spoon a thin film of jelly over each. Put to set in the refrigerator. Decorate as desired, spooning over a further thin film of jelly and allowing it to set (a couple of minutes).

7. Spoon over a third film of jelly. Leave to chill thoroughly. Serve with thin slices of hot wholemeal toast, passing extra butter if this is desired.

8. An alternative way to present the pâté: line a mould or loaf tin with plastic film, leaving plenty of overlap. Spoon in the first pâté, pressing it well into the corners. Put to chill.

9. Pour over a ⅛ inch layer of jelly and return the pâté to the refrigerator for the jelly to set. Spread in the second pâté. Put to chill. Finally, pour over the remaining jelly and refrigerate to set.

10. Just before serving, turn the double

*Chilled red pimento and ginger soup; Two mushroom pâté*

pâté on to a plate. To serve, dip a table knife into a jug of boiling water and cut thin slices.

# TERRINE OF DUCKLING WITH FOIE DE CANARD AND PISTACHIO NUTS

This terrine will freeze, but as it can be made three or four days in advance I prefer not to do this as freezing does tend to dry out the jellied juices.

---

*¾ lb streaky bacon, de-rinded*
*1 × 4 lb duck*
*1 duck's liver*
*2 pieces stem ginger, finely chopped*
*1 teaspoon ground ginger*
*4 tablespoons demerara rum*
*6 oz lean pork*
*6 oz pork fat*
*1 egg*
*3 teaspoons salt*
*1 level teaspoon pepper*
*1 teaspoon paprika*
*3 oz pistachio nuts, split or roughly chopped*
*1 × 5 oz tin foie de canard*

---

1. Lightly oil a 10–12 inch long iron terrine or seamless loaf tin.

2. With the back of a wetted knife, 'stretch' each rasher of bacon before lining the mould (this prevents shrinkage).

3. Remove the breasts from the duck (see recipe for Cold Pâté-stuffed Duck on page 75, but leave whole). Remove skin from breasts and discard. Remove legs and skin them. Cut meat from legs and any meat left on carcass.

4. Put the two duck breasts (whole) into a basin with the liver, the two gingers and the rum. Leave to marinate for 2 hours or more.

5. Put the leg meat, pork, fat, egg, salt, pepper, paprika and liquor from the marinade into a food processor and blend to a fine purée.

6. Turn the mixture into a basin, mix in the pistachio nuts and the liver, cut into smallish pieces.

7. Put one-third of the mixture into the bacon-lined mould, pressing well in with the back of a wetted spoon. Cut the foie de canard lengthways into 3 thick slices. Use a hot knife to do this. Lay these end to end in the terrine, trimming to fit your particular terrine.

8. Spread and press over another layer of the mixture. Lay in the two duck breasts, end to end. Cover with a final layer of the mixture, smoothing the top and pressing well into the corners. Cover with a lid or foil.

9. Cook in a bain marie of boiling water in a preheated oven, Gas Mark 6 (200°C, 400°F), for 1¼ hours.

10. Cool completely. Press with a piece of foil-covered board and a weight and refrigerate.

11. Leave to mature for a couple of days.

12. Serve cut in ¼ inch slices – no thicker – with Apple Sauce (see page 162) or Cumberland Sauce (see page 161). Serves 8–10 as a first course.

*Terrine of duckling with foie de canard and pistachio nuts*

# Salads

## MANGE-TOUT, ORANGE AND MEDITERRANEAN PRAWN SALAD

*2 pints chicken stock*
*juice of 1 lemon*
*16 Mediterranean prawns, defrosted*
*and shelled*
*4 oz mange-tout peas, topped and stringed*
*4 oz Kenya beans, topped, tailed,*
*stringed and cut in half*
*⅓ cucumber, peeled and seeded*
*2 navel oranges*

DRESSING:
*3 fl oz olive oil*
*1 fl oz orange juice*
*1 teaspoon finely grated orange zest*
*1 clove garlic, crushed*
*1 teaspoon mild French mustard*
*salt and freshly milled white*
*pepper*

GARNISH:
*plenty of freshly chopped chives and/or*
*parsley or basil*
*1 unshelled prawn per person*

1. Mix together the chicken stock and lemon juice and bring stock to the boil.
2. Plunge mange-tout peas and Kenya beans in turn into the stock for 2 or 3 minutes. Drain, cool and chill. Cut the cucumber into sticks the same size as the beans. Peel and segment the oranges, removing pith and membrane.
3. Chill all the ingredients well.
4. Make the dressing by shaking all ingredients together in a screw-top jar.
5. Toss vegetables, oranges and prawns together before tossing them in the dressing.
6. Pile on to a crisp lettuce leaf in individual bowls or plates. Sprinkle liberally with the herbs. Top with an unshelled prawn. Serves 4.

Note: black pepper leaves untidy specks on pale-coloured dishes. Freshly milled white pepper is not ordinary pepper, but whole white peppercorns milled in the usual way. These little details are important.

## STICK BEANS VINAIGRETTE

*1 lb stick, French or Kenya beans,*
*trimmed and stringed*
*light chicken stock to cover, use*
*stock cube if necessary*
*juice of ½ lemon*
*a little extra salt*
*1 small (1 oz) onion*
*2 whites of hard-boiled eggs*
*4 small cocktail gherkins*
*2 tablespoons chopped parsley*
*¼ pint French dressing*

1. Boil the beans in lemon-flavoured stock for 2–3 minutes only. Add a little extra salt. Drain, cool and chill.
2. Finely chop the remaining ingredients, add to the dressing and spoon over the cold beans. Serves 6 as part of an hors d'oeuvre.

*Mange-tout, orange and Mediterranean prawn salad*

# RUSSIAN SALAD

*2 medium-sized carrots*
*2 medium-sized waxy potatoes*
*1 (¼ lb) packet frozen peas, defrosted*
*chicken stock*
*¼ pint stiff mayonnaise*
*lemon juice*
*a little cream*

**1.** Cut the vegetables into minute dice. Cook the carrots and potatoes in chicken stock for a couple of minutes (they should still be somewhat crisp). Strain and use the stock to cook the peas for a minute. Strain and leave the vegetables to cool. Discard the stock or use for soup.

**2.** Mix the cold vegetables together and add a good squeeze of lemon juice. Bind with the mayonnaise adding a little cream if the mixture is too stiff. This salad can be served alone as a basis for egg mayonnaise or as a stuffing for Lobster Bellevue (see page 133).

# POTATO SALAD WITH SOUR CREAM DRESSING

An excellent accompaniment to cold roast meat. The hot potatoes absorb the flavour of the wine and oil. See photograph on page 91.

*1½ lb waxy or new potatoes, boiled*
*and slightly cooled*
*1 glass dry white wine mixed with*
*1 tablespoon olive oil*
*2 red-skinned onions, cut into rings*
*2 hard-boiled eggs, roughly chopped*
*salt and milled pepper*

DRESSING:
*½ pint soured cream*
*1 heaped teaspoon mild French or*
*English mustard (try Tewkesbury)*
*juice of ½ lemon*
*pinch of salt*

*Elegant 'chef's'
salad*

**1.** Skin the potatoes if you like, and cut

them into ¼ inch discs. Splash them with the wine and oil while they are still warm. Season lightly and leave to cool and absorb the liquid.

**2.** Mix with the onion rings (reserving some for a garnish) and the chopped hard-boiled eggs.

**3.** Make up the dressing and fold the potatoes into this in a large bowl. Chill for an hour, covered with plastic film. Garnish with extra onion rings before serving. Serves 5–6.

# ELEGANT 'CHEF'S' SALAD

Those of you who travel to America regularly will no doubt have tried 'chef's' salad, where strips of processed cheese, plastic ham and dry turkey are served on a mountain of Boston lettuce complete with a scarlet blob of their ubiquitous 'jello' on top! Here's my version, somewhat more refined, as you will see in the photograph opposite.

*4 oz smoked salmon, in 2 thick slices*
*2 cooked chicken breasts (home-poached if possible), cold*
*2 celery sticks*
*4 lettuce leaves, very finely shredded*
*4 oz cottage cheese*
*1 tablespoon chopped chives*

FRENCH DRESSING:
*¼ pint oil*
*⅛ pint red wine vinegar*
*1 level teaspoon mild French mustard*
*1 clove garlic, crushed (optional)*
*salt and freshly milled pepper*

**1.** Mix the dressing. Cut the salmon and chicken meat into 'sticks' and the celery into 'matchsticks'. Put a little 'chiffonade' of lettuce (which is what finely shredded lettuce is called) into individual bowls. Arrange the chicken meat, salmon and celery in attractive groups. Position a blob of cottage cheese strategically, sprinkle the whole with French dressing and add some chopped chives.

**2.** Each guest should turn out the salad on to his under-plate, mix it all together and enjoy it. Serves 4.

# TOMATO, CARROT AND ORANGE SALAD

*2 beefsteak tomatoes*
*2 large navel oranges*
*2 large carrots, peeled*
*lettuce leaves*

DRESSING:
*¼ pint olive oil*
*⅛ pint nut oil*
*juice and grated rind of 1 orange*
*1 tablespoon red wine vinegar*
*1 level teaspoon mild French mustard*
*1 level teaspoon caster sugar*
*salt and milled pepper*

**1.** Skin, seed and cut the tomatoes into petals. Knife-peel the oranges and cut into segments. Grate the carrots on the julienne blade of a food processor or on the coarse side of a grater.

**2.** Make up the dressing by combining all the ingredients. Arrange the fruit and vegetables on lettuce leaves in individual bowls. Dress before serving or pass the dressing separately. Serves 4.

# SPINACH, BACON AND MUSHROOM SALAD WITH CROÛTONS

See photograph opposite.

*12 rashers streaky bacon*
*4 slices white bread, ½ inch thick*
*butter for frying*
*1 lb spinach, washed and de-veined*
*8 oz very white tight-capped mushrooms*

DRESSING:
*¼ pint nut oil*
*1 teaspoon mild French mustard*
*juice of ½ lemon*
*salt and pepper*
*1 teaspoon caster sugar*
*⅛ pint single cream*

**1.** De-rind the bacon and cut into small pieces. Dry fry until really crisp. Remove the crusts from the bread and cut into ½ inch cubes. Either fry in the bacon fat, adding a little butter if necessary, or fry in butter alone for good flavour. Cool. The secret of a good nutty-flavoured, well-coloured croûton is very slow frying, adding enough butter or oil for them to absorb, and moving them about all the time they are frying – tedious, but well worth the effort. (Croûtons freeze well and can be kept in store for soups and other uses.)

**2.** Make up the dressing in the usual way, adding the cream last. Break up the spinach leaves into bite-sized pieces, and arrange a bed of these in individual bowls. Divide the bacon and croûtons evenly between the bowls. Wipe and thinly slice the raw mushrooms and pile these on top of each salad. Garnish with sprigs of parsley. Add the dressing at the table so that everything stays crisp. Serves 4.

# WINTER SALAD WITH GREEN AND RED PEPPERS AND CHEESE

The secret of this salad is in cutting the peppers and cheese into fine strips.

*2 green peppers*
*2 red peppers*
*8 oz Gruyère, Emmenthal or Tomme de Brevis cheese*

DRESSING:
*¼ pint olive oil*
*2 tablespoons white wine vinegar*
*1 clove garlic, crushed*
*1 level teaspoon mild French mustard*
*salt and freshly milled pepper*

GARNISH:
*1 red-skinned onion*
*1 tablespoon freshly chopped parsley*

**1.** Cut each pepper in half, remove any seeds *and pith* and cut away the stalk end. Cut the halves in half again and then

Clockwise from top left: *Tomato, carrot and orange salad; Dover sole and queen scallop salad in pimento mayonnaise (see page 132); Winter salad with green and red peppers and cheese; Waldorf salad; Spinach, bacon and mushroom salad with croûtons*

laboriously cut each piece into fine striplets about 1½ inches long, called 'julienne'. This salad can be made using a food processor but with the slicing blade not the julienne blade (the julienne blade is not a good idea with peppers). It will look different but will be almost the same.

2. Cut the cheese into the same sized strips as the peppers. Chill in separate containers. Mix together just before serving and toss in the dressing, mixed in the usual way, just before your guests sit down. Peppers have a very strong flavour and one which 'crosses' between other food very quickly. The idea here is to keep the cheese flavour 'separate' from the peppers until the point of eating is reached. Decorate with a few finely sliced onion rings and some freshly chopped parsley. Serves 6.

# AVOCADO SALAD WITH FOIE GRAS AND TARRAGON

*1 × 5–6 oz tin foie gras de canard au poivre vert*
*4 large ripe avocados*
*lemon juice*
*6 artichoke hearts (tinned will do)*
*1 × 8 oz tin hearts of palm*

DRESSING:
*⅛ pint rich olive oil*
*1 teaspoon tarragon mustard*
*juice of ½ lemon*
*salt and milled pepper*
*good pinch of caster sugar*
*1 tablespoon freshly chopped tarragon*

1. Put all the ingredients for the dressing into a screw-topped jar and shake until everything is emulsified.

2. Put the tin of foie gras into the refrigerator overnight to set. (Swiss Parfait can be used for a poor man's version of this salad.)

3. Cut 3 of the avocados in half and brush well with lemon juice. If you prepare them at lunchtime for the evening, pour the lemon juice into a shallow glass or china dish and stand the avocados, flesh down, in this.

*Avocado salad with foie gras and tarragon*

4. Quarter the artichoke hearts. Drain, rinse and drain again the hearts of palm. Cut into cubes, discarding any which are 'woody'.

5. Open both ends of the foie gras tin and push the contents out.

6. Using a knife dipped into boiling water, cut the chilled foie gras into cubes. Put on to a plate and leave in the refrigerator until you are ready to fill the avocados.

7. Using the small bowl of a melon baller, scoop out balls of the fourth avocado and toss in lemon juice. Cover with clingfilm until ready for use.

8. Half an hour before serving, bring all the ingredients together in a bowl and mix gently with the dressing. Pile into the avocado halves. Chill for 30 minutes. Serve with a teaspoon and small fork. An extra sliver of foie gras can be popped on top if your budget permits! Serves 6.

# PECORINO, CUCUMBER, TOMATO AND ORANGE SALAD WITH ANCHOVIES

See photograph on page 8.

*8 oz piece Pecorino cheese, cut into cubes*
*2 beefsteak tomatoes, skinned, seeded and cut into ½ inch chunks*
*1 small cucumber, channelled, seeded and cut in half, then into ½ inch chunks*
*1 dozen anchovies, rolled, for garnish*

DRESSING:
*¼ pint olive oil*
*juice and finely grated rind of 1 orange*
*1 teaspoon mild French mustard*
*salt and milled pepper*
*1 clove garlic, crushed (optional)*
*1 teaspoon caster sugar*

1. Put the dressing ingredients into a screw-topped jar and shake well.

2. Mix the salad ingredients in a large bowl and put to chill.

3. Dress the salad just before serving. Garnish with the anchovies. Serves 6.

# WALDORF SALAD

There is a modest difference between my Waldorf Salad and the classic version of the recipe: I use pecan nuts as they are sweeter and softer than walnuts, and I add a pear. See photograph on page 33.

---

*juice of 1 lemon*
*2 large Cox's apples*
*1 large ripe pear*
*4–5 white sticks of celery, cleaned*
*and crisped in ice-cold water*
*6 oz pecan nuts, plus a few for garnish*
*6 lettuce leaves, shredded*

DRESSING:
*¼ pint double cream*
*½ pint rich home-made mayonnaise*
*juice of ½ lemon*

---

**1.** Squeeze the lemon into a large bowl. Peel, core, quarter and cut into slices the fruits, and toss them in the lemon juice. Dry and then shred the cleaned and crisped celery and mix with the fruits.

**2.** To mix the dressing: whip the cream until it stands in soft peaks. Mix the mayonnaise and lemon juice, adding any juice that was left after tossing the fruits. Fold the cream into this.

**3.** Just before dinner, bind the fruits together with the dressing, adding the nuts. (Reserve a few slices of apple for the garnish.) Pile on to shredded lettuce leaves and decorate at will with extra pecan nuts and the odd slice of lemon-soaked apple. Serves 4.

# FENNEL, BLUE CHEESE AND RED CAVIAR SALAD

This salad makes an ideal first course on a hot summer's day.

---

*3 heads fennel, cleaned*
*1 bottle blue cheese dressing*
*1 small carton plain yoghurt*
*1 small glass red lump fish roe*

---

Shred the fennel as finely as possible on a mandoline or using the slicing blade of a processor. Mix the blue cheese dressing with the yoghurt. Toss all together, sprinkle with the red roe, and serve. Serves 5–6.

# OMELETTE AND BROCCOLI SALAD WITH WATERCRESS

---

*1 lb broccoli*
*1 pint chicken stock (use a cube)*
*juice of 1 lemon*
*3 bundles watercress*
*12 eggs*
*salt, pepper and nutmeg*
*butter for frying*

DRESSING:
*⅓ pint olive oil*
*juice of 1 large lemon*
*1 level teaspoon sugar*
*1 level teaspoon dry mustard*
*1 small clove garlic, crushed*
*salt and freshly milled pepper*

GARNISH:
*1 tablespoon each chopped chives and*
*finely chopped parsley*

---

**1.** Break the broccoli into 1 inch bits and boil, for 1–2 minutes only, in the chicken stock to which you have added the lemon juice. Drain and cool.

**2.** Wash and pick over the watercress which must be absolutely fresh. Pick the leaves from 2 of the bundles and put them through a blender with 6 of the eggs. Season well with salt, pepper and nutmeg.

**3.** Heat the omelette pan, add a knob of butter but do not let it brown. Make up thin omelettes (the mixture should make about 6–8), letting the egg mixture almost set before turning over with a large palette knife for a mere second; the omelettes must not be hard and tough. Turn on to a work surface and roll them up loosely. Do likewise with the remaining eggs, but this time do not use watercress, so that you end up with a mixture of green and yellow omelettes. Cut the rolls into ½ inch wide strips, diagonally.

4. Arrange the broccoli, omelette strips and sprigs of remaining watercress in a large salad bowl. Mix the dressing (this salad absorbs quite a bit), pour it over the salad ingredients, sprinkle over the chives and parsley, and serve immediately. Serves 6–8 as a starter.

# TANGY PEAR, SOUR CREAM AND RADISH SALAD

*juice of 2 lemons*
*1 bunch radishes*
*8 small pears*
*½ pint sour cream*
*¼ pint bland mayonnaise*
*salt and milled pepper*
*½ teaspoon ground cardamom*

1. Squeeze the lemons into a large glass bowl. Clean and slice the radishes into cold water. Peel and core the pears. Cut into long strips and toss them in the lemon juice.

2. Cover radishes and pears separately with plastic film and leave to chill and soak in the refrigerator for 2 hours.

3. Just before serving, mix the sour cream and mayonnaise together, seasoning with salt, pepper and cardamom.

4. Carefully fold in the drained pears. Pile into a serving dish. Pat the radishes dry, and arrange over the top of the salad.

Apples, pineapples – any fruit is good prepared this way and served with cold meats.

# MUSHROOMS IN MUSTARD MAYONNAISE

*8 oz tiny button mushrooms*
*4 fl oz amontillado sherry*
*5 fl oz bland mayonnaise*
*2 teaspoons mild French mustard*
*salt and pepper*
*a few cold mussels (optional)*

1. Trim, wash and drain the mushrooms, quartering them if they are too large but leaving the stalks on.

2. Put them into a pan with a tight fitting lid. Pour over the sherry and season sparingly. Fit the lid.

3. Bring to the boil and cook for 1 minute only, tossing them two or three times. Drain, retaining the liquid. Leave to cool.

4. Reduce the liquid to 1 tablespoonful. Leave to cool.

5. Mix this liquid with the mustard into the mayonnaise.

6. Just before serving, mix the cold mushrooms into the mayonnaise and mustard mixture. As a luxury, a few cold mussels can be added. Serves 6.

# BROWN RICE, MUSCATEL AND PEPPER SALAD

MARINADE:
*2 tablespoons rum*
*2 tablespoons soy sauce*
*3 tablespoons olive or groundnut oil*
*1 teaspoon ground coriander*
*1 teaspoon cinnamon*
*1 tablespoon grated orange rind*
*juice of 1 orange*

SALAD:
*4 oz stoned raisins, roughly chopped*
*8 oz 'quick' brown rice*
*chicken stock*
*2 red peppers*
*2 green peppers*
*salt and pepper if necessary*

1. Mix all of the marinade ingredients together. Add the raisins.

2. Boil the rice as instructed on the packet, using stock instead of water. While the rice is cooking, seed the peppers and dice or cut them into fine julienne strips. Drain the rice (reserve the liquor for a soup or gravy), and add while still hot to the marinade mixture. Stir in well and add extra salt and pepper if liked.

3. Just before serving, mix in the chopped peppers. Serves 8–10.

# Egg Dishes

## BUTTERED EGGS IN THE SHELL

A good enough reason to use an antique egg cruet, this dish makes a novelty for Easter Sunday brunch or a first course at a dinner party.

---

*4 eggs*
*salt and milled white pepper*
*pinch of nutmeg or ground coriander*
*⅛ pint single cream or top of the milk*
*1½ oz butter*

GARNISH (OPTIONAL AND VARIABLE):
*1 small jar caviar or lumpfish roe*
*1 tomato, skinned, seeded and diced*
*4 small mushrooms, chopped, seasoned with nutmeg and briefly sautéed in a knob of butter*

---

**1.** Have the garnish ready, as described. Using a small, fine saw-edged knife or steel nail file, very gently saw off the top of each egg at the pointed end, about quarter of the way down. Rest the egg on a crumpled towel and don't apply any pressure with the knife or your fingers. Do not attempt to saw right through until you have sawn a groove right round. This way you will get a clean break.

**2.** Beat the 4 eggs together well, season, adding a touch of nutmeg or ground coriander for a change. Stir in the cream or top of the milk.

**3.** Melt 1 oz butter in a small pan and, over a low heat, 'draw' the mixture across the bottom of the pan with a spatula until it is beginning to set. Dab over the remaining butter with a teaspoon, fill the shells and garnish. The eggs should be soft. Serves 4.

## EGGS TABBOULEH WITH RIPE FIGS

The idea for this dish came to me when I was offered – as a salad – tabbouleh in the home of a Lebanese friend.

Burghul, or cracked wheat, as it is known in our health food shops, is delicious and, as a salad mixed with spring onions, parsley and the all-essential mint, goes well with cold lamb or chicken.

I have piled it on to halved, lightly hard-boiled eggs, and added a third dimension in the form of ripe figs. See photograph on page 42.

---

*6 hard-boiled eggs*
*French dressing*
*6 ripe figs (optional)*

TABBOULEH:
*8 oz cracked wheat*
*cold chicken stock*
*¼ pint good olive oil*
*2 level teaspoons mild French mustard*
*juice of 1 large lemon*
*2 tomatoes, skinned, seeded and chopped*
*1 bunch spring onions, trimmed (but the green left on) and finely chopped*
*1 teacup freshly chopped parsley*
*1 teacup freshly chopped mint*
*salt and milled black pepper*

---

**1.** Soak the wheat for an hour in the cold stock (if you are a vegetarian you can use cold water). It will swell. Drain, and squeeze out surplus moisture. Spread the soaked wheat on a clean tea towel to dry a little.

**2.** Mix the oil, mustard and lemon juice together. Then, in a large bowl, mix all the

*Buttered eggs in the shell*

rest of the tabbouleh ingredients in. Cover and refrigerate until ready for use.

3. Shell and cut the hard-boiled eggs in half. Splash with a little French dressing (about 1 teaspoon on each).

4. Arrange in a dish. Pile the tabbouleh on top of each half.

5. Arrange the figs in and amongst if used. Serves 6.

# CODDLED EGGS

Coddling eggs is a singularly pleasant English habit which is enjoying a renaissance. Coddlers usually come in two sizes, single and double. The double is more useful as it means there is room for adding extra ingredients. Into a pan pour exactly the amount of water needed to come up to the neck of the coddlers. Bring to a rolling boil. Butter the inside and rims of the coddlers.

### SIMPLE CODDLED EGGS:
¼ teaspoon unsalted butter
1 egg
salt, and pepper or nutmeg
teaspoon single cream (optional)

### CODDLED EGGS WITH TONGUE PURÉE:
4 large eggs
2–3 oz tongue, puréed or
finely chopped
2 teaspoons chopped chives
4 good teaspoons thick cream
4 teaspoons butter

1. To make simple coddled eggs: butter the coddler and break in the egg. Season and add the cream. Screw the lid on, checking that the thread isn't twisted.

2. Immerse in the boiling water for 7–8 minutes. Check to see if they are done: they ought to be soft.

3. To make coddled eggs with tongue purée: butter the double-sized coddlers. Divide the tongue equally between them. Break in the eggs. Season lightly, sprinkle with chives and add cream.

4. Coddle in boiling water for 10–12

minutes. Serve with toast or muffins. Serves 4.

Note: minced cooked ham, seasoned, minced *raw* chicken breast, cooked smoked haddock, chopped spinach – almost anything can be used.

# EGGS IN CASES

### RICH SHORTCRUST PASTRY FOR THE CASES:
1 egg
2 fl oz milk
1 teaspoon salt
8 oz flour
5 oz butter

### FILLING:
12 button mushrooms
6 tablespoons amontillado sherry
salt and milled pepper
4 oz boiled ham, minced
1 heaped tablespoon chopped chives
and parsley
1 oz butter, softened
12 eggs
12 asparagus spears, cooked
6 tablespoons single cream

1. To make the pastry: beat the egg with the milk. Add the salt to the flour and rub the butter into the flour until sand-like in texture. Mix in the milk mixture with a large fork and knead lightly. Rest the pastry in a cool place for 1 hour.

2. Line six 3 × 1 inch loose-bottomed tart tins with the pastry. Stand them on a baking sheet and line with paper or foil and pastry pebbles. Bake these blind at Gas Mark 6 (200°C, 400°F) for 20 minutes.

3. Cook the mushrooms in a small, lidded pan with the sherry, tossing them constantly. Season lightly.

4. Mix the ham with the herbs and softened butter. Season if necessary, but ham is usually salty enough. Divide the mixture evenly between each pastry case, spreading it over the base.

5. Carefully break 2 eggs into each case. Garnish with the asparagus and mushrooms. Dribble over each a spoonful of cream and season lightly.

*Eggs in cases*

**6.** Reduce the oven temperature to Gas Mark 4 (180°C, 350°F). Bake for 15 minutes or until the eggs are just set but the yolks are still soft. Serve immediately. Serves 6.

# SIMPLE STUFFED EGGS

Creamy butter and fresh herbs make these perfect.

---

*8 hard-boiled eggs*
*3 oz softened butter*
*1 heaped teaspoon tarragon*
*mustard or other mild French mustard*
*salt and freshly milled white pepper*
*1 tablespoon freshly chopped parsley*

---

**1.** Halve the eggs lengthways and scoop out yolks. Mix the yolks, butter and mustard together. Press through a hair sieve. Season well.

**2.** Mix in the parsley. Pipe or fork into the halved whites.

# EGGS WITH WALNUT MAYONNAISE

---

*6 hard-boiled eggs*

WALNUT MAYONNAISE:
*4 egg yolks*
*1 level teaspoon dry mustard*
*1 level teaspoon salt*
*¼ teaspoon milled pepper*
*¼ pint walnut oil*
*¼ pint olive or arachide oil*
*2 tablespoons red wine vinegar*
*4 oz walnut halves, well crushed*
*extra walnut halves (optional garnish)*

---

**1.** Mix the yolks, mustard, salt and pepper with a balloon whisk until thick and sticky. Mix the two oils together. Add a droplet of oil to the yolk mixture and whisk in well.

**2.** Now gradually add the remaining oil, ensuring that the mixture remains stiff all the time.

*Spiced crab-stuffed eggs; Eggs with walnut mayonnaise; Eggs tabbouleh with ripe figs*

**3.** After a third of the oil has been added, whisk in half the vinegar. Add the remaining oil and vinegar alternately.

**4.** Adjust the thickness of the mayonnaise to 'coating' consistency with a little cold water. Fold in the crushed walnuts.

**5.** Shell and slice the eggs. Coat with the walnut mayonnaise.

**6.** Garnish with extra walnuts if you wish. (This sauce can be made entirely in a blender.) Serves 6.

# SPICED CRAB-STUFFED EGGS

---

*12 eggs, hard-boiled*
*wholewheat bread or toast*

FILLING:
*6 oz butter, softened*
*1 small freshly dressed crab (about 8–10 oz) weighed after dressing*
*2 oz freshly grated Parmesan cheese*
*1 heaped teaspoon Colman's tarragon mustard*
*2 heaped teaspoons Baie Roses (pink peppercorns in brine)*
*1 clove garlic, crushed*
*2 good dashes tabasco sauce*
*1 level teaspoon salt*
*good squeeze of lemon juice*
*2 heaped teaspoons tomato purée*
*1 tablespoon freshly chopped tarragon (or parsley)*
*1 level teaspoon milled black pepper*

---

**1.** Cut a small piece off the top and bottom of each egg. Empty the eggs with an apple corer by gently plunging it down the centre from top to bottom. Put all the filling ingredients plus the hard-boiled egg yolks into a blender or food processor. Mix until smooth. Press through a hair sieve.

**2.** Using a large rose tube fitted into a piping bag, pipe the mixture into the eggs. Fit a 'cap' of egg white. Spread any remaining mixture on to circles of wholewheat bread or toast. Stand an egg on top of each circle.

**3.** Serve at room temperature. Serves 6.

# Other Dishes

## 'BRYE FAVORS'

When made small enough these savoury parcels are ideal for cocktail parties. Make them either square (1 inch) or cut them with a small fluted pastry cutter.

When used as a first course or savoury, serve a simple tomato coulis as an accompaniment.

---

*6 oz wedge of Brie (fairly ripe but not oozing)*
*1 tablespoon olive oil*
*1 clove garlic, crushed*
*1 tablespoon lemon juice*
*salt*
*1 lb flaky pastry (bought or home-made)*
*beaten egg*
*oil for frying*
*1 oz grated Parmesan cheese*

TOMATO COULIS:
*12 oz tin plum tomatoes*
*1 tablespoon lemon juice*
*salt and pepper*

---

**1.** To make the 'brye favors': cut the cheese (including rind) into ½ inch cubes. Mix the oil, garlic, lemon juice and ¼ teaspoon salt in a glass or china bowl. Toss the cheese in this. Leave to marinate while you roll out the pastry.

**2.** Cut the pastry into equal halves. Roll out evenly and thinly into rectangles of the same size, about ⅛ inch thick. Place cubes of the cheese at 1½ inch intervals on one rectangle, leaving enough room for sealing the pastry between the rows.

**3.** Brush between the rows of cheese with beaten egg. Carefully lay over the second rectangle of pastry. Press well between the rows and cut into 1 inch squares or rounds.

**4.** Deep fry in lightly smoking oil until crisp and puffed up. Drain on crumpled kitchen paper. Dredge lightly with Parmesan and a smidge of salt. Serve on a clean napkin.

**5.** To make the tomato coulis: press the tomatoes through a hair sieve. Reduce to ½ pint by boiling rapidly. Add the lemon juice and salt and pepper to taste. Makes about 16–20 'favors' to serve 4 as a first course.

## WENSLEYDALE SOUFFLÉ TARTS

---

*12 oz shortcrust pastry to line*
*6 (3 inch) loose-bottomed tart tins*
*4 oz cooked ham, minced and mixed*
*with 1 teaspoon mild French mustard*

SOUFFLÉ MIXTURE:
*1½ oz butter*
*1 oz plain white flour*
*scant ½ pint milk*
*4 oz Wensleydale cheese, grated*
*salt, milled white pepper or nutmeg*
*4 egg yolks, beaten*
*5 egg whites*

---

**1.** Bake the pastry shells blind (the day before if you like). Return them to their tins and spread the ham mixture equally between the six.

**2.** Make up the basic sauce in advance: melt the butter, stir in the flour, gradually add the cold milk, stirring briskly until you have a smooth white sauce. Add the grated cheese

*'Brye favors'*

and cook for 2–3 minutes. Season well, remembering to allow for the bulk of the beaten egg whites.

3. Remove from the heat and gradually add the beaten yolks. Leave to cool covered with a circle of buttered paper to prevent a skin forming.

4. Whisk the egg whites until they *just* stand in peaks. Mix one-third thoroughly into the sauce. Cut and fold in the remainder with a slotted spoon.

5. Pour or ladle the mixture into the tarts, filling them. Bake in a preheated oven Gas Mark 7 (220°C, 425°F) for 15 minutes or until risen, golden brown and set. These tarts are also nice when cold. Serves 6.

# WALTON'S DOUBLE CRAB MOUSSE

### DARK MEAT MIXTURE:
*2 leaves gelatine soaked (or 1
teaspoon crystals)
½ lb fresh dark crab meat
6 oz cream cheese
pinch of allspice
1 fl oz dry sherry
juice of ½ small lemon
6 fl oz double cream
8 fl oz aspic jelly (see below)*

### WHITE MEAT MIXTURE:
*2 leaves gelatine, soaked (or 1
teaspoon crystals)
½ lb fresh white crab meat
1 dessertspoon freshly grated
Parmesan cheese
1½ fl oz dry white vermouth
¼ teaspoon ground mace
pinch of cayenne pepper
juice of ½ small lemon
½ pint double cream
8 fl oz aspic jelly (see below)*

### SPECIAL ASPIC JELLY MIX:
*1 oz commercial (flavoured) aspic
crystals
5 leaves gelatine, soaked (or 2 heaped
teaspoons gelatine crystals)
a large measure of Pernod
1 teaspoon paprika*

*Walton's double
crab mousse*

1. To make the aspic jelly: bring 24 fl oz water to the boil. Add the aspic crystals and the gelatine. Stir until dissolved, away from the heat. Divide equally into three. Add the Pernod and paprika to one portion. Leave all three to cool, but not set.

2. To make the mousse mixtures: dissolve the gelatine in 2 tablespoons water in a cup, standing it in a pan of simmering water.

3. Blend all the ingredients for the dark crab mixture, except the cream, adding the melted gelatine. Sieve. Stir in the double cream and then one unflavoured portion of aspic jelly. Do exactly the same for the white crab mixture, but do not sieve.

4. To mould the mousse: lightly oil a seamless loaf tin or other mould. Pour in a thin layer of the Pernod jelly and leave to set. Pour in the dark crab mixture and leave to set. Pour over a further thin layer of the Pernod jelly and leave to set. Pour over the white crab mixture and leave to set. Pour over a final film of Pernod jelly and refrigerate overnight.

5. To unmould: run a hot palette knife round the sides. Quickly pass the base of the mould over a low flame (or immerse in boiling water, briefly). Invert on to a dish. Serves 8–10.

# COTTAGE CHEESE MOUSSE

*½ pint chicken stock
2 sachets gelatine crystals
1½ lb cottage cheese
1 level teaspoon black pepper
1 heaped teaspoon paprika
1 level teaspoon salt
juice of ½ lemon
½ pint double cream,
whipped to soft peak
2 egg whites, stiffly beaten*

1. Bring the chicken stock to the boil. Turn off the heat. Sprinkle in the gelatine crystals and stir until dissolved. Leave to cool but not set.

2. In a blender or food processor, blend the cheese with all the seasoning, cooled chicken

stock and lemon juice. Transfer to a large bowl.

**3.** Incorporate the whipped cream thoroughly. Cut and fold in the stiffly beaten egg whites. Pour the mousse into a ring mould or glass bowl. Cover this with clingfilm. Put to set overnight.

# CHEESE GLAZED MUSHROOMS WITH RUM AND LEMON

*1 oz butter*
*1 lb baby white button mushrooms,*
*quartered or sliced*
*2 fl oz Jamaica rum*
*½ pint double cream*
*1 teaspoon flour mashed with 1 heaped*
*teaspoon soft butter*
*juice of ½ lemon*
*¼ teaspoon ground mace*
*¼ teaspoon salt*
*1½ oz freshly grated Parmesan cheese*

**1.** Melt the small amount of butter in a large frying pan, swirling it round to ensure even browning. Tip in the mushrooms and stir them round over a high heat for a minute.

**2.** Pour in the rum and ignite by tipping the pan to the flame (or using a taper). Allow the flames to die down. Pour in the cream. Allow to bubble for half a minute. Whisk in enough of the flour and butter paste *just* to cohere the sauce.

**3.** Season with the lemon juice, mace and salt. Divide the mixture into individual fireproof ramekins. Dredge with the cheese. Glaze under a hot grill. Serve with butter-fried croûtons. Eat with a teaspoon.

Note: the mushrooms can be prepared two or three days before, in which case before filling the ramekins bring the mixture to boiling point over a low heat, and *if* it 'oils' out, add a dash of rum or cold water to restore the emulsion which has broken down. Serves 4–6.

# SAMOSAS

These little parcels from India make ideal starters or are perfect cocktail food. If you don't want to make your own pastry, buy flaky or Greek filo. I give two alternative fillings below.

*8 oz wholewheat flour*
*3 large tablespoons nut or vegetable oil*
*1 level teaspoon salt*
*oil for frying*

MEAT STUFFING (KHEEMA):
*2 tablespoons ghee (or vegetable oil)*
*¼ teaspoon ground cloves*
*4 cloves garlic, crushed*
*1 piece green ginger, shredded or*
*finely chopped, or 1 level teaspoon*
*ground ginger*
*½ teaspoon garam masala*
*¼ teaspoon cinnamon*
*2 chillies, well crushed*
*1 heaped teaspoon ground coriander*
*1 teaspoon turmeric*
*¼ teaspoon ground bay leaf*
*1 level teaspoon ground black pepper*
*1 teaspoon salt*
*1 heaped teaspoon medium hot curry*
*powder*
*1 large onion, finely chopped*
*1½ lb minced lamb (or beef)*
*4 tomatoes, skinned and seeded*
*8 oz frozen peas*

QUICK VEGETABLE FILLING:
*1 tablespoon olive oil*
*4 onions, chopped*
*1 dessertspoon mild (or hot if you*
*prefer it) curry powder*
*6 waxy potatoes, cooked and diced*
*6 oz peas, cooked*
*4 oz green beans, cooked and diced*
*4 oz cooked haricot beans*
*2 tomatoes, skinned and seeded*

**1.** Combine the flour and oil and rub in. Add the salt. Use enough water (about ½ pint) to mix to a firm dough. Knead very well with the heel of the hand for 10 minutes and form into a ball. Rest it for half an hour.

**2.** Flour a work surface. Divide the dough into 16–20 (or for smaller cocktail samosas

20–30) balls and roll into 3½–4 inch circles. Cut each circle in half and form into a cone. Wet the edges and pinch them together with the fingers working inside and the thumb outside. Fill each one ¾ full with your chosen mixture. Moisten and seal the top edges, pressing them well together.

**3.** Deep fry at 185–195°C (360–380°F). The samosas reheat well in a low oven, Gas Mark 2 (150°C, 300°F), for 15–20 minutes, so they can be made in advance.

**4.** To make the meat stuffing: heat the ghee or oil in a large frying pan. Add all the spices and fry for a few seconds, stirring well and briskly. Add the onion, stir in and fry.

**5.** Add the meat a little at a time, stirring in and frying well. Add the tomatoes.

**6.** Blanch peas in boiling water for 2 minutes and drain.

**7.** Transfer everything but the peas to an ovenproof pot. Pour over ¼ pint water. Cook in the oven at Gas Mark 5 (190°C, 375°F) for an hour. Ten minutes before the end of the cooking time, add the peas.

The mixture should be very thick – almost dry. Take off any excess fat and leave to cool completely.

To make the quick vegetable filling: heat the oil and soften the onion. Scatter over the curry powder and fry for 5 minutes over a medium heat. Add the remaining cooked vegetables. Stir in well, remove from heat and cool.

# MUSHROOMS IN SNAIL BUTTER

*12 inch-diameter tight-capped mushrooms*
*3 oz butter*
*1 small onion, grated*
*2 oz white breadcrumbs*
*nutmeg for seasoning*
*juice of 1 lemon*

SNAIL BUTTER:
*1 large clove garlic, crushed*
*1 small onion, finely chopped*
*2 tablespoons freshly chopped parsley*
*4 oz butter, creamed*
*salt and freshly milled pepper*
*tabasco sauce*

**1.** To make the snail butter: pound the garlic, onion and parsley well. Beat into the creamed butter, seasoning it liberally with salt and pepper and a small dash of tabasco sauce.

**2.** Form into a ½ inch 'pipe', or pipe rosettes on to wax paper. Chill well.

**3.** Prepare the mushroom caps. Wipe them clean and remove the stalks. Finely chop the stalks and fry them in a modicum of the butter.

**4.** Melt 2 oz of the butter in a frying pan. Add the grated onion and fry over a low heat until softened and golden brown. Add the breadcrumbs and fry for 2 minutes, stirring well. Season liberally with salt, pepper, nutmeg and a squeeze of lemon juice. Mix in the chopped mushroom stalks.

**5.** Toss the mushroom caps in lemon juice and season lightly.

**6.** Butter a suitable ovenproof dish and arrange the caps in it. Fill them with the mixture and bake at Gas Mark 7 (220°C, 425°F) for 15–20 minutes. Serve the mushrooms topped with the snail butter. Serves 4.

# SMOKED SALMON AND ASPARAGUS TARTLETS

*1 lb shortcrust pastry*
*1 (8 oz) tin soft green asparagus tips*
*4 eggs, beaten*
*8 oz smoked salmon off-cuts*
*¾ pint single cream*
*1 bay leaf, crumbled*
*1 small onion, chopped*
*salt and milled pepper*

**1.** Roll out the pastry and line the tartlet tins. Bake blind at Gas Mark 7 (220°C, 425°F) for 10 minutes.

**2.** Drain the asparagus, cut into small pieces and put a couple of pieces into each pastry shell.

**3.** Machine blend the beaten eggs and smoked salmon.

**4.** Put the cream, bay leaf and onion into a pan over a very low heat, season, and let these infuse for 30 minutes. Bring to the boil and strain over the salmon and egg mixture, whisking briefly until all is incorporated.

**5.** Fill the tartlets and bake at Gas Mark 4 (180°C, 350°F) until golden brown and puffed up. Quantity makes up to 24 small tartlets.

# AVOCADO PEBBLE MILL

I concocted this dish to celebrate the one thousandth edition of the BBC's popular magazine programme 'Pebble Mill at One'. It is probably one of the richest first courses you will ever taste, so serve before a very modest and plain main course and an even more modest pudding.

---

*2 ripe avocado pears*
*4 eggs*
*juice of 1 lemon*
*½ pint chicken stock*
*freshly ground black pepper*
*½ pint quick béarnaise sauce*
*(ingredients and method below)*
*1 oz Parmesan cheese, grated*

QUICK BÉARNAISE SAUCE:
*6 oz butter*
*4 egg yolks*
*¼ chicken stock cube dissolved in 2 tablespoons tarragon or wine vinegar*
*1 level teaspoon Dijon mustard*
*¼ level teaspoon salt*
*freshly ground white pepper*
*1 tablespoon tarragon, freshly chopped*
*1 teaspoon lemon juice*

---

**1.** Make up the quick béarnaise sauce: select a round-bottomed basin which will sit comfortably over a pan of gently rolling water. The basin should stand proud of the pan rim by about 2 inches so that you can grip it firmly and safely, the bottom of the basin being in contact with the water.

Cut the butter into cubes and, in a small pan and over the lowest heat, let this melt and get hot. It must not brown. Stand the pan at the back of the stove to keep hot.

Whisk yolks, vinegar stock, mustard, salt and pepper together in the basin and place over the boiling water. Have a folded kitchen cloth at the ready to protect your hand when you come to lift the basin out of the pan. Also have some cold water in a large bowl nearby.

Using a small balloon whisk, gently stir the egg mixture over the heat until it thickens. Whisk over the bottom and around the sides of the basin, gradually changing to a figure-of-eight movement with the wrist.

As soon as the sauce starts to thicken and there is a definite trail left by the whisk, lift the basin from the pan and stand it in the cold water for a moment or two, whisking gently all the time to rid the yolk mixture of any residual heat, which might scramble it.

Take the basin from the cold water and stand it on a folded damp dish cloth to hold it firm. Start by whisking in a scant dessertspoon of the hot melted butter. Whisk briefly. Incorporate each addition of butter thoroughly before adding the next.

Add the tarragon. Check the seasoning, adding the lemon juice to 'lift' the flavour and give a slight edge to the sauce.

Stand the finished sauce in a basin over a pan of warm, not boiling, water to keep warm. Remember this is a warm, not a hot sauce.

**2.** Poach or lightly boil the eggs. Cut the avocado pears in half, remove the stone and rub the exposed surface with lemon juice.

**3.** Select a shallow pan just large enough to contain the pears face down. Bring the stock to the boil, together with the juice of half a lemon and pour round the pears in the pan. Heat through over a modest heat (approximately 5 minutes).

**4.** Arrange each pear in an individual dish. If you use lightly boiled eggs (easier), shell them and pop one egg into each stone pit. (The eggs can be boiled or pan-poached earlier in the day and kept in cold water. Warm through in hot, not boiling, chicken stock.) Sprinkle over a little extra lemon juice for astringency and a little freshly milled black pepper.

**5.** Coat with the sauce already made, dredge lightly with the grated Parmesan, glaze lightly under a spanking hot grill and serve immediately with fingers of dry wholemeal toast. Serves 4.

*Oignons monégasques; Avocado Pebble Mill*

# POTTED SMOKED TROUT

---

*8 oz smoked trout, skinned and boned*
*2 oz butter, softened*
*4 oz cream cheese*
*2 tablespoons soured cream or natural*
*yoghurt*
*juice of ½ lemon*
*2–3 dashes of tabasco*
*½ teaspoon ground mace*
*salt and pepper*
*2 oz clarified butter*

---

1. Purée the trout in a blender.
2. Mix in the remaining ingredients except the clarified butter in short, sharp bursts.
3. Spoon into a pretty pot or dish and pour over a film of clarified butter. Leave to set.
4. Take out of the refrigerator at least 1 hour before serving. Serve with hot, dry brown toast. Serves 6.

# POTTED SALMON

You might like to try the original way of potting our king of fish.

---

*1 lb piece of salmon*
*1 level teaspoon mace*
*1 slice of lemon*
*pinch of ground clove*
*¼ teaspoon ground bay leaf, or one*
*bay leaf broken into bits*
*salt and freshly milled white pepper*
*7 oz butter*

---

1. Skin and slice the fish into thinnish pieces. Put into an earthenware pot just large enough to contain it, seasoning well with the herbs and spices as you arrange the pieces, and dispersing 4 oz butter amongst the fish pieces.
2. Put a lid on the pot and stand this in a container of hot water.
3. Bake at Gas Mark 6 (200°C, 400°F) until the fish is cooked (about 45 minutes). Cool completely. Make a purée in a food processor or blender. Pack this purée, having adjusted

the seasoning if necessary, into an attractive china container. Chill well.
4. To clarify butter: put 3 oz butter into a pan and add about ½ pint water. Bring to the boil, leave to cool, then put to set in the refrigerator. Remove the 'set' butter and wipe the underside clean with paper towel. Melt this butter again without it getting too hot. Pour over the chilled salmon purée and return the dish to the refrigerator to set again. Serve like a pâté. Serves 6–8.

# BROCCOLI AND LOBSTER FLAN

---

PASTRY:
*6 oz plain white flour*
*2 oz butter*
*2 oz lard*
*1 level teaspoon salt*
*1 egg yolk beaten with 3 tablespoons*
*iced water*

FILLING:
*12 oz broccoli*
*chicken stock (from a stock cube)*
*juice of ½ lemon*
*3 lobster tails or the equivalent in*
*crayfish or jumbo prawns*
*4 large eggs, beaten*
*salt and freshly milled pepper, plus*
*good pinch of mace*
*12 fl oz single cream*

---

1. Make up the pastry and line a 1½ inch deep flan ring. Bake the flan case blind at Gas Mark 6 (200°C, 400°F) for 15 minutes.
2. Break the broccoli into tiny florets and poach for 1 minute in chicken stock, acidulated with lemon. Drain and cool.
3. Slice the lobster tails into manageable pieces.
4. Season the beaten eggs. Bring the cream to the boil and pour over the eggs, whisking well as you do this. Arrange the lobster tails attractively in the base of the flan. Disperse the broccoli florets amongst the lobster. Pour over the savoury custard.
5. Bake at Gas Mark 3 (170°C, 325°F) for 35 minutes, or until custard is set.
6. Serve hot, warm or cold. Serves 8.

*Potted smoked*
*trout*

# AVOCADO WITH STEM GINGER

*2 large avocados (the Hass variety,*
*if available)*
*juice of 1 large lemon*

DRESSING:
*juice and grated rind of 1 small orange*
*level teaspoon dry mustard*
*¼ teaspoon ground ginger*
*1 teaspoon honey*
*2 tablespoons rich olive oil*
*1 clove garlic, crushed (optional)*
*2 pieces stem ginger, sliced or chopped*

GARNISH:
*1 level tablespoon chopped chives*

1. Make up the dressing a day in advance. One hour before serving, peel and pit the avocados: cut into long slices, toss in lemon juice, cover with plastic film and refrigerate.

2. Arrange the slices in small dishes, spoon over the dressing, sprinkle with chives if available and serve.

3. Alternatively, the avocados can be served simply, cut in half, pitted and the dressing passed in a china boat.

# MUSHROOM CREAMS

*¾ lb tiny white button mushrooms*
*2 oz unsalted butter*
*4 tablespoons brandy or dry madeira*
*¾ pint single cream*
*salt and milled white pepper*
*1 teaspoon gelatine crystals*
*1 teaspoon freshly chopped oregano*
*(or pinch dried)*
*½ pint aspic jelly (commercial variety)*
*¼ pint double cream*

1. Clean and slice the mushrooms. Heat butter till foaming and 'almondy'. Quickly fry mushrooms in batches.

2. Pour over brandy and ignite. When the flames have died down pour in single cream, season lightly. Cook for 1 minute only.

3. Strain. Reserve half the cream. If any butter has risen to the surface of the reserved cream this can readily be removed when the cream is cold and the butter set.

4. Stir gelatine into the other half of the hot brandy/cream in a pan until dissolved. Add oregano. Return mushrooms to the pan. Leave to cool, but not set.

5. Line 4 individual moulds with ⅛ inch aspic jelly. Put to set.

6. Spoon in the mushroom mixture. Put to set. Turn out and serve with the reserved cream mixed with the half-whipped double cream. Makes 4.

# VEGETABLE TARTLETS

CHEESE PASTRY:
*5 oz butter*
*7 oz flour*
*2 oz freshly grated Parmesan cheese*
*2 egg yolks*
*squeeze of lemon juice*

FILLING FOR 6 × ¾ INCH
TARTLETS:
*8 oz carrots*
*8 oz potatoes*
*well-seasoned chicken stock*
*2 tablespoons lemon juice*
*1 oz butter*
*8 oz petits pois*
*1 scant teaspoon sugar*
*salt and milled white pepper*
*¾ pint stiff mayonnaise*

GARNISH:
*extra mayonnaise*
*3 hard-boiled eggs, cut into quarters*
*1 tomato, blanched, seeded and cut*
*into 6 'petals'*
*sprigs of watercress*

1. To make cheese pastry: rub butter into the flour and mix in the cheese. Beat together egg yolks, lemon juice and 2 tablespoons cold water. Stir this mixture into the flour until a dough is formed. Let it relax for an hour. Roll out and line individual tart tins with the pastry. Freeze for 2 hours.

2. Cover pastry with buttered foil pads or paper and dried beans. Bake blind at Gas

Mark 6 (200°C, 400°F) for 15 minutes. Remove foil, continue baking at Gas Mark 4 (180°C, 350°F) until golden brown and crisp. Allow to cool for 2–3 minutes. Remove the pastry shells from their tins and cool completely on a wire rack.

3. To make filling: cut the carrots and potatoes into minute dice. Cook each separately but in the same chicken stock for no more than 2–3 minutes. The vegetables must still be quite crisp in texture.

4. Drain well and, while still hot, toss each in a tablespoon of lemon juice. Cool. Melt the butter in a small pan, add the frozen peas, sugar and a seasoning of salt and pepper. Toss the peas over a low heat to defrost, and simmer for 2 minutes. Drain and cool.

5. Mix the three vegetables together before binding with the mayonnaise. Pile into the cheese pastry shells. Decorate with extra swirls of mayonnaise, wedges of egg, tomato petals and bunches of watercress. Serves 6.

6. Variations: any combination of vegetables can be used. Try adding diced peppers, cucumber or minute cauliflower florets. Tiny cubes of ham or salami, flaked smoked fish, shrimp and poached mussels can all 'extend' these tartlets, elevating them to a grander position in the menu.

## SMOKED SALMON ICE

½ lb smoked salmon
1 lb tomatoes, skinned and seeded
juice of ½ lemon
2–3 dashes tabasco sauce
teaspoon gelatine crystals dissolved
in 1 tablespoon boiling water
milled white pepper and salt

TO GARNISH:
½ lb tomatoes, skinned and seeded
1 cucumber, peeled and seeded
striplets of smoked salmon

1. Make a purée of the smoked salmon and the tomatoes in a blender, adding the rest of the ingredients as you go along. Go sparingly on the salt.

2. Allow the gelatine to cool before adding to the purée; push through a fine sieve.

3. Freeze the mixture in a domestic ice-cream maker or put it in a plastic bowl in the freezer compartment of your refrigerator or deep freezer. Stir the mixture every half hour until a 'soft set' has been achieved.

4. To serve: using a melon baller or large teaspoon dipped into boiling water scoop the ice into chilled glasses. Decorate with tomato and cucumber balls and rolls of salmon. Serve with crisp brown toast and lemon butter.

5. To make tomato balls: cut tomatoes in half downwards, and remove stalks. Cut away hard core. Place each half in the corner of a clean cloth; gather the fabric and twist the tomato into a tight compact ball about ¾ inch diameter. Sprinkle with salt, pepper and lemon juice before garnishing the ice.

## OIGNONS MONÉGASQUES (SWEET AND SOUR ONIONS)

See photograph on page 51.

1 lb tiny pickling onions
4 fl oz red wine vinegar
4 fl oz olive oil
3 oz tomato purée
2 bay leaves
½ teaspoon dried thyme
parsley stalks (optional)
6 oz seedless raisins or sultanas
1 oz brown sugar
salt
freshly milled pepper
fresh basil (optional garnish)

1. Peel the onions and put in a pan with all the remaining ingredients and 6 fl oz water. Cover, bring to the boil and simmer for 15–20 minutes, until the onions are tender but not collapsed. If the sauce is not thick enough remove the onions with a draining spoon and boil the sauce rapidly until it is viscous. Cool, chill in the refrigerator.

2. Serve in individual ramekins or glasses with a small wedge of lemon and French bread and butter. If, in the summer months, you have some fresh basil, use a little chopped and sprinkled over the onions. Serves 6–8.

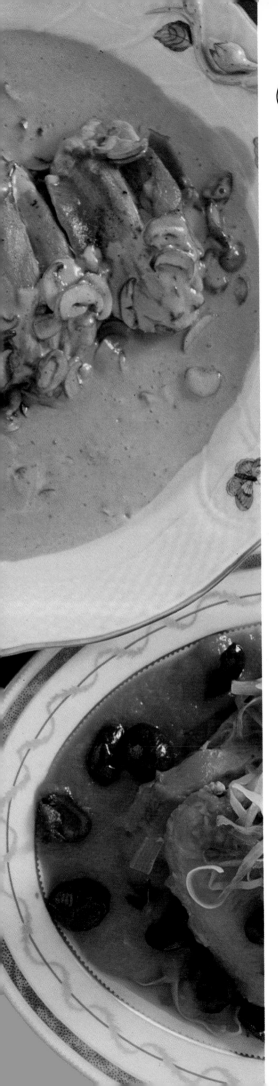

# Main Course

Entertaining habits have changed so much over the last ten years that it is now possible to serve almost any type of dish as a main course. Whereas, at one time, only a roast, game or poultry would have been considered acceptable, today fish, a handsome vol au vent, a ragoût – even a pasta or a home-made savoury pie – are welcomed.

At lunchtime, or for a summer supper served in the garden, the best main dishes can often be found in the first course section. An elaborate salad, served in generous portions, will be just as acceptable in its new place at the heart of the meal. For many people, especially the figure-conscious, a light main course is a welcome respite from heavy meat dishes; terrines, quiches and other such delicacies, often seen only in small quantities as an hors d'oeuvre, can be appreciated in full.

While breaks with tradition are fine and stimulating, what we must not forget is that for a lot of people cooking is a pleasure and dinner party-giving a highlight in their social life. It is the host – who enjoys giving a great deal of consideration to a meal as a whole, its content and presentation – who appreciates the importance of those last small details: the fragrant flower arrangement, the clutch of candles casting a soft glow over shimmering glass and silver. This book is really to be seen as an aid towards this sentiment.

So, whichever dish you choose to serve as a main course, and the variety is wide, think about its presentation. Be bold. Dress up a simple dish of lasagne with an under-plate decorated cheerfully with a colourful napkin. Pop two or three flowers alongside the vegetable or salad. The element of surprise can come anywhere provided it is striking enough to make an impression.

Select recipes which you know you can tackle without too much trepidation. A calm hostess is important, and your confidence *will* grow as your expertise increases. Remember, you still have the third act, the pudding, to come. But I suspect you will be preoccupied with this section for a while. I hope so.

Top row: *Mange-tout peas; Lapin aux deux moutardes;* bottom row: *(Fried rabbit); Sauce maltaise*

# Poultry and Game

## GLAZED POUSSINS WITH BEAUMES DE VENISE

*8 poussins*
*½ bottle Beaumes de Venise*
*4 oz pine kernels, browned in*
*1 oz butter*
*12 oz seedless grapes or skinned and*
*pipped larger grapes*

PASTE:
*6 oz butter*
*2 teaspoons celery seeds*
*4 teaspoons sesame seeds*
*1 tablespoon green cardamoms, crushed*
*2 cloves garlic, crushed*
*1 heaped teaspoon salt*
*milled pepper*

**1.** Make a paste with the listed ingredients and spread this over and inside the poussins. Truss the birds and roast at Gas Mark 7 (220°C, 425°F) for 45 minutes; remove them to a warm serving dish. Allow the pan juices to settle and pour away any excess fat.

**2.** Pour in the wine and reduce, by boiling rapidly, to ¼ pint. Spoon a little of this glaze over each bird. Sprinkle over some of the pine kernels and grapes and serve the rest in the sauce separately. It is a good idea to hand finger bowls to guests as you need to use your hands when eating poussins. Serves 8.

## BREASTS OF CHICKEN FLORENTINE

See photograph on page 60.

*1½ lb leaf spinach*
*salt*
*ground nutmeg*
*2 oz butter*
*4 chicken breasts*
*milled pepper*
*½ pint single cream*
*1 level teaspoon mild French mustard*
*4 oz Dutch cheese, coarsely grated*
*2 egg yolks*
*1 oz freshly grated Parmesan cheese*

**1.** Pick over and de-vein the spinach. Wash in plenty of cold water. Drain.

**2.** Bring to the boil ½ inch salted water in a large pan. Pack the spinach in and cover with a lid. Boil over a high heat for 3 minutes, shaking the pan two or three times. Drain the spinach well. Chop roughly. Press away any surplus liquid. Season with salt, a pinch or two of ground nutmeg and a good 1 oz butter. Arrange the spinach in the bottom of a warm fireproof dish and keep warm.

**3.** To cook the chicken breasts: cut the breasts away from the rib-cage but leave the wing-bone intact if possible.

**4.** Melt 1 oz butter in a sauté pan until an

*Glazed poussins with Beaumes de Venise*

even light brown and foaming. Brown the chicken on both sides.

**5.** Season fairly liberally, with salt, pepper and nutmeg, pour over all but 2 tablespoons of the cream, reduce the heat and simmer the chicken for 5–6 minutes, turning at half time. Remove the breasts and place on top of the spinach. Put to keep warm.

**6.** Boil the cream rapidly for ½ minute. Whisk in the mustard. Stir in the grated cheese. Simmer until the cheese has melted.

**7.** Mix the egg yolks with the remaining 2 tablespoons cream. Remove the cheese sauce from the heat. Whisk in the egg and cream liaison. Strain over the chicken breasts. Sprinkle with the Parmesan cheese. Glaze until golden under a hot grill. Serves 4.

# CHICKEN AND LEEK PIE

*4 oz shortcrust pastry*
*4 oz puff pastry*
*8 leeks, washed, trimmed and*
*finely sliced*
*3–4 oz butter*
*salt and pepper*
*2 chicken breasts, about 12 oz in all*
*½ teaspoon ground mace*
*1 dessertspoon soy sauce (optional)*
*1 egg, beaten*

THICK WHITE SAUCE:
*1 oz flour*
*1 oz butter*
*½ pint milk infused with a piece of*
*onion, bay leaf and sprig of thyme*

**1.** Butter a lipped 9–10 inch diameter, 1½ inch deep, loose-bottomed tin and line with the shortcrust pastry. Bake blind. Roll out puff pastry and cut a lid to fit.

**2.** Make up ½ pint thick white sauce: melt the butter, stir in the flour and gradually add the milk after infusing it with onion, bay leaf and thyme for 30 minutes over a low heat.

**3.** Soften the sliced leeks in 2 oz butter in a lidded pan, stirring occasionally. Check seasoning and set aside.

**4.** Cut the chicken breasts into ½ inch cubes. Season with salt and mace.

*Breasts of chicken florentine*

**5.** Melt 1 oz butter in a large frying pan until it is lightly browned and foaming. Fry the chicken in two batches for a couple of minutes only. Add extra butter if necessary. Bring the fried chicken together, splash over the soy sauce and mix well, coating each bit lightly. Remove with a slotted spoon.

**6.** Mix the leeks with the white sauce. Mix in the chicken cubes, fill into the pie case and wet the edges. Fit the pastry lid. Brush with beaten egg, and decorate as desired. Bake at Gas Mark 7 (220°C, 425°F) for 30 minutes until the pastry is puffed up, crisp and golden brown. Serve hot or cold. Serves 5–6.

# MINI CHICKEN AND APRICOT KEBABS

*2 large chicken breasts*
*4 apricots (fresh, tinned or*
*reconstituted dried)*
*2 small onions, quartered*

MARINADE:
*2 tablespoons olive oil*
*1 tablespoon medium dry sherry*
*1 tablespoon soy sauce*
*1 level teaspoon ground mace*
*1 level teaspoon ground ginger*
*finely grated rind and juice of 1 small*
*orange*
*salt*

**1.** Combine all the ingredients for the marinade in a glass or china bowl.

**2.** Cut each chicken breast into 8–10 pieces. Quarter the apricots. Split the onion quarters into 'leaves'. Marinate all these for up to 4 hours.

**3.** Spike alternative items on to 6–8 slim wooden skewers. Protect the tips from burning by wrapping with foil if necessary. Grill for 3–4 minutes under a hot grill, turning them halfway through. Serves 3–4.

For Mini Brochettes of Scallops, Bacon and Pear, toss 4 scallops and a pear, all cut into equal pieces, in oil and lemon juice. Thread on a skewer with 4 rashers of streaky bacon cut into pieces and grill for 4–5 minutes, turning.

# CHICKEN VOL AU VENT WITH ASPARAGUS AND OYSTER MUSHROOMS

*2 large (12 oz) packets of frozen*
*puff pastry*
*beaten egg*
*1 × 4 lb chicken*
*8 oz oyster mushrooms or ordinary*
*large, quartered white caps*

STOCK:
*2 sticks celery*
*2 carrots, cleaned and cut into pieces*
*2 leeks, trimmed and cleaned*
*1 onion, peeled*
*6 peppercorns*
*a good sprig of thyme*
*1 fresh bay leaf*
*a little salt*
*¼ pint dry white wine*

SAUCE:
*2 oz butter*
*1½ oz plain white flour*
*¾ pint chicken stock (see above)*
*6 fl oz single cream*
*5 fl oz amontillado sherry*
*salt if necessary*

GARNISH:
*12 spears of fresh asparagus, cooked*

1. Leave the pastry to thaw. On a well-floured surface, very carefully and *evenly*, roll each block of pastry into equal-sized rectangles, approximately 10 × 6 inches. Place the first rectangle on a wetted baking sheet. Brush all over with beaten egg, taking care to avoid any egg getting on the sides as this will inhibit the rising of the pastry.

2. Cut an oblong piece out of the second rolled block of pastry, leaving a border about 1 inch wide. Carefully lift this border and lay it on the egg-washed pastry on the baking tray. Brush the top surface of this with egg. Bake the oblong piece of pastry that was cut from the centre, at the side of this large vol au vent. Bake in a preheated oven, Gas Mark 8 (230°C, 450°F) for 20 minutes. Lower the temperature to Gas 6 (200°C, 400°F) and bake for a further 20 minutes. Remove from the oven and carefully cut and scrape away any risen pastry in the central oblong hole. Return the shell to the oven to get crisp right through. The 'lid' should be OK.

If your particular oven starts to scorch pastry, you must obviously lower the temperature accordingly, but *do* ensure the pastry is crisp and cooked right through. It should be quite brittle. Don't worry if it isn't evenly risen: it will still taste good.

3. For the filling: make up the stock and cook the whole chicken, following the recipe for Chicken Creams with Tarragon (see page 71). Remove the flesh from the bird and cut into bite-sized pieces. Put to keep warm in a lidded casserole at Gas Mark ½ (130°C, 250°F). Make up the sauce as instructed on page 71, omitting the tarragon. Add the oyster mushrooms at the same time as the cream and sherry.

4. Put most of the chicken into the centre of the vol au vent. Spoon over the sauce and add a few asparagus spears for garnish. Cut the vol au vent into 4 or 6 portions. Serve any remaining chicken in the sauce separately. (A rectangular vol au vent is the simplest to make but, if you wish, you can make it oval-shaped, as shown opposite, or round.) Serves 4–6.

# CHAFING DISH CREAM-CURRIED CHICKEN BREASTS

*6 chicken supremes (breasts), skinned,*
*boned and cut into small strips*
*2 oz butter*
*1 teaspoon mild curry powder*
*1 clove garlic, crushed*
*salt and milled pepper*
*finely shredded zest of 1 orange*
*·2 fl oz whisky*
*¼ pint double cream*
*2 oranges, peeled, pith removed*
*and segmented*

1. Melt the butter until it is foaming and quiet.

*Chicken vol au vent with asparagus and oyster mushrooms*

**2.** Fry the chicken striplets in one batch. Sprinkle with the curry powder and stir well in. Add the crushed garlic. Season well with salt and pepper. Add the shredded orange zest to the mixture.

**3.** Pour over the whisky (this may not ignite due to an excess of juices – it *will* over a high heat). Stir in the cream. Bubble for 5 minutes, until the sauce has cohered.

**4.** Serve the chicken striplets garnished with the orange segments with rice, noodle twists, or on slices of hot, crisp buttered toast.

**5.** If the sauce 'oils' (which will depend very much on the fat content of your cream – this varies from dairy to dairy), add a squeeze or two of orange juice. Serves 4–5.

# CHICKEN, NOODLE AND MELON SALAD WITH PEANUT CREAM SAUCE

*1 × 4–5 lb capon or chicken*
*1 leek*
*1 carrot*
*1 onion*
*1 bay leaf, sprig of thyme, 12 black peppercorns, 12 coriander seeds tied in a piece of muslin*
*½ lemon*
*12 oz Chinese noodles or vermicelli*
*chicken stock or water (see step 4)*
*salt*
*2 tablespoons peanut or other ground nut oil*
*1 small charentais melon*
*1 small ogen melon*

PEANUT DRESSING:
*½ jar smooth peanut butter*
*⅓ cup chicken stock (see step 2)*
*2 tablespoons soy sauce*
*2 cloves garlic, crushed*
*2 × 1 inch pieces ginger root, grated*
*1 tablespoon caster sugar*
*1 tablespoon lemon juice*
*2 dashes tabasco sauce*
*½ pint single cream*
*spring onions for garnish (optional)*

*Chicken, noodle and melon salad with peanut cream sauce*

1. Wash and rinse the capon under cold running water. Bring the vegetables and spices and herbs to the boil in a large pan with 2 pints water. Reduce the heat and simmer for 15 minutes. Put in the capon and make sure the thighs are just covered with liquid. Simmer the bird until the thighs are just tender, about 50 minutes to an hour.

2. Remove the bird to cool. Strain the stock into a second pan reserving a pint. Boil the rest rapidly to reduce to about a teacup. Cool and retain for the peanut sauce.

3. Before the capon is entirely cold, strip the meat from the carcass and either cut into bite-sized pieces or carve into slices, depending on whether you are standing or sitting to eat this dish (a fork lunch or a seated supper).

4. Boil the noodles or vermicelli for 7–8 minutes, or for the time given on the packet, in chicken stock. Use that left over from cooking the capon or make some up with a cube. Salt sparingly. Drain and turn into a bowl, stir in a couple of tablespoons of peanut oil and leave to cool.

5. Knife-peel the melons, seed them and cut into neat pieces.

6. Using a blender, or food processor fitted with the plastic blade, blend together all the dressing ingredients except the cream. Scrape the mixture out of the blender and stir in the cream to form a dressing.

7. To assemble the salad: arrange the cold noodles on a large platter. Lay the capon and melon on top, dribble over a little of the sauce and serve the rest in a sauceboat. Garnish with strips of spring onion if wished. Serves 6–8.

# TANDOORI-STYLE CHICKEN

Strictly speaking, this Indian way of cooking chicken should be in a *tandoor*, a special clay oven that was at one time peculiar to the north-west frontier but is universally popular today. Also, small whole birds are considered the proper thing to use. However, since it is so good and simple to do, I have adapted a traditional recipe for regular household use, using an ordinary domestic grill. Of course, in the summer Tandoori-style Chicken is ideal for outside barbecuing, where the aroma of meat cooking makes a mouthwatering prelude to its delicious spicy flavour. The only ingredient I haven't included is fine weather.

---

*4 large whole chicken breasts*

MARINADE:
*1 onion, chopped roughly*
*3 cloves garlic, crushed*
*1 small carton yoghurt*
*2 tablespoons lemon juice*
*4 tablespoons olive oil*
*1 teaspoon salt*
*½ teaspoon milled or cracked pepper*
*1 level teaspoon ground ginger*
*1 teaspoon turmeric*
*½ teaspoon mace or ¼ teaspoon nutmeg*
*1 heaped teaspoon ground coriander*
*1 teaspoon mild paprika*
*¼ teaspoon cayenne (hot) or 2 good dashes tabasco*
*1 level teaspoon garam masala*
*¼ teaspoon ground cinnamon*
*orange, or a mixture of red and yellow colouring (optional)*
*halved lemons for serving*

---

1. Start the day before you want to serve the chicken. Whether or not you remove the chicken skins is up to you, but leave in the rib-cage bones. Trim or snip off the wings as they get in the way when using a domestic grill. Make three or four deep incisions in the flesh, cutting diagonally across each breast to allow the marinade to get right into the flesh, and also to speed up the cooking process without drying out the meat.

2. Mix together all the ingredients for the marinade in a shallow dish and marinate the chicken overnight.

3. Preheat the grill to spanking hot. Brush the rack or pan with oil and the chicken pieces with the marinade and place on the bars. Grill at a good heat for 5 to 6 minutes on each side. Lower the grill pan or, if outside, lift it a notch or two away from the heat source. Continue cooking for a further 10 to 12 minutes on each side, turning *frequently* and basting with a little of the marinade.

4. It is almost impossible to give even a nearly accurate cooking time as grills and

*Tandoori-style chicken*

barbecues vary so much in structure. If in doubt, use a sharp knife and cut into the *thick* part of the flesh and have a peek. Remember that chicken legs if used take longer than breasts. Serves 4.

# GINGERED CHICKEN WITH HONEYED ALMONDS AND RASPBERRIES

Inventing dishes is one of the nicest parts of the cook's game. The idea of putting the raspberries actually into the sauce in this recipe came after Michael Boys and I had finished the photograph. It is a vast improvement on my original concept, and for most, who enjoy the sweet and sour marriage, will become a winner, I'm sure.

This dish is delicious served cold. In which case, stir an extra ⅛ pint double cream into the sauce when it is cold.

---

*4 oz amamiele or whole, blanched almonds, honeyed (see method)*
*3 oz butter*
*2 teaspoons ground ginger*
*1 teaspoon salt*
*1 clove garlic, crushed (optional)*
*1 × 4 lb roasting chicken*

SAUCE:
*1 level teaspoon plain flour*
*1 sherry glass Amaretto liqueur (or amontillado sherry – different, but an option)*
*juice of ½ lemon*
*2 tablespoons raspberry vinegar*
*⅓ pint double cream (6 fl oz)*
*2 × 4 oz punnets raspberries (or the equivalent in unsugared frozen raspberries)*
*salt*
*chicken stock or water*

---

**1.** You can sometimes buy amamiele (honeyed almonds) in specialist food shops – they are delicious eaten with cream cheese and toast or crackers. If not, substitute whole blanched almonds bathed in a little honey. To make amamiele: wash whole almonds. Put into a jar, pour over hot honey. Cool and seal. Store for 6 months or longer.

**2.** Make a paste of the butter, ginger, salt and garlic. Put a good knob of this inside the chicken, rubbing it well into the cavity. Spread the rest over the chicken breasts and legs. Roast at Gas Mark 5/6 (190/200°C, 375/400°F) for about an hour, or until cooked. Remove the chicken to a warm serving dish. Let the pan juices settle.

**3.** Pour away all but a tablespoon of the fat, but take care to retain the juices and sediments.

**4.** Stand the roasting pan over a low heat and, using a wooden spatula, work in the modest amount of flour, letting it take on a good tan colour. Pour in the liqueur, lemon juice and vinegar. Give it a gentle bubble for a minute or two.

**5.** Pour in the cream and one punnet of raspberries. Cook until pulped. Check seasoning. Press through a fine sieve (not a blender or food processor as this produces too foamy a consistency). If the resulting sauce looks a little oily, whisk in a good tablespoon of chicken stock or water.

**6.** Reheat and quarter the chicken (or leave whole and carve in the usual way). Pour over the sauce, garnish with the remaining raspberries (cold) and honeyed almonds. Serve with buttered noodles. Serves 4.

# CHICKEN, WALNUT AND PINEAPPLE MAYONNAISE

---

*2 chicken breasts, cooked*
*1 small pineapple*
*a squeeze of lemon juice*
*salt*
*milled pepper*
*3 oz walnut halves*
*3 good tablespoons rich home-made mayonnaise*
*a little cream*

---

**1.** Slice the chicken breasts. Using a grapefruit knife, carefully cut out the pine-

*Gingered chicken with honeyed almonds and raspberries*

apple flesh in one piece. Cut this in half. Core and quarter the halves before cutting into smaller pieces.

2. Season the pineapple pieces with a squeeze of lemon juice, salt and milled pepper. Reserve some pieces as a garnish and toss the rest with the walnuts and chicken. Mix the mayonnaise with a little cream and fold in the chicken, fruit and nut mixture.

3. Pile back into the empty pineapple shell, garnish with the reserved pineapple and chill.

4. Serve as a first course or as a summer main course with a tossed salad of lettuce, radicchio and curly endive dressed with lemon juice and walnut oil. Serves 4.

# CHICKEN CREAMS WITH TARRAGON

The breasts of chicken will be used for this recipe and the legs and carcass are needed for the sauce. The cooked leg meat, which is not used, can be served in a chicken mayonnaise or salad.

---

*1 × 4 lb fresh chicken*
*2 eggs*
*1 bunch freshly picked tarragon*
*10 fl oz double cream, chilled*
*salt and freshly milled white pepper*

STOCK:
*2 sticks celery*
*2 carrots, cleaned and cut into pieces*
*2 leeks, trimmed and cleaned*
*1 onion, peeled*
*6 peppercorns*
*a good sprig of thyme*
*1 fresh bay leaf*
*a little salt*
*¼ pint dry white wine*

SAUCE:
*2 oz butter*
*1½ oz plain white flour*
*¾ pint chicken stock (see above)*
*6 fl oz single cream*
*5 fl oz amontillado sherry*
*2 tablespoons freshly chopped tarragon*
*salt if necessary*

*Chicken creams*
*with tarragon*

1. First make the stock, either early in the day or the previous day. Remove the breasts from the chicken. Put the carcass and legs into a pan with the listed ingredients and enough cold water to cover (at least 2–2½ pints). Bring to the boil, take off any scum, and simmer the chicken until the legs are tender (about 45 minutes). Remove the legs (not needed in this recipe) and continue simmering the stock for another hour.

2. Strain the stock into a clean pan through a sieve lined with a clean handkerchief or kitchen paper. Let this stand until the fats have risen to the surface. Skim off the fat layer and discard. Now reduce the stock to ¾ pint by boiling.

3. Meanwhile, remove the skin from the raw chicken breasts. Cut the flesh into pieces and weigh out 10 oz. Put through a food processor or blender, using the eggs as the liquid to achieve a very fine purée. (If you have the energy, press this purée through a wire sieve – this is a refinement and is not essential.) Put this purée into a large bowl and chill in the refrigerator for 2 hours until quite cold.

4. To make the sauce: melt the butter without browning. Stir in the flour. Add the stock, bring to the boil, lower the heat and simmer for 5 minutes. Add the cream and sherry and continue simmering for a further 20 minutes. If the sauce looks 'oily' towards the end of the cooking time, add a spoonful of hot water and whisk in to restore the consistency. Strain and stir in 2 tablespoons of freshly chopped tarragon, but reserve enough tarragon to decorate each ramekin. Check the seasoning and add salt if necessary.

5. To make the chicken creams: butter 6–8 ramekins well and place a good sprig of tarragon in the bottom of each. Remove the chilled chicken purée from the refrigerator. Add the double cream a little at a time, beating well to maintain a good thick consistency. Divide the mixture between the ramekins. Level the tops. Stand these in a roasting tin of hot water (bain marie) and cook at Gas Mark 6 (200°C, 400°F) for 30 minutes. Turn out on to a clean cloth to absorb any surplus juices. Quickly move each mousse to a warm plate, coat with the sauce and serve immediately. Enough for 6 medium-sized (3 inch) ramekins or 8 smaller.

# CHICKEN, APPLE AND WALNUT MAYONNAISE

*1 × 4–5 lb capon or chicken*
*½ pint French dressing*
*3 red-skinned apples*
*juice of 1 lemon*
*6 oz walnut halves, roughly crushed*
*¾ pint mayonnaise (home-made or bought)*

STOCK:
*2 carrots, cleaned and cut*
*into pieces*
*2 sticks celery*
*1 onion, peeled*
*1 bouquet garni*
*salt as necessary*

GARNISH:
*stuffed eggs (see Simple Stuffed*
*Egg recipe on page 43)*
*2 oz walnut halves*
*freshly chopped parsley*
*cress*

1. First cook the bird, either early in the day or the previous day. Try to avoid over refrigerating it once cooked as this does tend to dry out the meat. Unless the weather is exceptionally hot, it can be left covered in a cool larder, overnight.

2. Put the bird in a pan with the stock ingredients and enough cold water to cover (at least 2 pints). Bring to the boil, take off any scum and simmer for about 1–1½ hours.

3. Leave to cool, then skin, bone and cut the meat into bite-size pieces. Splash with Fresh dressing before it is completely cold.

4. Quarter and core the apples but do not peel them. Cut into small pieces. Toss in lemon juice to prevent discolouring. Mix with the chicken and crushed walnuts.

5. Bind the chicken, apple and nut mixture with the mayonnaise. If home-made mayonnaise is too stiff, whisk in a spoon or two of water before adding to chicken.

6. Pile the mixture into serving dishes and garnish. Serves 8.

# OLD ENGLISH DUCK PIE WITH FORCEMEAT BALLS AND CHESTNUTS

Have your poulterer cut the duck into eight pieces, removing excess carcass bones for stock for soup.

*1 × 4 lb duck*
*oil for frying*
*1 teaspoon flour*
*8 oz bacon, cut into sticks*
*1 onion, chopped*
*8 oz oyster or field mushrooms, quartered*
*rind and juice of 1 orange*
*½ bottle red wine*
*½ tin plus, duck or game consommé*
*salt and pepper*
*1 sprig or 1 teaspoon dried sage*
*1 sprig or 1 teaspoon dried thyme*
*1 clove garlic, crushed*
*1 × 1 oz tin chestnuts in brine or fresh*
*roasted chestnuts*
*1 × 12 oz packet flaky pastry, or 12 oz*
*home-made rough puff or shortcrust pastry*

FORCEMEAT BALLS:
*6 oz lean pork or veal, cut up*
*4 oz pork fat, cut up*
*the duck's liver, diced*
*1 level teaspoon nutmeg*
*2 tablespoons medium sherry*
*1 egg, beaten*
*2 teaspoons salt*

1. To make the forcemeat balls: put the pork and fat twice through the fine blade of a mincer.

2. Mix in the rest of the ingredients. This can be done in a food processor, mixing in the duck liver last to retain texture.

3. Form into 12–14 small flattish balls or 'cakes'. Brown quickly in a little smoking oil. Set aside.

4. Brown the duck pieces a few at a time in a very little smoking oil. Transfer to an ovenproof dish. Sprinkle over the flour. Mix in well.

5. In the pan oils, brown the bacon sticks, onion and mushrooms. Add to the ovenproof

*Old English duck pie with forcement balls and chestnuts*

pot using a draining spoon. Add the orange rind and juice, red wine and enough consommé just to cover. Add salt, pepper, the herbs and garlic. Fit the lid.

**6.** Cook in the oven at Gas Mark 6 (200°C, 400°F) for 45 minutes. Remove the duck pieces to a deep pie dish (about 10 × 7 × 4 inches). For those who don't like the rich duck skin, this can be taken off now. Disperse the chestnuts and forcemeat balls amongst the duck pieces. Skim excess fat from the sauce and pour over the contents of the pie dish. Leave it to cool.

**7.** While the duck filling is cooling, roll out the pastry and rim the pie dish. Cut a lid and fit with any decorations such as circles, leaves, etc. Brush the pie all over with beaten egg before baking at Gas Mark 8 (230°C, 450°F) for 15 minutes, then at Gas Mark 4 (180°C, 350°F) for a further 45 minutes. Serves 5–6.

# COLD PÂTÉ-STUFFED DUCK

This rich way of preparing cold duck is popular in Denmark which is where I originally came across it many moons ago. There it forms part of their famous *koldbord* or cold table. I suggest you serve it as a first course, with slivers of bresaola, smoked loin of pork, smoked chicken or goose. Parma ham, even silverside or pastrami, could be part of the medley.

---

*1 cold roast duck*

FILLING:
*1 × 12 oz tin Swiss Parfait*
*6 oz unsalted butter*
*1 level teaspoon nutmeg*
*1 level teaspoon black pepper*
*squeeze of lemon juice*
*3 tablespoons whisky or rum*

---

**1.** Cut the breasts off the duck by cutting down either side of the breast bone, following the wishbone round. Carefully lift each breast away, cutting where it adheres to the carcass. Lay the breasts side by side on a

*Cold pâté-stuffed duck*

cutting board and, holding the knife at an angle of 45 degrees, cut diagonal pieces ½ inch thick. You should get 7–8 slices from each side.

**2.** Combine the pâté ingredients and fill a piping bag fitted with a rose tube with half the mixture. Spread the remaining pâté on the bared breast and lay it back where it came from! Finally, pipe a column of rich pâté down the centre of the breasts, using any left over as you please. Serves 8 as a first course, 4 as a main course.

# WILD DUCK STUFFED WITH CRANBERRIES AND CELERY

---

*1 brace wild duck*

STUFFING:
*2 oz butter*
*2 rashers bacon, chopped*
*1 small onion, chopped*
*4 sticks celery, chopped*
*1 (8 oz) packet cranberries*
*1 teaspoon grated orange rind*
*1 level teaspoon salt*
*milled black pepper*
*½ teaspoon ground rosemary*

PASTE:
*4 oz butter*
*grated rind of 1 orange*
*1 level teaspoon ground thyme*
*1 level teaspoon ground rosemary*
*salt and milled pepper*
*1 clove garlic, crushed*

GRAVY:
*½ chicken stock cube*
*small glass of red wine*
*sherry glass of port*
*juice of 1 orange*

---

**1.** To make the stuffing: melt the butter in a skillet and fry the bacon until it begins to crisp. Remove to a plate with a slotted spoon while you fry the onion and celery in the pan residues over a low heat until softened. Add the cranberries and seasonings and turn these over a moderate heat until the berries plump

up but don't actually burst. Leave this to cool before filling into the wild ducks.

**2.** Make a paste with the listed ingredients and rub this well into the skin of the duck. Stand the birds on a rack in a roasting tin and roast at Gas Mark 8 (230°C, 450°F) for 50 minutes basting the birds at 10-minute intervals. The meat should still be pink and somewhat bloody.

**3.** To make a little gravy for the ducks: remove the ducks to a warm serving dish. Crumble the stock cube into the residue in the roasting tin, add a small glass of red wine, a sherry glass of port and the juice of an orange. Simmer for 2–3 minutes, strain into a small pan, leave to settle, skim off any excess fats, return the sauce to the boil, check the seasoning and pour into a warm sauce boat.

**4.** The ducks can be served cut in half or carved. Serves 4.

# MARINATED BREASTS OF DUCK WITH STIR-FRIED VEGETABLES

I hasten to say that this dish is by no means authentic Chinese cookery! But none the less, it is very good. Serve as part of a Chinese meal.

*2 duck breasts (from a 3–4 lb duck)*
*1 red pepper, seeded*
*1 green pepper, seeded*
*1 bunch spring onions*
*2 tablespoons soy, arachide or other nut oil*
*2 pieces stem ginger, sliced*
*4 oz brown rice, cooked as instructed on the packet, but in chicken stock using a stock cube*

MARINADE:
*2 cloves garlic, crushed*
*2 tablespoons soy sauce*
*2 tablespoons Jamaica rum*
*2 teaspoons paprika*
*2 teaspoons salt*
*3–4 dashes tabasco*
*¼ teaspoon ground nutmeg*

*Marinated breasts of duck with stir-fried vegetables*

1. Mix all the ingredients for the marinade together in a china or glass pie dish. Cut the breasts into ½ inch diagonal strips, and marinate for 24 hours, covered with clingfilm. (The duck legs can be grilled for another meal or cooked in a cook-in-one sauce!)

2. Cut the peppers and onions into 1 × ¼ inch strips.

3. If you possess a wok then use it: if not, use a large heavy-based frying pan. Heat 2 tablespoons oil until it is smoking heavily and the heat is quite searing. Toss the marinated duck – allowing whatever marinade clings to it to do so – in the smoking oil for a minute or two; longer if you like the duck crispy and well-cooked.

4. Add the ginger and put duck on one side. Repeat the process, tossing the vegetables around for a minute or two, and add the rice, tossing this around until it is hot through. Add a couple of spoonfuls of the remaining marinade, and stir well in while the rice is heating.

5. Pile the rice mixture into Chinese bowls and arrange the duck pieces on top. Serves 3–4.

# A GOOD DUCK GRAVY

*1 teaspoon plain flour*
*4 fl oz amontillado sherry*
*½ chicken stock cube*

1. Carefully decant away all excess fats from the roasting pan, holding back any dark juices and residues. Sprinkle over the flour and work this in well, using a straight-edged wooden spatula. Place the pan over a medium heat and let everything brown a little more if the vegetable mixture (see next recipe) is not already well browned.

2. Pour in the amontillado sherry. Crumble in half a chicken stock cube, then add ¾ pint cold water. Bring everything to the boil, lower the heat and simmer for 30 minutes.

3. Strain everything through a fine-meshed strainer into a small pan.

4. Reduce this gravy or sauce to ½ pint by boiling rapidly. It will now be shiny or glossy and, hey presto! you'll have the best and brightest duck gravy in the land.

# ROAST DUCKLING WITH WALNUT, APRICOT AND RAISIN STUFFING

The texture of this recipe can be changed – rougher or smoother – by adjusting the texture of the walnuts. If you like them crunchy, halve the quantity of juice. This quantity of stuffing is enough for 2 small ducklings or 1 large duck.

*1 carrot, cleaned and sliced*
*1 celery stick, sliced*
*1 leek, washed and sliced*
*½ onion, quartered*
*1 teaspoon tomato purée*
*1 large duck*

STUFFING:
*1 onion, chopped*
*½ small head of celery, knife-shredded*
*2 oz butter*
*6 oz walnuts, pulverized or roughly crushed*
*6 oz dried apricots, diced*
*1 clove garlic, crushed*
*4 oz seedless raisins, whole*
*1 level teaspoon salt*
*1 level teaspoon black pepper*
*grated rind and juice of 1 orange*
*grated rind and juice of 1 small lemon*

1. To make the stuffing: soften the onion and celery in the butter in a pan over a low heat. Cool. Combine all the ingredients and pack into the duck or duckling.

2. Put all the vegetables into a roasting tin, add the tomato purée and sit the duck on top. Roast at Gas Mark 6 (200°C, 400°F) for 30 minutes and then at Gas Mark 5 (190°C, 375°F) for an hour or until cooked. Test by piercing under the leg – the juices should run clear. Leave to rest on a hot serving dish for 20 minutes while you make the gravy. Serves 4.

*Roast duckling with walnut, apricot and raisin stuffing*

# ROAST GROUSE

*2 brace of grouse*
*1 onion, quartered*

PASTE:
*1 level teaspoon ground bay*
*4 oz softened butter*
*1 level teaspoon salt*
*1 level teaspoon ground thyme or large*
*sprig fresh thyme, chopped*
*1 tablespoon brandy*

*4 rashers fat bacon*
*4 oz butter*

GRAVY:
*giblets from the grouse*
*1 teaspoon white flour*
*sherry glass of brandy*
*wine glass of red wine*
*¾ pint light chicken stock (use half*
*a stock cube)*
*gravy browning*

**1.** Preheat the oven to Gas Mark 9, yes 9! (240°C, 475°F).

**2.** Make a paste of the listed ingredients and rub this all over the birds, leaving about a teaspoonful to go inside them with the piece of onion and a little extra bay and thyme. Wrap a rasher of bacon over the breasts, and tie down with linen thread.

**3.** In an iron skillet, or some other receptacle which will go into the oven as well as on top, melt a further 4 oz butter until foaming and giving off an almond smell.

**4.** Brown each bird on all sides for a minute or two. Now stand them all the right way up in the skillet and transfer this to the oven, roasting them for no more than 35 minutes if you like your game bloody, for longer if you prefer things more well done. Transfer the birds when cooked to a warm serving dish to let them 'set'.

**5.** To make the gravy, put the giblets into the roasting pan, sprinkle over a teaspoon of plain white flour and stir in well. Allow the flour to take on a good brown colour — almost to burning point.

**6.** Pour over a sherry glass of brandy and flame it. Pour into the pan a wine glass of claret or other red wine and ¾ pint light

chicken stock. Simmer this for 45 minutes: strain. Leave to settle at the side of the stove for 5 minutes when any excess fat will rise to the surface. Skim this off. If the gravy is not of a good rich brown colour, add one or two drops of pure caramel or gravy browning, which *is* pure caramel. You should end up with about ⅓ pint of gravy, fairly thin, rich and bright.

**7.** Grouse are served whole and can have the added luxury of being served on top of a heart-shaped croûton (see following recipe) spread with a little pâté. Serves 4.

# BUTTER-FRIED BREADCRUMBS

*8 slices white bread,*
*crusts removed*
*4 oz unsalted butter*

**1.** Laboriously pick or pluck the bread into crumbs. You can use a grater for this job if you like, but the result is different.

**2.** Melt the butter evenly in a heavy-bottomed skillet. Add the crumbs and, over a low heat, fry them until a lovely golden brown. You must stir them and turn them all the time or they will burn at the edges and won't become evenly browned all over.

**3.** The crumbs can be heated through in the oven on a shallow baking tray before being transferred to a heated boat for serving.

# GAME CHIPS

**1.** Waxy potatoes are best for game chips. Allow 1 medium-sized potato per person. Peel, wash and slice them as thick as a 5p piece, either using a mandoline (a piece of board-like equipment with two blades set into the flat surfaces, one crenellated, the second plain, both adjustable for differing thickness) or a sharp knife. To make 'basket-weave' chips, the potato is cut over the crenellated blade of the mandoline, turning it a quarter turn between each cut. A food

*Roast grouse;*
*Butter-fried*
*breadcrumbs;*
*Game chips*

processor can be used but the size of the chips will be somewhat reduced.

2. Wash the cut potatoes well in cold water then, using nut or vegetable oil, fry them in small batches at 160°C (325°F). Drain them on a rack, then fry them again in very hot oil 190°C (375°F) until crisp and golden.

3. Salt them lightly. These can be made days in advance. All you then have to do is heat them up in the oven for a minute just before serving. Serve them on a folded linen napkin.

# CONYNGS IN GREKE WINE

A conyng (coney or rabbit) was very popular in medieval England, so much so that it was a prominent dish at the coronation feast of Henry IV in 1399. I find it somewhat ironical that 580 years later this rich English dish with its highly spiced sauce, having been lost for centuries in our culinary archives, should now slot into our modern cuisine.

Preparations should begin a day in advance, not because they are complex – in fact far from it – but because the dish is better with marinating.

---

*1 rabbit, portioned*
*seasoned flour*
*olive oil for frying*

MARINADE:
*½ pint sweet Greek red wine or sweet white wine*
*3 tablespoons red wine vinegar*
*6 oz muscatel raisins (seedless)*
*6 oz dried apricots*
*3 large pieces stem ginger, sliced*
*1 tablespoon syrup from the stem ginger*
*1 teaspoon ground ginger*
*1 teaspoon ground cinnamon*
*1 teaspoon ground cloves*
*12 juniper berries (optional)*

---

1. Put all the ingredients for the marinade in a glass or china bowl. Cover and leave overnight.

2. The next day, arrange the rabbit portions on a dish and pour over the marinated fruit and wine. Leave for a further 5 or 6 hours. Remove the rabbit portions and dry them.

3. Dredge the pieces in well-seasoned flour and fry until golden in gently smoking oil. Drain off excess oil.

4. Pour over the fruit marinade, cover and simmer for 30–40 minutes, or until the largest pieces are tender. Back fillets will be cooked first.

5. Remove the rest of the rabbit pieces and keep warm while you reduce the sauce until thick and cohered, by boiling rapidly for 10–15 minutes. Serve with Saffron Rice (see page 141). Serves 4.

# ROAST PHEASANT WITH MADEIRA CREAM SAUCE, BUTTERED ALMONDS AND GLAZED CHESTNUTS

---

*1 brace pheasants*
*1 level teaspoon ground bay or*
*4 small pieces fresh bay leaf*
*4 oz softened butter*
*1 level teaspoon salt*
*1 level teaspoon ground thyme*
*or large sprig fresh thyme*
*1 tablespoon brandy*
*4 rashers fat bacon*
*4 oz butter*

SAUCE:
*2 oz button mushrooms, sliced*
*1 clove garlic, crushed*
*1 level teaspoon flour*
*¼ pint dry madeira*
*½ pint double cream*

GARNISH:
*2 oz butter*
*4 oz sweet flaked almonds*
*salt*
*1 × 8 oz tin whole chestnuts in brine*
*2 oz lard*
*2 tablespoons caster sugar*

---

*Conyngs in Greke wine*

1. Prepare the pheasants as for Roast Grouse (see page 81) and cook them in exactly the same way, allowing up to one hour in the oven, but lowering the temperature after 30 minutes to Gas Mark 6 (200°C, 400°F).

2. While the pheasants are roasting prepare the buttered almonds by melting the butter in a heavy-bottomed skillet; before it browns add the flaked almonds and stir and turn them continuously until they are an even golden brown. Tip them into a sieve and lightly salt them. Keep them warm in a small container until you are ready to serve the pheasants.

3. To glaze the chestnuts: drain them and wash them under cold water. Drain again and pat them dry with paper kitchen towels. Melt the lard in a heavy skillet until it is smoking.

4. Add the caster sugar. Swirl the pan round until you see the sugar form a pool of caramel. This will be very obvious. Carefully slide the chestnuts into the pan and shake them around until they are coated with the caramel and are hot right through. Use kitchen tongs to remove them from the pan and to the serving dish or they will all stick together!

5. Dissect the birds into two breast and two leg portions. Remove as many of the rib-cage bones as you can manage easily. Put the portions into an ovenproof dish to keep warm.

6. Add the sliced mushrooms to the juices in the roasting pan, and fry these for a minute or two until they soften. Add the crushed garlic. Sprinkle over the flour and stir in well. Pour in the madeira and deglaze the pan, working any brown residues into the liquid with a wooden spoon. Add the cream and simmer for 10 minutes.

7. Strain the sauce into a small pan. Leave to settle for 5 minutes. If the sauce 'oils', and this will depend very much on the quality of the cream you are able to purchase in your particular area, then add a tablespoon of hot water to restore the emulsion to its creamy state. Skim off any excess fats which come to the surface. Bring to the boil and pour over the waiting pheasant pieces. Sprinkle over the almonds and garnish the finished dish with the glazed chestnuts. Serves 4.

# GAME PIE

FILLING:
*1 hare*
*1 small grouse or half a pheasant*
*6 oz pork fat (taken from the loin)*
*2 lb venison pieces*
*1 lb extra pork fat*
*¼ pint Jamaica rum*
*8 fl oz red wine (Burgundy-type)*
*1 level teaspoon ground ginger*
*1 clove garlic, crushed*
*1 egg, beaten*
*salt and freshly milled pepper*

CRUST:
*4 oz lard*
*2 oz butter*
*1 lb plain white flour*
*1 oz icing sugar*
*1 level teaspoon salt*
*½ teaspoon freshly ground pepper*
*1 level teaspoon ground mace*
*1 teaspoon finely grated orange rind*
*beaten egg for glazing*

ASPIC JELLY:
*commercial aspic crystals*
*gelatine crystals*
*¼ pint dry sherry*

1. To make the filling: bone the hare, cutting the back fillets into ½ inch cubes. Bone the game bird, cutting the breasts into equal-sized pieces. Cut the loin fat into ¼ inch cubes.

2. Put the venison, boned *leg* meat of the hare and game bird, and the extra pork fat through the coarse blade of a mincer.

3. Mix in the other ingredients, then add the cubes of meat and the cubed pork fat. Leave to marinate for 3–4 hours or overnight.

4. To make the pie crust: bring 7 fl oz water, the lard and butter to the boil in a pan.

5. In a large bowl sieve the flour, sugar, salt, pepper and mace together. Add the orange rind. Make a well in the mixture.

6. Pour in the hot liquid butter and lard mixture at one fell swoop. Mix it to a soft dough with a fork and leave to cool a little.

7. Butter a deep loose-bottomed cake tin (about 8–10 inches in diameter). Chill.

8. Knead the dough lightly on a floured work surface. Cut off one third and retain for the lid of the pie.

9. Roll the remaining dough into a large circle as big as the base of your tin plus the height of the sides. Fold this dough into four, place in the bottom of the tin and unfold, pressing into place up and somewhat over the edge of the tin.

10. Spoon the filling into the pastry shell, pressing well into the corners. Any spare filling can be baked in a separate dish and served as a pâté, or it can be formed into small meat cakes and fried.

11. Wet the edges of the pastry. Roll out a lid and fit this, pinching the edges together. Decorate with pastry shapes. Make a hole in the centre and fit a foil funnel to allow the steam to escape.

12. Stand the pie on a tray and bake in a preheated oven, Gas Mark 6 (200°C, 400°F) for 1 hour. Lower the temperature to Gas Mark 4 (180°C, 350°F) and bake for a further hour.

13. Remove the outside of the cake tin, but not the base. Brush the pie with beaten egg and return it to the oven for a further 30 minutes to brown all over. Leave to cool.

14. When the pie is quite cold, make up 1 pint of commercial aspic jelly following the instructions on the packet but substituting plain gelatine crystals for half the aspic crystals and using ¾ pint boiling water and ¼ pint dry sherry for extra flavour. Leave this to cool to the point where it is just beginning to thicken but not gel. Remove the foil funnel from the pie and pour the jelly in through the hole in the lid using a small kitchen funnel. The amount of jelly required will depend on how much the meat has shrunk during cooking. Serve cold. Serves 8–10.

# LAPIN AUX DEUX MOUTARDES

See photograph on page 56.

*1 oz butter and 2 tablespoons olive oil*
*1 English rabbit or 2 packages*
*frozen Chinese rabbit (2 hind legs*
*and 2 good back portions)*
*2 oz onion, sliced*
*2 oz white mushrooms, sliced*
*salt and freshly ground white pepper*
*1 clove garlic, crushed*
*¾ pint chicken stock, with ½ stock cube*
*to ¾ pint water*
*½ pint dry white wine*
*beurre manié*
*½ teaspoon made-up English mustard*
*2 heaped teaspoons Dijon mustard*
*¼ pint thick cream*
*squeeze lemon juice*
*1 tablespoon freshly chopped*
*tarragon or parsley*

1. Heat olive oil and butter in a heavy sauté or frying pan with a lid.

2. When oil and butter are lightly smoking, brown the rabbit portions all over, turning them at intervals. Work over a strong heat.

3. Remove the pieces to one side. Lightly brown the onion and then the mushrooms in the same fat. Strain away surplus fat before returning the rabbit to the pan in one layer.

4. Season very lightly with salt and ground pepper and add the crushed garlic. Pour the stock and wine over the rabbit; it should barely cover the pieces. Cover and gently simmer until the rabbit is tender (about 30 minutes).

5. Remove the rabbit pieces to a warm serving dish. Strain the liquid into a second pan and reduce by boiling rapidly until you have about ¾ pint.

6. To make *beurre manié*: mix 2 level tablespoons of butter with 1 of plain flour to a smooth paste. Whisk in little bits of *beurre manié* to thicken the sauce, allowing it to boil well between each addition. Use only enough to reach desired consistency. Store the remainder, covered, in the refrigerator.

7. The sauce at this stage should be no thicker than single cream. Whisk in the two mustards, adding more Dijon if you like a good mustardy flavour. Pour in the thick cream and allow the sauce to boil rapidly for 2–3 minutes. Check the seasoning, adding a good squeeze of lemon juice which will 'lift' the flavours.

8. Strain the finished sauce over the rabbit and sprinkle the finished dish with freshly chopped tarragon or parsley. Serves 4.

# COLD PÂTÉ-STUFFED QUAIL

If you decide to luxuriate and serve the quail on cold butter-fried croûtons, then you must increase the quantity of the stuffing mixture by 50 per cent as each croûton should be spread with a little of this before standing each bird atop. Allow 2 quail per serving. See photograph opposite.

*8 quail*
*½ clove garlic, crushed*
*4 oz butter, well-softened*
*1 tablespoon brandy*
*salt and milled white pepper*
*¼ teaspoon ground mace*

STUFFING:
*1 small (6 oz) tin real or mousse de foie gras*
*3 oz good butter*
*1 tablespoon dry sherry or madeira*
*2–3 drops lemon juice*
*more salt if liked*

GARNISH:
*8 croûtons*
*8 walnut halves, warmed through in the oven and lightly salted, then cooled again*
*truffle slices (optional)*

1. Beat the garlic, 4 oz butter, brandy, seasoning and mace together in a basin. Rub over the skins of the quail. Put a small amount inside each bird. Stand the birds on a rack in a roasting tin. Roast at a high temperature, Gas Mark 8 (230°C, 450°F) for 15 minutes. If they are not brown enough, slide the tin under a spanking hot grill for a moment or two. Leave the quail to cool completely while you make the stuffing.

2. Blend all the ingredients for the stuffing in a blender until smooth. With a sharp pointed knife remove the breasts from each bird.

3. Fill the stuffing into a piping bag fitted with a star tube (¼ inch size). Pipe swirls of this on to the exposed breast bone of each bird. Lay the breast meat back on top. Pipe a decorative 'seam' down the 'join'. Garnish. Serves 4.

*Cold pâté-stuffed quail*

# ELEGANT RABBIT PIES

No, you cannot miss out the forcemeat balls, so it is a good idea to prepare them first. The quantities here fill one 4 pint dish or 4–5 smaller ones.

---

FORCEMEAT BALLS:
*6 oz gammon steak soaked in cold water for 2 hours if salty
fat for frying
2 oz onion, finely chopped
½ clove garlic, crushed
2 oz fresh white breadcrumbs
1 tablespoon fresh chopped basil or
2 level teaspoons dried sweet basil
salt and freshly ground pepper
3 tablespoons olive oil and 1 oz butter for frying
1 egg, beaten*

PIE FILLING:
*2 legs and 2 whole back pieces rabbit
1 small (2½ lb) chicken or 4 chicken joints
1½ tablespoons flour, seasoned with salt and freshly ground black pepper
2 tablespoons olive oil for frying
1 large onion, finely sliced
½ head of celery, finely sliced
a little butter
2 good sprigs basil or a bouquet of herbs
2 teaspoons sea salt
¾ pint chicken stock, made from carcass or stock cube
½ bottle dry white wine*

PASTRY:
*1 lb shortcrust or puff pastry
beaten egg*

---

1. To make forcemeat balls: cut the gammon into 1 inch cubes and brown lightly on all sides. Remove the pieces with a draining spoon and put on one side to cool.

2. In the same fat fry the onion until soft and pale gold. Add the garlic.

3. Mince the gammon, transfer it to a bowl and mix with the breadcrumbs, herbs, seasonings and frying juices. Bind mixture with beaten egg.

*Elegant rabbit pies*

4. Divide into 18 equal portions of about a heaped teaspoonful, and roll into balls on a floured work surface.

5. Heat the olive oil in a heavy-bottomed frying pan, add the butter, swirl it round and, as soon as it becomes quiet, fry the forcemeat balls. Turn them two or three times to ensure even browning.

6. Transfer them as they are ready, to drain on crumpled kitchen paper. Leave on one side while you prepare the pie filling.

7. To make pie filling: dredge the rabbit and chicken pieces in seasoned flour in a large plastic bag. Retain the surplus flour.

8. Heat the oil until lightly smoking and quickly brown the pieces on both sides. Transfer pieces to a casserole.

9. Lightly brown the onion and celery, adding a little butter if necessary. Transfer to the casserole. Sprinkle with the surplus flour, add the herbs and salt. Pour over the wine and stock. Cover and cook at Gas Mark 4 (180°C, 350°F) for 50 minutes.

10. Halfway through cooking time adjust the seasoning, adding more sea salt if necessary.

11. Remove the rabbit and chicken pieces and leave until cool enough to handle. Bone and strip the skin and sinew and cut the meat into 1 inch pieces.

12. Roll out pastry. Edge and cut a lid for 1 large or 4–5 small pie dishes. Cut decorations from the trimmings, such as circles, leaves or diamonds.

13. Fill 1 large pie dish or evenly distribute the meat and forcemeat balls between 4–5 smaller ones. Ladle over the gravy, celery and onions from the casserole.

14. Brush the edges with beaten egg and fit the lids. Pinch or fork shortcrust edge; with puff pastry cut nicks ½ inch apart. Brush all over with more beaten egg, add any decorations and brush these as well.

15. For puff pastry, bake at Gas Mark 8 (230°C, 450°F) for 45–50 minutes. Lower the heat a little if crusts are getting too brown after half the time, but puff pastry must be very crisp.

16. For shortcrust pastry, start at Gas Mark 7 (220°C, 425°F). Lower the temperature slightly if tops get too brown. Bake for 45–50 minutes. Serve with a simple tossed green salad or buttered mange-tout peas. Serves 4–6.

# Beef and Lamb

## ROAST FILLET OF BEEF

The tenderest, and the most expensive of joints! But also the most succulent when roast 'to a turn'.

*2 lb middle fillet of beef*
*suet*
*4 oz butter*
*1 teaspoon dry mustard*
*1 teaspoon salt*
*½ teaspoon milled pepper*
*1 tomato, cut up*
*1 carrot, sliced*
*1 small onion*
*1 clove garlic, crushed*

**1.** Have your butcher trim off all sinew and tie a 2 lb piece of middle fillet, wrapping a good-sized piece of suet across the top as he does so.

**2.** Liberally spread this with the butter mashed to a paste with the dry mustard, salt and pepper.

**3.** *Preheat* the oven to Gas 9 (240°C, 475°F) – yes, as hot as that!

**4.** Stand the fillet on a bed of tomato, carrot, onion and garlic.

**5.** Roast for 25 minutes if you like beef rare, 35 for 'rosé', or longer for well done. There will be a deal of smoke, so have the kitchen door closed and the extractor on full blast! Turn the fillet once during the roasting time, and baste it.

**6.** Carve into ¼ inch slices and serve with Béarnaise Sauce (see page 159).

## POT-ROAST TOPSIDE OF BEEF IN RED WINE

See photograph on page 92.

*olive oil for frying*
*4 lb piece topside*
*2 medium-sized onions, quartered*
*4 carrots, peeled and sliced*
*½ head of celery, cleaned and sliced*
*2 leeks, cut into pieces*
*1 lb tomatoes, each one quartered*
*2 cloves garlic, crushed*
*bouquet garni*
*salt and milled pepper*
*½ bottle red wine*

THICKENING AGENT FOR GRAVY:
*1 heaped teaspoon flour, mashed with 1 tablespoon softened butter*

**1.** In a cast iron pot large enough to contain the piece of meat plus the vegetables, heat 4 tablespoons olive oil until it is smoking. Sear the meat on all sides until it is very well browned, using a cook's fork to help turn it over and around.

**2.** Remove the sealed meat to a kitchen tray while you brown the onions, carrots and celery in three batches, removing each batch to a side dish while you brown the next lot, adding a little more oil if necessary. Work over a high heat and use a spatula to move the vegetables to ensure even colouring.

**3.** Return the browned vegetables to the pot. Add the other vegetables and herbs, season well, stand the piece of meat on the bed of vegetables and pour the wine and ½ pint water around. Cover with a lid and

*Roast fillet of beef; Potato salad with sour cream dressing*

transfer the pot to the oven, Gas Mark 8 (230°C, 450°F), for 45 minutes; the beef will be done but very rosy inside. If you like your meat well done, then lower the temperature to Gas Mark 5 (190°C, 375°F) for a further hour or so.

**4.** Remove the bouquet garni. Transfer the meat to a warm serving dish, then either strain the vegetables out and serve them separately, and then make the gravy or sauce, or simply whisk in the flour and butter paste to liaise the sauce lightly. The rich gravy from this pot roast is a wonderful accompaniment to Yorkshire puddings. Serves 8.

# SLICED BRISKET OF BEEF WITH PINK PEPPERCORNS AND SAVOURY JELLY

*4–5 lb brisket, tied*
*handful of parsley*
*small jar pink peppercorns in brine*
*2 cloves garlic, sliced*
*1 bottle dry white wine*
*1 large sprig fresh thyme, or 1 teaspoon*
*rubbed thyme*
*3 bay leaves (or 1 teaspoon dried*
*powdered bay)*
*1 teaspoon powdered coriander*
*1 large onion, peeled and quartered*
*1 large carrot*
*2 dessertspoons salt*

FOR THE JELLY:
*3 egg whites*
*2 sachets gelatine crystals*

**1.** You are going to stuff 'holes' in the brisket so, using a sharp longish pointed knife, plunge this into the brisket going right through. Slide a palette knife down the side of the ordinary cook's knife. Remove the cook's knife leaving the palette knife in place. Use this as a means to open a gash into which you can pack plenty of parsley, peppercorns and the odd sliver of garlic, carefully sliding the palette knife out when the gash is packed full. Do this in about six places.

**2.** Now stand the brisket in a pan large enough to take it with the lid on. Pour over the wine and just enough water to cover. Put in all the other ingredients, using plenty of salt. Bring to the boil, lower the heat and simmer for 1½–2 hours (15 minutes per lb).

**3.** Leave to cool for an hour in the liquid. Strain the liquid into a bowl through a hair sieve lined with kitchen paper. Leave the liquid to chill until the fat is set. Remove this and discard.

**4.** Slacken the egg whites with ¼ pint cold water and whisk into the chilled stock. Bring gradually to the boil, over a very low heat, stirring most of the time. Sprinkle the gelatine crystals in and stir until dissolved.

**5.** Draw the pan to one corner of the heat so that the liquid is just moving. Leave, without stirring again, to simmer for 45 minutes, when the stock will be clear. Leave to cool.

**6.** Carefully decant the liquid through a paper-lined sieve into a clean bowl. *Do not* attempt to force or press the liquid through. Encourage speed by tapping the edge of the sieve sharply with a ladle.

**7.** Put the clear liquid to set into jelly. Turn on to a clean board. Chop with a hot knife (this keeps things crystal clear). Serve a little of the jelly with wafer-thin slices of spiced brisket carved 'across'. Serves 6–8.

# PAN-FRIED CHÂTEAUBRIAND

A châteaubriand steak is taken from the heart of the fillet and is, in fact, a double fillet steak gently pressed and beaten into one large round steak. Grilled or pan-fried, it is carved in thin slices cut across the grain.

Béarnaise Sauce (see page 159) is the most usual accompaniment, but almost any sauce would be good, from a rich onion purée – called Sauce Soubise – through the whole gamut of the egg-based sauces, of which Béarnaise is but one, to the rich red wine sauces such as Sauce Périgueux, Sauce Bordelaise or a simple Sauce Madère.

Sauce Foyot, which I often serve, is from the egg-based sauce family. These are *warm* sauces; they cannot be served really hot or

*Pot-roast topside of beef in red wine*

they would curdle. See page 158 for the well-known Hollandaise Sauce, which is the 'mother' or 'base' sauce, with a number of simple derivatives to try at your leisure.

---

*1–1¼ lb châteaubriand steak*
*2 tablespoons olive oil*
*salt*
*milled or cracked black pepper*
*1 teaspoon dry mustard*
*glass of amontillado sherry (optional)*

---

1. To pan-fry the steak: having pressed the meat with the heel of the hand, give it three or four very firm bangs with a wetted rolling pin or metal meat cleaver. Re-form the steak into a circle about 6–7 inches across and tie string round its waist.

2. Heat 2 tablespoons good olive oil in a heavy-bottomed frying pan until it is searing hot and smoking well. Seal the steak for a minute on both sides. There will be a deal of smoke and palaver, but this is necessary to form a good brown crust which will seal in all the juices.

3. Having sealed the meat over this very high temperature, lower the heat for the rest of the cooking time – about 3–4 minutes on each side, depending on the size of the steak. Obviously you must cook it longer if you want the meat well done (which you don't, do you?).

4. Towards the end of the cooking time, season both sides well with the salt, black pepper and dry mustard, all mixed together.

5. Remove the steak to a board or dish and cut away the string. Only slice the meat when you are ready to eat and enjoy it.

6. I often pour a glass of amontillado sherry into the pan, swirl this round over a high heat, and strain it into a small sauceboat. A teaspoon of this juice is very good, dribbled over each slice of meat. Serves 2.

# MINCED BEEF COBBLER PIE

I have always been fond of savoury mince pie. I also like a 'cobbler'. Here I have combined the two, making a hearty dish for an impromptu Sunday lunch party. It is a rich filling which should only be made with best mince (you will notice I call for minced rump or braising steak). The light suet crust removes the need for potatoes – in fact the ubiquitous tossed green salad is all you need serve. The mince mixture freezes. The topping doesn't – at least, I haven't tried it.

---

*6 oz shortcrust pastry*

FILLING:
*2 fl oz oil (or butter and oil)*
*1 onion, finely chopped*
*4 middle sticks celery, finely chopped*
*1 clove garlic, crushed*
*2 lb rump steak, minced*
*4 oz tomato purée*
*1 oz plain flour*
*salt, pepper and nutmeg*
*½ bottle red wine*
*6 oz mushrooms, sliced*

COBBLER TOPPING:
*6 oz self-raising flour*
*3 oz suet*
*1 tablespoon chopped parsley*
*level tablespoon chopped chives*
*salt and pepper*
*1 whole egg, beaten with 2–3 tablespoons of cold water*

---

1. The day before: heat a little of the oil in an enamelled iron or steel oven pot. Fry the onion and celery until lightly browned and soft. Add the garlic and continue frying for a minute or two. Remove. Fry the mince in batches over a good heat for a minute or two. Mix in the celery and onion. Stir in the tomato purée, then the flour. Lower the heat and let all this take on a little colour. Season with salt, pepper and nutmeg.

2. Remove the meat mixture to a dish. Deglaze the pot with the red wine, working all the brown residue into the wine with a wooden spatula. Return the mince to the pot. Add the sliced mushrooms. Mix all together well. Cover with a lid. Cook in the oven at Gas Mark 4 (180°C, 350°F) for an hour.

3. Remove the lid. Check the seasoning. Skim off any fat on the surface and leave to cool overnight.

4. On the day: line an 8–9 inch diameter,

*Pan-fried châteaubriand*

2 inch deep, loose-bottomed tin with the pastry. Fill with the mince mixture.

5. Toss all the dry ingredients for the topping together. Mix to a soft dough with the egg and water.

6. Press or roll out to ½ inch thickness. Cut 2 inch discs with a scone cutter or glass and arrange on top of the meat, slightly overlapping, fitting in a circle.

7. Bake at Gas Mark 7 (220°C, 425°F) for 25 minutes or until the cobbler top is risen and baked through. Serves 8–10.

## BOEUF TARTARE

Boeuf Tartare, a luxurious dish enjoyed by French and Italians alike, need not be restricted to the luncheon or dinner menu. My special recipe, which includes red, green and yellow peppers, I use as a covering on ryebread or pumpernickel cut into inch-size pieces to serve with pre-prandial drinks.

---

*3 peppers (if possible 1 yellow, 1 red, 1 green)*
*1 large onion, sliced*
*3 tablespoons olive oil*
*knob of butter*
*1½ lb minced fillet of beef*
*3 teaspoons fresh parsley, chopped*
*juice of 1 lemon*
*1 teaspoon mild French mustard*
*salt and pepper*
*small tin anchovy fillets*
*capers or olives*

---

1. Wash, seed and slice the peppers. Put them into a frying pan together with the sliced onion, some olive oil and a knob of butter. Fry gently until all is tender and cooked (about 30 minutes). Allow to cool and chop finely.

2. Mix enough of the above ingredients, according to taste, with the minced meat, adding olive oil, parsley, lemon, mustard, salt and pepper.

3. Serve on individual plates, flattening

with a fork to cover the whole of the plate, garnished with anchovy fillets and olives or capers. Serves 5–6.

## BOEUF EN DAUBE BORDELAISE

---

*3–4 lb rump steak, in a piece*
*salt and pepper*
*1 bottle red Bordeaux wine (claret)*
*1 tablespoon wine vinegar*
*bouquet garni*
*2 sprigs fresh tarragon or 1 level teaspoon dried tarragon*
*4 cloves garlic, peeled and halved*
*1 oz butter*
*6 oz fat salt pork, diced*
*8 oz button or pickling onions*
*2 fl oz cognac or armagnac*
*orange segments and parsley for garnish*

---

1. Put the steak (trimmed of excess fat) into a large flat dish and season.

2. Pour over the wine and vinegar, and add the bouquet garni, tarragon and garlic. Leave to marinate for 24 hours, turning the meat every 2 hours throughout the day.

3. Next day, remove the steak, drain and pat dry with paper towels. Heat a large frying pan, melt the butter, add the diced salt pork and onions and fry until lightly golden. Remove these with a draining spoon while you brown the steak well on both sides.

4. Transfer everything to a large ovenproof casserole, cover with the marinade and cognac or armagnac. Cook in the oven for 5 hours at Gas Mark 2 (150°C, 300°F). This recipe calls for long slow cooking, so do not stint on the time.

5. Check the seasoning. Remove the meat. Slice it thinly and arrange on a large shallow platter (check to see that this will fit in your refrigerator; if not, use two smaller ones as the meat should be arranged in one layer, only slightly overlapping).

6. Strain over the cooking liquor and refrigerate. The juices should set. Garnish as wished. Serves 6–8.

*Boeuf Tartare;*
*Boeuf en daube*
*bordelaise*

# SWEET AND SOUR BARBECUED BEEF

*1½ lb rump steak, in a thick slice*
*1 red pepper, seeded*
*1 green pepper, seeded*
*1 medium onion, peeled and quartered*
*2 thick slices fresh pineapple*
*oil*
*12 button mushrooms*

MARINADE:
*3 tablespoons honey*
*2 tablespoons soy sauce*
*1 tablespoon Worcestershire sauce*
*3 tablespoons good olive oil*
*2 tablespoons lemon juice*
*2 teaspoons each salt, milled pepper and*
*ground mace*
*2 cloves garlic, crushed*

**1.** Trim the steak of all fat and sinew and cut into 1½ inch cubes. Quarter and cut the peppers into eights. Break the onion into 'petals'. Cut the pineapple into equal pieces.

**2.** Mix the marinade ingredients in a large china or glass bowl. Put the meat cubes into this marinade and leave overnight or for 4–5 hours. Marinate the rest of the ingredients for an hour. Oil some metal skewers.

**3.** Spike on cubes of meat, alternating them at random with the rest of the ingredients, and pushing everything well together.

**4.** Seal the skewered meat over a high heat (or near the heat source, depending on whether you're in the kitchen or out in the garden). Lower the heat or raise the grill grid on the barbecue and continue cooking for 20–30 minutes, turning the skewers frequently and brushing every now and then with any remaining marinade or extra oil. Serve with a rice pilaf and a tossed salad. Serves 4.

# BOILED RIBS OF BEEF WITH CAPER CHIVE SAUCE

When one thinks of boiled beef and carrots with caper sauce, memories of robust meals from our grandparents' tables spring to mind. Try my way of cooking this English dish: the meat will (or should) be tender and succulent, the sauce rich, yet light, and flavourful. The quality of the dish will depend on the quality of the meat. It should not be a sin to boil ribs of beef, it should be a late-twentieth-century virtue and there will be enough of the wine-flavoured beef stock to make an excellent consommé.

BEEF:
*1 onion*
*1 carrot*
*1 bottle dry white wine*
*1 sprig of thyme (or 1 level teaspoon*
*dried thyme)*
*1 bay leaf*
*2 teaspoons salt*
*12 peppercorns*
*1 × 5–6 lb ribs of beef, boned and rolled*
*carrots, cauliflower and any other*
*accompanying vegetables*

SAUCE:
*2 oz butter*
*1 teaspoon flour*
*¾ pint beef stock (see method)*
*¾ pint double cream*
*salt and pepper*
*juice of ½ small lemon*
*3 oz plump capers*
*1 bunch chives, chopped*

**1.** In a pan just large enough to contain the beef, bring to the boil all the ingredients for the boiled beef except the meat, carrots and cauliflower. When boiling, add the beef and enough boiling water just to cover. Cook at a very gentle roll for 1½ hours. The meat will be pink.

**2.** Remove the beef on to a warm serving platter and cover with a damp cloth. Boil the carrots in the stock until tender. Cook the vegetables separately.

**3.** Strain the stock through a sieve lined with a clean cotton handkerchief. (Many people say strain through kitchen paper, but this takes forever!)

**4.** To make the sauce: melt the butter in a heavy-bottomed pan, stir in the flour, pour in the stock, bring to boiling point and add the cream. Simmer over a low heat for 20–30 minutes, by which time the sauce will be bright and will have reduced to about ¾ pint.

**5.** Check the seasoning, adding the lemon juice. Add the capers and chives. Serves 6–8.

# BEEF AND HAM MOULD

*1 lb best braising steak*
*1 lb green gammon*
*4 slices white bread, made into crumbs*
*1 heaped teaspoon gelatine crystals*
*1 level teaspoon ground mace*
*1 level teaspoon freshly milled*
*black pepper*
*a little salt if necessary*
*2 eggs, beaten*
*1 teacup dry sherry*

**1.** Butter a 2 pint pudding basin.

**2.** Trim the steak of all fat. De-rind the gammon, retaining the fat. Put both steak and gammon once through the coarse blade of a mincer. Mix with the breadcrumbs. Sprinkle over the gelatine crystals and seasoning, salting very sparingly as the ham may well be quite salty.

**3.** Bind with the beaten eggs and mix in the sherry.

**4.** Press well into the basin, cover with buttered foil, tie down with string and steam over water at a steady rolling boil for 2 hours.

**5.** Leave to cool. Chill. Turn out of the basin and serve cut in ¼ inch slices.

**6.** This mould can be made more economical by adding as many breadcrumbs again, and substituting water for the sherry. Serves 12–16 good slices.

# HERBED AND HONEYED LAMB CUTLETS

*lamb cutlets*
*salt and pepper*
*acacia or lime flower honey*
*freshly chopped herbs (apple- or*
*gingermint, spearmint or peppermint,*
*chives, golden oregano, parsley)*

**1.** Select only the choicest cutlets. Trim off 2 inches of the fat from the bone and all but a ¼ inch of fat round the 'eye' of the meat. Gently flatten the cutlets with a wetted rolling pin or cutlet bat. This breaks down the fibres a little and makes the cutlets look more attractive.

**2.** Brush the grill rack with a little oil or butter. Grill under a fierce heat to seal and brown them, and also to ensure they are juicily rosy inside. Season lightly with salt and pepper.

**3.** Heat some acacia or lime flower honey by standing the jar in a pan of simmering water. Dribble a modicum of this over the cutlets when they are in a serving dish. Sprinkle with freshly chopped herbs which should include one or other of the mints such as apple- or gingermint, spearmint or peppermint; some chives and perhaps a little golden oregano. Parsley is all right to use but can be overpowering, so use sparingly.

Note: if your grill rack is not of a design which leaves an attractive criss-cross pattern, this can be done by heating the tines of a cook's fork, or steel knitting needle, until glowing red. It takes but a minute or two and adds a rather nice burnt flesh flavour to the cutlets.

# 'PILLOW' OF RICE

*4 rashers of bacon, finely diced*
*1 onion, finely chopped*
*2 sticks of celery, diced*
*2 cloves of garlic, finely chopped or*
*crushed*
*2 tablespoons olive oil (if needed)*
*4 oz mushrooms, finely chopped*
*8 oz patna rice*
*1 pint chicken stock*
*salt and milled pepper*

*2 oz butter*
*3 oz freshly grated Parmesan (or 'dry'*
*Gruyère)*
*1 tablespoon thick cream*
*1 tablespoon freshly chopped parsley*

**1.** Dry-fry the bacon until almost crisp and transfer to an ovenproof pot.

**2.** Fry the onion and celery in the bacon dripping until soft, adding the garlic as you finish and a little oil if necessary. Add the mushrooms and fry for 1–2 minutes. Add the rice and do likewise.

**3.** Transfer all this to an ovenproof pot. Bring the stock to the boil, pour over the rice mixture and stir well, seasoning with salt and pepper to taste.

**4.** Cook in a preheated oven Gas Mark 7 (220°C, 425°F) for 20 minutes, when the rice will be cooked and all the liquid absorbed. Just before serving, stir in the butter, cheese and cream and garnish with parsley. Serves 6–8.

# CROWN OF LAMB WITH TURMERIC, THYME AND BAY

A roast crown of lamb can only be successfully roast if *un*stuffed: I cut away a good deal of the excess fat inside the crown and insert a tin (which has had lid and base cut away). This transfers heat up the centre, cooking the fat which so often appears almost raw.

I make a stuffing which can be cooked separately, and be added just before serving.

BUTTER PASTE:
*3 oz butter, softened*
*1 level teaspoon salt*
*1 level teaspoon ground thyme*
*1 level teaspoon ground bay leaf*
*2 level teaspoons turmeric*
*1 level teaspoon ground black pepper*

LAMB:
*5–6 lb crown of lamb (12–16 bones)*
*2–3 cloves of garlic, skinned and cut into slivers (optional)*

PASTRY BAUBLES FOR CROWN OF LAMB:
*½ lb packet of puff pastry*
*beaten egg with a pinch of turmeric*

**1.** Make the butter paste by mixing all the ingredients together.

**2.** With a sharp-pointed knife, make incisions deep into the flesh of the meat and slide a sliver of garlic down the blade into the hole. Use as much as you like (or none at all). I suggest starting with 9 slivers.

**3.** Rub the butter paste inside and between the cutlets – you can even melt the butter if you like. Cover the bone tips with 1 inch or so of foil.

**4.** Roast at Gas Mark 9 (240°C, 475°F) for 30 minutes. Lower the temperature to Gas Mark 6 (200°C, 400°F) for a further 30 minutes or longer if you like your lamb well cooked. Remove the foil tips 15 minutes before the end of the cooking time.

**5.** To make the pastry baubles: roll out the pastry thinly. Cut out twice as many fluted circles as there are cutlet bones. Brush 2 circles of pastry with egg and press them together on each bone tip. Return the lamb to the oven until the pastry is crisp and golden.

**6.** Stand the lamb on a warm serving dish while you make the gravy (below). Serves 6–8.

# HERB-ROAST SHOULDER (OR LEG) OF LAMB WITH SAFFRON GRAVY

*3–4 lb shoulder or leg of lamb*
*3 cloves garlic, peeled and thinly sliced*
*2 large sprigs rosemary or thyme or lavender*
*2 oz butter*
*salt and pepper*
*good sprig of thyme or*
*1 level teaspoon ground thyme*
*1 large carrot, cleaned and sliced*
*1 onion, peeled and sliced*
*1 tomato, sliced*

GRAVY:
*1 dessertspoon flour*
*5 fl oz red wine*
*½ pint stock (or use a stock cube plus ½ pint water)*
*2 sachets of 'Zaffy' saffron powder or 1 teaspoon turmeric*
*salt and pepper if necessary*

*Crown of lamb with turmeric, thyme and bay*

**1.** Make 10 or 12 deep incisions in the fleshy part of the shoulder with a small sharp-pointed knife. Slide a sliver of garlic into each hole and push a small sprig of rosemary and/or thyme into alternate holes (if you like a stronger flavour, then put in more rosemary).

**2.** Rub the skin with the butter, season well with salt, pepper, and dried rubbed (or chopped fresh) thyme.

**3.** Put a cushion of the vegetables in the bottom of a roasting tin and stand the lamb on this.

**4.** Roast at Gas Mark 9 (240°C, 475°F) for 45 minutes to an hour, longer if you prefer lamb well done (in which case lower the temperature to Gas Mark 7 (220°C, 425°F) after 20 minutes) and continue roasting.

**5.** To make the saffron gravy: decant away all but 2 tablespoons of the pan fats. Stir in the flour: let this fry over a low heat in the roasting tin. Pour over the wine and stock. Sprinkle in the saffron. Check the seasoning.

**6.** Let the sauce bubble gently for 10 minutes. Strain. Boil down to ½ pint to give strength to the sauce. (The saffron is optional, as it is so expensive, but the subtle tones are very provocative and worth the expense.) Serves 4.

# BUTTERFLIED LAMB

Serve the lamb cut in long thin succulent slices with Brandied Cheese Potatoes (see page 148) and a tossed salad with plenty of bite in the dressing.

*8–9 lb leg of lamb, boned and skinned*

MARINADE:
*¼ pint good olive or arachide oil*
*¼ pint white wine*
*juice and pared peel of 1 lemon*
*juice and pared peel of 1 orange*
*1 level teaspoon each of dried rosemary,*
*bay, marjoram and thyme*
*2–3 large juicy cloves garlic,*
*crushed*
*2 teaspoons cracked pepper*
*2 teaspoons salt*

**1.** Mix together all the ingredients for the marinade in a large shallow dish.

**2.** Wet a heavy rolling pin and gently, but firmly, bash the lamb to break down the tissues. The wetting prevents the flesh from dragging. With a very sharp knife make long diagonal incisions right across the fat side of the lamb about ¼ inch deep to allow the marinade to get right into the flesh. Leave the meat to marinate overnight.

**3.** Arrange the large flat piece of meat in a square basket grill, or tie it between two cooling trays or even two oven racks. Preheat the grill to red hot. Grill the meat for 10 minutes on each side under this fierce heat. Obviously, if you have a total aversion to rare meat then you must grill the lamb for longer. If your grill is on the small side you will have to cut the lamb in half and grill it in two sessions. It is well worth the trouble. The meat is deliciously succulent. Serves 8–10.

*Butterflied lamb*

# Pork and Ham

## PARCELS OF HAM AND CHICKEN MOUSSELINE

*6 oz raw lean gammon*
*6 oz raw chicken breast*
*¼ teaspoon ground nutmeg*
*1 level teaspoon salt*
*1 level teaspoon finely grated lemon rind*
*½ teaspoon milled white pepper or*
*¼ teaspoon ground ginger*
*2 eggs, beaten*
*¼ pint double cream*
*24 Chinese cabbage leaves*
*chicken stock (use carcass or a stock cube)*

*SAUCE:*
*2 large egg yolks*
*¼ teaspoon salt*
*juice of 1 lemon*
*4 oz butter, melted and kept hot*
*2 fl oz double cream, warmed*
*6 spring onions, washed and finely shredded*

1. Purée the ham and chicken meat in a food processor, adding all the seasonings. Mix in the eggs, scrape the mixture into a bowl and beat in the cream. Chill very well (overnight or all day).

2. Wash the Chinese cabbage leaves. Bring a pan of lightly salted water to the boil and blanch the leaves, a few at a time, for 30 seconds. Rinse under cold water and pat dry.

3. Clear a work surface. Arrange two leaves in a cross and put a spoonful of the purée in the centre. Wrap the stalk ends over first, then the green ends. Tie with fine string or linen thread. Make in advance to this stage and refrigerate.

4. Place the parcels in a shallow pan, barely cover them with stock and poach for 15–20 minutes. Remove the string before serving.

5. If necessary, these will keep warm in the oven, Gas Mark 1 (140°C, 275°F), for about 20 minutes. If doing this, place the parcels on a warm dish and cover with a clean napkin, dipped in scalding water and wrung out.

6. To make the sauce: mix the egg yolks, salt, lemon juice and 1 tablespoon water in a Pyrex bowl. Stand the bowl over a pan of hot water and whisk gently until the mixture thickens. Remove the bowl from heat.

7. Dribble in the hot melted butter whisking hard and allowing the emulsion to thicken as you do this. Stir in the cream. Add the raw spring onion before serving. Do not reheat. Serves 4–6 as a main course (2–3 parcels each).

## PORK AND CRANBERRY PIE

The addition of butter and icing sugar makes the pastry somewhat crisper than is usual for raised pies. I also add a pinch of an appropriate flavour to the pie I am making; in this case, orange zest and ground mace. A less expensive version of the pie can be made with sausagemeat.

*Parcels of ham and chicken mousseline*

*2½ lb lean pork meat, coarsely minced*
*¾ lb pork fat, coarsely minced*
*1 teaspoon grated orange zest*
*1 level teaspoon ground mace*
*1 good teaspoon salt*
*1 level teaspoon milled pepper*
*6 oz Ocean Spray cranberries*

PIE CRUST:
*4 oz lard*
*2 oz butter*
*1 lb plain white flour*
*1 oz icing sugar*
*level teaspoon salt*
*¼ teaspoon milled pepper*
*1 level teaspoon ground mace*
*1 teaspoon finely grated orange zest*

JELLY:
*aspic crystals*
*gelatine crystals*
*¼ pint amontillado sherry·*

1. To make the pie crust: bring 4 oz lard, 2 oz butter and ⅓ pint water to the boil in a pan.

2. In a large bowl, sieve the flour, sugar, salt, pepper and mace together (but not the orange zest; add this after sieving). Make a well.

3. Pour in the liquid butter and lard mixture at one fell swoop. Mix it to a soft dough with a fork and leave to cool a little. Butter an 8 inch round, 2 inch deep, loose-bottomed tin.

4. Knead the dough lightly on a floured work surface. Cut one-third off and retain for the lid of the pie. Roll out the larger piece to a circle 14–15 inches in diameter. Fold into four and place in the tin. Unfold and press into place, up and over the edge of the tin.

5. Mix the meat, fat, zest, mace, salt and pepper together well. Then mix in the cranberries.

6. Spoon the filling into the pastry case. Fold over the edge. Wet the edges. Roll and fit the lid, pinching the edges together. Apply any decorations, such as leaves, circles and flutes. Make a small hole in the centre and fit a foil funnel to allow steam to escape.

7. Stand the tin on a tray and bake in a preheated oven, Gas Mark 6 (200°C, 400°F) for 1 hour. Lower the temperature to Gas

Mark 4 (180°C, 350°F) and bake for a further 1 hour.

8. Remove the ring but not the base. Brush the pie all over with beaten egg. Return it to the oven for a further 30 minutes. Leave it to cool before removing the metal base.

9. When the pie is quite cold, make up 1 pint of commercial aspic jelly, following the instructions on the packet but substituting half the aspic crystals for plain gelatine crystals and using ¾ pint boiling water and ¼ pint amontillado sherry for extra flavour.

10. Leave this to cool to the point when it is just beginning to gel, then pour into the pie through the hole in the lid, using a small funnel. The amount of jelly to pour through the funnel depends on how much your pastry lid has or has not risen and how much your meat has shrunk. Serve hot or cold. Serves 8–10.

# PYT I PANNA

The ingredients in this Scandinavian speciality are cooked separately, unlike most hashed dishes.

*1 lb bacon, cut into small dice*
*2 large onions, cut into small dice*
*a little butter*
*2 tablespoons oil*
*6 medium-sized waxy potatoes, cut into small dice*
*any cold meat, cut into small dice (optional)*
*extra salt and milled pepper (these may not be needed)*
*1 tablespoon chopped chives and/or parsley*
*1 fried egg or 1 egg yolk per serving*

1. Fry the bacon until crisp. Remove with a slotted spoon and set aside.

2. Fry the onions in the bacon fat, adding a little butter if necessary. When they are a golden brown remove with a slotted spoon and set aside.

3. Strain the fat into a clean frying pan, add the oil and, when it is smoking, add the potatoes (patted dry with paper towel).

*Pyt i panna*

**4.** Fry them over a good heat until they, too, are brown and cooked through (about 15–20 minutes). Discard any surplus oil. Bring the above ingredients together in one pan with any cold meat and make thoroughly hot. Check the seasoning.

**5.** Divide into serving portions on hot dinner plates or serve in one dish. Sprinkle with the herbs, top with a fried egg or sit an egg yolk in its shell on top to mix in on the plate. Serve while piping hot. Serves 4–5.

# SALAMI, RAISIN AND PEANUT TOPPING

This is enough for a 5–6 lb loin or leg of pork.

*8 oz Italian or Danish salami, diced*
*1 large onion, chopped and softened*
*in 1 oz butter*
*12 oz seedless raisins, roughly chopped*
*1 clove garlic, crushed*
*grated rind and juice of 1 lemon*
*8 oz peanuts*
*2 eggs, beaten*
*salt and milled pepper*

BASTING MIXTURE:
*juice of 1 lemon*
*1 teaspoon dry mustard*
*salt and milled pepper*
*1 teaspoon caster sugar*

**1.** Mix together the first six ingredients. Put one-third of the mixture through a food processor, blender or mincer, adding the beaten eggs at this stage. Check the seasoning: salt may not be necessary as the nuts and salami may be salty enough.

**2.** Mix the minced and unminced mixtures together. Prepare the basting mixture by mixing all the ingredients together.

**3.** Half an hour before the end of the roasting time, remove the meat from the oven. Take off the crackling. Make ¼ inch deep incisions diagonally across the cushion of fat now exposed. Brush and spoon the basting mixture over the fat.

*Roast pork with salami, raisin and peanut topping; Potato latkes*

**4.** Press the salami mixture over the roast into an even cushion about ¾ inch thick, depending on the size of your joint. Cover with a piece of lightly buttered foil. (If you manage to get the crackling off in one piece, then you can use this.) Return the joint to the oven and continue roasting for a further 35–40 minutes at Gas Mark 6 (200°C, 400°F), when the topping will be cooked through.

**5.** Serve with Potato Latkes (see page 144) and Special Apple Sauce (see page 162).

# BAKED HAM CRUSTED WITH GROUND ALMONDS AND HYMETTUS HONEY

*8–10 lb piece of ham*

GLAZE:
*8 oz ground almonds*
*8–10 oz Hymettus or other fine-flavoured honey*
*grated zest of 1 orange*
*½ teaspoon salt*
*½ teaspoon milled pepper*

OPTIONAL PARTY TIME EXTRA:
*8 pieces of candied pineapple, or slices of fresh pineapple, or drained tinned pineapple rings*
*8 glacé apricots (or tinned or dried)*

**1.** Having boiled or baked your piece of ham, remove the skin, and some of the fat if there is a heavy cushion of this, whilst still hot.

**2.** Mix the ingredients for the glaze to a stiff paste, and spread this over the surface.

**3.** Stand the ham on a rack or piece of foil, and return it to the oven at Gas Mark 6 (200°C, 400°F) for 25–30 minutes or until the glaze is well browned and cooked through. Leave to cool completely overnight. Note: almonds burn easily, so keep an eye on things!

**4.** Arrange the optional extras on top of the glaze before baking. Fix with wooden cocktail sticks. Dribble over a little extra honey, and sprinkle with salt and pepper. When carving ham it is easier to remove the fruit decorations first, cutting them into pieces to pass with each slice. Serve with Cumberland Sauce (see page 161).

# THE SMITH BURGER

Louis' in New Haven, Connecticut, claims to be the originator of the hamburger in America back in the 1880s. Still in full swing today, this tiny family-run business uses the original nineteenth-century vertical gas grills for cooking and, more interestingly, the finished burger is served in toasted bread, not the soft pappy sesame roll we have come to expect. I, too, prefer mine in toast. Makes eight 3 inch burgers.

*1 lb green gammon, coarsely minced*
*1 lb white raw chicken meat, coarsely minced*
*salt and white pepper*
*pinch of mace*
*16 toasts, cut into rounds with a large pastry cutter, buttered or dry*

Mix the meats, season and shape. Grill or pan-fry the burgers. Serve with relishes of your choice: tomato sauce, apple chutney, sweetcorn or onions.

*The Smith burger*

# Offal

## TIMBALES DE RIS DE VEAU À LA CRÈME

Individual hot moulds of sweetbreads served with a madeira cream sauce.

SWEETBREAD FILLING:
*8 oz calves' sweetbreads
or frozen lambs' breads
squeeze of lemon juice
1 oz good butter
2 fl oz madeira
½ pint cream sauce (see below)
salt and milled pepper*

STOCK FOR SAUCE:
*2½–3 lb fresh roasting chicken
1 onion, peeled and quartered
1 carrot, peeled and quartered
1 bay leaf
1 sprig thyme
5–6 peppercorns*

SAUCE:
*stock (as above)
1 good oz of French or Dutch butter
½ oz flour
salt and freshly milled white pepper
½ pint double cream
good squeeze of lemon juice*

TIMBALE LINING:
*8–10 oz of prepared chicken breast meat
(see below)
2 whole eggs, beaten
½ pint chilled double cream
melted butter
salt and milled white pepper*

**1.** To blanch and trim sweetbreads: put the sweetbreads into a basin and leave under gently running cold water for an hour. Put them into a pan with cold water, a little salt and a good squeeze of lemon juice. Bring them to the boil *slowly*, simmer for 2–3 minutes, skimming away any scum. Drain and cool under running cold water. Trim away any strange bits and gently peel off all skin and membrane. Press between two dinner plates with a weight on top.

**2.** To make the stock: remove the breasts from the chicken and reserve these for making the chicken mousse with which to line the timbales. Cut off the chicken legs and crush or chop the carcass. Pack all this into a pan with the other stock ingredients. Add a good pinch of salt – not too much at this stage as the stock is going to be reduced. Pour over 2 pints cold water. Bring to the boil, uncovered, reduce the heat and simmer for 45–50 minutes.

**3.** Remove the legs as they will be cooked, and reserve these for some other use. Simmer the rest of the carcass bones for a further 30 minutes. Strain through a sieve lined with muslin or kitchen paper. Reduce this stock to a good ½ pint by boiling rapidly.

**4.** To make the sauce: melt the butter in a heavy-bottomed saucepan without it getting too hot. Stir in the small amount of flour, whisk in the stock, allow to bubble away gently for 2–3 minutes, reduce the heat, add the cream and continue simmering for 10–15 minutes. Adjust the seasoning with salt if necessary and lemon juice. Strain again. Cover with a thin film of butter or a circle of buttered paper and leave on one side.

**5.** To prepare sweetbread filling: cut the

Top: *Calves' brains in black butter;* right: *Timbales de ris de veau à la crème;* bottom: *Ragoût of veal kidneys*

blanched and trimmed breads into ¼ inch cubes. Melt the butter in a large, heavy-bottomed skillet or frying pan until it is a golden brown colour. Toss in the cubed breads and over a high heat fry them for a minute or so, stirring them round with a wooden spatula. Pour over the madeira and ignite. When the flame has died down pour over ½ pint of the prepared cream sauce, stirring it in well. Reserve remaining cream sauce for reheating and coating the cooked timbales. Reduce the heat and simmer for 2–3 minutes when the breads will be tender. Leave to cool completely. Chill until ready for filling the timbales.

6. To line the timbales: in a food processor or blender, make a fine purée of the chicken and beaten eggs. Transfer the mixture to a bowl and put to chill well for 2 hours. Then gradually beat in the cream, beating well after each addition and seasoning lightly as you proceed. The mixture should be stiffish. Put to chill while you butter each timbale or mould well, using a pastry brush and melted butter. (Castle pudding tins are ideal for this recipe. If you don't have any of these then use teacups.)

Put these buttered moulds into the refrigerator to set the butter, so that the chicken doesn't slide down the sides when you line them.

7. Scoop up small amounts of the chicken mixture with a teaspoon, and spread it into each mould, pressing it into the bottom and round and up the sides. This is easy if you continually dip the spoon into a small bowl of cold water which will prevent the mixture from 'dragging'. The hardened butter will stop it from sliding down. The coating should be no thicker than ¼ inch yet with no thin patches. Fill with the cold sweetbread mixture. Top with more of the chicken mixture, a little thicker coating this time, pressing and sealing the edges with the wetted spoon. The moulds should be filled completely. Draw the edge of a palette knife across the top of each to level things off evenly.

8. Stand the timbales in a bain marie and bake, uncovered, in the oven at Gas Mark 6 (200°C, 400°F) for 25–30 minutes, when they will have golden brown tops and will be risen and somewhat puffed up. Turn out on to individual warm plates, pour over a small amount of the remaining cream sauce and serve immediately.

If there is a delay, the timbales will 'hold' for 15 minutes or so if you turn the oven down to Gas Mark 1 (140°C, 275°F). (Electric ovens keep their heat, so the door may have to be propped open an inch or two.) Serves 4.

# SHERRIED BEEF, KIDNEY AND MUSHROOM TARTLETS

*12 oz rich shortcrust pastry*

FILLING:
*1 medium-sized onion, finely chopped*
*3 tablespoons olive oil for frying*
*1 lb best mince (totally fat-free)*
*6 oz button mushrooms, finely chopped*
*1 tablespoon tomato purée*
*2 level teaspoons white flour*
*½ pint dry sherry*
*salt and milled pepper*
*1 level teaspoon ground nutmeg*
*4 lambs' kidneys, cut into small pieces*
*1 oz butter*

1. Make up the pastry and line and make lids for a dozen deep tart tins.

2. Brown the onion lightly in 2 tablespoons hot oil in a large heavy-bottomed frying pan. Remove to a casserole with a slotted spoon. Turn the heat up and fry the mince in small batches, adding a little more oil if necessary. Add the mushrooms, tomato purée and flour.

3. Stir everything well together and allow a crust to form over a low heat in the bottom of the pan. Remove everything to the casserole.

4. Pour in the sherry and deglaze the bottom of the pan until it is quite clean. Pour all this into the casserole and stir well in. Add the salt, pepper and nutmeg. Cover with a lid and cook in a preheated oven Gas Mark 6 (200°C, 400°F) for 40 minutes.

5. Meanwhile, cook the kidneys. Melt 1 oz butter and 1 tablespoon olive oil in a heavy-bottomed pan: leave until this gets

quite hot and the butter starts to foam. Add the kidneys and fry until cooked. Season lightly.

**6.** Remove the casserole, skim off any surplus fat, stir in the kidneys and leave everything to cool overnight.

**7.** Fill the tartlets with the cold meat mixture. Wet the edges of the pastry and fit the lids. Pierce a small hole in each lid and bake at Gas Mark 6 (200°C, 400°F) for 20 minutes.

**8.** Leave to cool a little before transferring carefully to a cooling tray.

# CALVES' BRAINS IN BLACK BUTTER

See photograph on page 113.

---

*12 oz calves' brains*
*chicken stock*
*5 oz butter*
*salt and pepper*
*juice of ½ lemon*
*chopped parsley*
*Spanish capers*

---

**1.** Soak brains in cold water for one hour. Remove blood and membrane. Poach whole in enough chicken stock to cover, for 15 minutes. Drain and cool.

**2.** Cut brains into serving portions. Melt 2 oz butter until foaming. Fry brains for 2–3 minutes. Season lightly with salt and pepper.

**3.** In a second pan melt remaining butter until it is foaming, with an almond aroma. Black butter is in fact brown; squeeze in lemon juice to arrest further darkening.

**4.** Pour black butter over cooked brains. Sprinkle with fresh chopped parsley and

garnish with whole Spanish capers, obtainable from delicatessens. They are sweeter than the English bottled kind. Serves 4.

# RAGOÛT OF VEAL KIDNEYS

This eighteenth-century ragoût is good as a main dish, as a patty filling or served on buttered toast. If you halve the quantities and chop the kidneys small, it makes a superb sauce for veal escalopes or roast veal. See photograph on page 113.

---

*6 calves' kidneys*
*4 oz button mushrooms*
*2 oz butter*
*¼ teaspoon powdered rosemary or ginger*
*salt and freshly ground pepper*
*2 tablespoons madeira or medium dry sherry*
*¼ pint double cream*

---

**1.** Skin and trim kidneys of all fat then either cut them in half or slice them thinly. Wipe and slice the mushrooms.

**2.** Melt the butter in a frying pan until it foams and fry the kidneys until they are tender. If your pan is not very large, it is better to do this in two batches. Season the kidneys lightly with rosemary or ginger, salt and pepper and remove them to a warm serving dish.

**3.** Toss the mushrooms in the remaining pan juices, adding a little more butter if necessary. Pour over the madeira and the cream and cook until the sauce has a good consistency. Pour over the kidneys ready in a warm dish and serve. Serves 4–6.

# Fish

## INSALATA DI MARE

Sambuca is my favourite London Italian restaurant. Here is Signor Sandro's recipe for their Insalata di Mare – mixed seafood salad.

*6 medium-sized squid*
*salt*
*½ lemon*
*6 scallops*
*½ lb jumbo scampi, peeled*
*2 pints fresh mussels*
*½ pint fresh clams (or small tin)*
*½ lb peeled prawns*
*1 green pepper*
*1 red pepper*
*8 gherkins*
*¾ pint olive oil*
*juice of 4/5 lemons*
*ground black pepper*
*1 tablespoon capers*
*1 teaspoon oregano, basil or parsley*
*1 clove garlic, crushed*
*8 whole red chillies*

GARNISH:
*½ lb prawns in their shells*
*slices of lemon*

1. Pull the tentacles of the squid from the bodies. Wash and clean the bodies carefully, removing the purplish membrane skin and the quill-like backbones. Cut the tentacles from the head in one piece. Boil the bodies for 20 minutes, and the tentacles separately for 10 minutes longer in salted water with the juice of half a lemon.

2. When cooked, slice the fish into rings, and split the tentacles. Rewash and dry. Reserve the liquid.

3. Split the scallops in two and put in the fish liquid with the scampi. Bring to the boil, remove from the heat immediately and allow to cool in the liquid.

4. Immerse the mussels in boiling water and cover, adding a little salt. As soon as the mussels open, remove from the heat and allow to cool. Separate the mussels from the shells.

5. Cook clams in the same way as the mussels, but leave in their shells.

6. Slice the peppers and gherkins in julienne strips. Mix all the fish in a large bowl with the oil and lemon juice, add salt and pepper and the herbs and spices. Leave the chillies whole. Mix well and taste. If the dressing is not sharp enough, add more lemon juice.

7. Allow the mixture to marinate for a few hours, remixing before serving. Arrange the prawns in their shells around the serving dish with the slices of lemon. Serves 8.

## CHILLED CREAMED COD

Delicious for a fork luncheon on a warm spring or summer's day. It looks marvellous as a finished dish. Present it to your guests as shown in the photograph (page 119), and not as a dollop on a plate!

*Insalata di mare*

*3 lb cod fillet, skinned*

COURT BOUILLON:
*1 onion, sliced*
*½ pint dry white wine*
*juice and zest of 1 lemon*
*salt*
*8–10 peppercorns*

DRESSING:
*½ pint soured cream*
*½ pint single cream*
*12 oz cottage cheese*
*salt and milled white pepper*
*juice of ½ lemon*
*1–2 dashes tabasco*
*cold, strained cooking liquor*

GARNISH:
*1 cucumber, peeled, halved, seeded*
*and cut into ¼ inch segments*
*4 hard-boiled eggs, segmented*
*freshly chopped dill, parsley, chives*
*or any fresh green herbs*
*shrimps or prawns*

**1.** Bring the ingredients for the court bouillon to the boil with 1 pint water and simmer for 10 minutes. Cut the cod into pieces, add to the court bouillon, simmer for 5 minutes, covered.

**2.** Leave to cool in the liquor for half an hour. Drain, retaining the liquor. Remove any bones. Flake coarsely with your fingers. Cool completely. Chill, covered with plastic film.

**3.** Using a metal spoon, fold first the soured cream then the single cream into the cheese. Season well with salt, milled white pepper, lemon juice and the odd dash of tabasco. If necessary, add a little of the cold liquor to arrive at a loose but not runny consistency.

**4.** Carefully fold in the chilled flaked fish. Pile the mixture into a china or glass serving dish and garnish as illustrated on page 119 using the ingredients listed above, or as desired.

**5.** If the dish has to wait a while before being served, cover lightly with a plastic film or a clean napkin wrung out in cold water, and store in the refrigerator. Do not leave fish dishes standing in a warm room or outside in the sunshine. Serves 6–8.

Left: *Chilled creamed cod;* right:
*Scallops à l'indienne*

## SALMON CUTLETS FLAMED WITH PERNOD

*2 (1 inch) thick middle cut Scotch salmon
cutlets, about 1¼ lb in total weight
1½ oz butter for frying
salt and milled white pepper*

SAUCE:
*2 oz butter
1 tablespoon lemon juice
1 tablespoon finely chopped fresh parsley
¼ tablespoon chopped fennel fronds or
tarragon leaves
3 fl oz Pernod
2 oz pine kernels – or mixed
pine kernels and Macadamia nuts*

**1.** Halve the cutlets. Melt the butter until foaming. Fry the salmon for 1–1½ minutes on each side. Season. Transfer to a warm serving dish.

**2.** To make the sauce: melt the butter in a clean frying pan but do not brown. Add the lemon juice, parsley and tarragon. Add the par-cooked salmon cutlets.

**3.** Baste with the herby butter and season with a little more salt and pepper. Pour in the Pernod, baste and continue cooking for a further 2 minutes or so – it will depend on the thickness of the cutlets as to just how long this takes, so test your own portion!

**4.** Sprinkle over the nuts. Tip the pan to the flame and ignite. Baste until the flames subside. Serves 4.

## GRILLED SCAMPI WITH PARMESAN

*6 good-sized scampi
2 oz freshly grated Parmesan cheese
a little butter*

MARINADE:
*juice and finely grated rind of ½ orange
2 tablespoons olive oil
¼ teaspoon ground mace
salt and freshly milled pepper*

*Salmon cutlets flamed with Pernod*

1. Split the scampi in half, taking care not to cut right through. Remove the 'vein'.

2. Mix the juice and rind of the orange with the olive oil and mace, and add the salt and pepper.

3. Arrange the scampi on a platter. Spoon over the marinade and leave for an hour in a cool place.

4. Preheat the grill. Cook the scampi about 6 inches away from the element, for about 2 minutes on each side, and basting the 'open' side with any remaining marinade.

5. Dredge the grilled surface of the fish with the Parmesan cheese, dot with butter and continue grilling until the cheese is golden brown. Can be served on a bed of mixed peppers.

6. To make the pepper bed: soften an onion in 3 fl oz oil. Add 3 peppers, each a different colour and cut into strips, a little seasoning, $\frac{1}{4}$ teaspoon ground ginger and a clove of garlic, crushed. Fry the mixture quickly until the peppers are just soft. Serves 6.

## CANAPÉ OF SMOKED EEL

This makes a nice light main course at lunch. Use the larger Danish or Dutch eels: if these are not available then mini-eels or even tinned ones will do.

---

*1 level teaspoon mild French mustard*
*squeeze of lemon juice*
*4 slices Danish rye bread or German*
*Vollkornbrot*
*2 oz butter*
*4 pieces smoked eel, cut the same*
*length as the bread*

SAVOURY CUSTARD:
*2 whole eggs*
*1 extra egg white*
*salt and milled pepper*
*$\frac{1}{4}$ pint milk*
*a little butter*

GARNISH:
*snipped chives or freshly chopped*
*parsley*
*lemon wedges*

---

1. First make the savoury custard. Beat the eggs and white, season and pour in the milk. Butter a small oblong or square seamless tin or mould (a foil freezer container is ideal). Pour in the mixture. Stand the receptacle in a pan of cold water. Bring to the boil. Simmer until set and firm. Cool. Turn out and cut into suitable lengths for garnishing.

2. Cream the butter and mustard. Add a squeeze of lemon juice. Spread liberally on the rye bread.

3. Skin, trim and bone the eel. Arrange on bread. Decorate with a slice of the custard and sprinkle with the chives or fresh parsley. Hand lemon wedges separately. Serves 4.

## LANGOUSTINES FLAMED IN WHISKY

I cannot imagine you will want to cook these from live, but if you can buy live langoustines then I recommend you do so. Defrosted Mediterranean prawns will do equally well, or crayfish tails or prawns. Just how many fish you fry at one time will depend on the size of your pan. Let's assume your pan holds 10–12 langoustines or prawns. Allow 2 oz butter, 1 clove of garlic and 2 fl oz whisky for each batch.

---

*5–6 fish per serving*
*butter for frying*
*crushed garlic*
*whisky for flaming*
*salt and pepper, to be added by each*
*guest*

---

1. Melt 2 oz of butter to foaming point. Add the garlic and stir this round. Add the fish to the mixture. Turn and stir them until hot (or cooked if raw) right through.

2. When all is hot and sizzling, pour in 2 fl oz whisky. Lean away from the pan, tip it to the flame. The flame should shoot heavenwards!

3. Repeat the process until all your fish are cooked.

4. There is little point in attempting to eat these fish in any other way but with the fingers. Pass the allotted number to each

*Langoustines flamed in whisky*

guest, basted with the pan juices, together with a lemon wedge, large napkin and finger bowl.

# DRESSED CRAB

Unless, of course, you buy the crab live, this job is invariably done by your fishmonger. Serve dressed crab lightly chilled, with a boat of creamy blandish mayonnaise, some chopped hard-boiled egg, salt and milled pepper, letting the guests make their own crab mayonnaise as they please. A little grated orange zest goes well with crab. Allow one ¾–1 lb crab per serving.

# GOUJONS OF FISH WITH SAUCE CHORON

*2 largish Dover or lemon soles, skinned and filleted*

BATTER:
*4 oz self-raising flour
1 level teaspoon salt
½ teaspoon baking powder
¼ pint milk
1 dessertspoon olive oil
2 oz nib almonds (optional)*

MARINADE:
*1 tablespoon olive oil
1 small clove garlic, crushed
juice of 1 lemon
salt and pepper*

SAUCE CHORON (see page 159):
*½ pint Hollandaise Sauce
1 dessertspoon tomato purée
1 good dessertspoon freshly chopped tarragon*

1. Sieve together the dry ingredients for batter. Mix to a smooth consistency with the milk. Add the oil. Mix in the nib almonds.
2. Cut the sole fillets into long diagonal strips about ½ inch thick. Put in a glass or china bowl, pour over the small amount of marinade and mix well together. Cover with plastic film and leave in the refrigerator for 2

hours or so. Make up the Sauce Choron (see page 159).
3. When ready, put the fish into the batter and coat well. Deep-fry in small batches until crisp and brown. Drain on kitchen paper.
4. Serve on a crisp linen napkin lined with a dish paper, accompanied by the sauce. Serves 4–5.

# 'BOIL'D SOALS'

This delicious way of cooking Dover sole is my version of an eighteenth-century recipe where the word 'poach' was not used. Whilst boiling sounds drastic, when qualified, as it was in cookbooks in those days, to read 'boil without movement' – it means poached!

*8 fillets Dover sole, skinned and trimmed
salt and milled white pepper
1 heaped tablespoon freshly chopped mixed herbs (parsley, thyme, tarragon, basil)
a very little rubbed rosemary
1 teaspoon grated orange rind
a little butter
½ pint thick bland mayonnaise
¼ pint double cream, half-whipped*

SPECIAL COURT BOUILLON:
*½ bottle light German wine or Yugoslav Riesling
1 small bay leaf
1 small onion, sliced
juice of 2 oranges
1 clove garlic, crushed
2 inch piece orange rind
1 carrot, cleaned and roughly chopped
the sole bones, washed and cut up*

GARNISH:
*2 navel oranges, segmented
8 anchovy fillets, cut into striplets
1 tablespoon capers, roughly chopped
extra chopped parsley and/or other fresh herbs
gherkin fans*

1. Put the ingredients for the court bouillon into a stainless steel or enamel pan with ½ pint cold water. Bring to the boil and simmer for

*'Boil'd soals'*

20 minutes. Strain, discarding the solids, and allow to cool completely.

2. Meanwhile, with a wetted rolling pin, gently pat the fish fillets without crushing the flesh. Lay them out flat, insides uppermost. Season lightly with salt and pepper. Sprinkle with the mixed herbs, rubbed rosemary and the orange rind. (You can use rubbed dried herbs, but go sparingly.) Fold the fillets in half, or roll them up starting at the tail.

3. Arrange them in a buttered shallow enamel or stainless steel pan. Pour over the cold court bouillon. Cut a circle of grease-proof paper to fit the surface, butter this and lay it directly on the fish fillets (this will collect any dirt or scum). Fit a lid.

4. Bring to the boil slowly and simmer for 3 to 4 minutes. Leave to cool in the liquid for an hour.

5. Remove the fillets and leave them to drain and cool completely. Strain the liquid through a fine sieve. Bring this back to a good rolling boil and reduce to one coffee cup. Leave to cool completely before whisking this fishy essence into the mayonnaise.

6. Add enough cream to give the cold sauce a good coating consistency.

7. Arrange the fillets in two or three rows in a long serving dish. Spoon over the sauce. Add the garnish just before serving, as the orange juice will spoil the consistency of the sauce if added too early. Serves 4.

## FILLETS OF DOVER SOLE CAPRICE

*4 large fillets of Dover sole, skinned*
*1 heaped tablespoon white flour*
*salt and pepper*
*2 'straight' bananas*
*lemon juice*
*2 oz butter for frying*
*2 tablespoons good chutney, sieved*

1. Using a wetted rolling pin to prevent the flesh dragging, gently flatten each fillet without crushing it.

2. Sieve the flour, salt and pepper on to a large dinner plate. Dredge each fillet through this, shaking away any surplus flour.

3. Peel the bananas. Cut in half length-ways. Brush with lemon juice to keep them white. Melt the butter in a large (12 inch) heavy-bottomed frying pan, turning and swirling it around to ensure even colouring.

4. When the butter is foaming and giving off an almondy aroma, fry the fillets (rounded side first) on both sides until golden brown and cooked. Remove to a warm serving platter and keep warm while frying the bananas.

5. Next, fry the bananas until nicely brown, adding some lemon juice when you have first turned them. Season lightly with salt and milled pepper.

6. Arrange the bananas on top of the sole fillets. Warm the chutney in a small pan and dribble a little of this over the fillets. Serves 2.

## FILLETS OF RAINBOW TROUT WITH CRANBERRY/ VERMOUTH SAUCE

This dish can be served hot or cold.

*2 × 10 oz rainbow trout*
*6 fl oz dry white vermouth*
*salt and milled white pepper*
*small pieces onion, sliced*
*5–6 tarragon leaves, plus extra for garnish*
*1 heaped tablespoon cranberry jelly or compôte or 2 tablespoons fresh cranberries for a sharper sauce*
*good squeeze of lemon juice*

1. Cut off the heads and tails of the trout. Wash the fish well.

2. Place them side by side in a shallow sauté pan. Pour over the vermouth. Season lightly. Scatter over the pieces of onion and the tarragon.

3. Cover with a circle of buttered paper, then with a lid. Bring to the boil and simmer for 3–4 minutes.

4. Remove the trout, leave to cool a little, then remove the skin.

*Fillets of Dover sole caprice*

**5.** Reduce the pan liquid by half by boiling rapidly, uncovered. Add the cranberry jelly or fresh cranberries. Simmer until incorporated or the fresh cranberries are pulped. Sieve finely. Add lemon juice. Check the seasoning.

**6.** Cover with plastic film and leave to cool. When the trout are cold, fillet them by cutting down the centre back and lifting away the two top fillets. Trim off any untidy bits. Invert these on to a plate or dish. Gently lift out the backbone. Invert the bottom two fillets on top of those already in the dish. Pour around a little of the sauce. Garnish with extra blanched tarragon leaves, or a little freshly chopped tarragon. Serves 2.

# GRILLED MACKEREL WITH ANCHOVY CAPER BUTTER

---

*1 × 4 lb mackerel*
*white wine for marinade*
*few sprigs of fresh rosemary, thyme*
*and oregano*

SAVOURY BUTTER:
*1 (2 oz) tin anchovy fillets*
*2 level tablespoons capers*
*8 oz butter, softened*
*¼ teaspoon milled black pepper*
*2 tablespoons anchovy essence*
*1 tablespoon raspberry vinegar or*
*Vieux Vinaigre du Vin*
*anchovy fillets, capers and lemon*
*slices for garnish*

---

**1.** To make the savoury butter: finely chop first the fillets and then the capers. Blend the rest of the ingredients together, then mix in the chopped items. As texture is desirable for this butter avoid using a traditional blender. Form the butter into a roll and chill well. Cut into discs.

**2.** Marinate the mackerel in white wine for 4 hours, having made three or four diagonal ¼ inch deep slashes down both sides in order to counteract the natural oiliness of the fish. Put a few sprigs of fresh rosemary, thyme and oregano in the fish's belly for added aroma.

*Grilled mackerel with anchovy caper butter*

**3.** Brush the grill rack or basket with a little oil and 'dry grill' it for 15 minutes each side under a good heat, turning it if there is a tendency to scorch. Test to see if cooked by pressing the flesh in the thickest part with the thumb. It will 'give' readily when cooked. Serve with the anchovy caper butter on top and extra anchovies, capers and lemon slices for a garnish. Serves 4–5.

# SALMON AND EGG PIE WITH A GOUGÈRE TOPPING

---

SHORTCRUST PASTRY:
*6 oz plain white flour*
*2 oz butter*
*2 oz lard*
*salt*

SALMON AND EGG FILLING:
*1 lb flaked cooked fish, salmon, tuna,*
*haddock, or tinned salmon*
*3 hard-boiled eggs, roughly chopped*
*2 tablespoons chopped parsley, fresh*
*basil or tarragon or all three mixed*

SAUCE:
*1 oz flour*
*2 oz butter*
*¾ pint milk, with onion, bay leaf*
*and thyme for infusing*

CHOUX PASTRY TOPPING:
*3 oz good butter*
*4 oz plain strong white flour*
*½ teaspoon salt*
*4 small eggs, well beaten*
*4 oz Dutch or other melting cheese,*
*cut into ¼ inch dice*

---

**1.** Make the pastry in the usual way. Line a 10 inch, 2 inch deep, loose-bottomed pie tin with the pastry. Bake blind at Gas Mark 7 (220°C, 425°F) for 20 minutes.

**2.** To make the filling: mix fish, chopped eggs and herbs in a large bowl. Include the juice from tinned fish or a little stock if you have poached your own.

**3.** To make the sauce: infuse the milk with the onion, bay leaf and thyme over a low heat for 30 minutes. Melt the butter, stir in the flour and add the milk gradually, after straining it.

4. To make the choux pastry: sieve the flour and salt on to a paper. Boil the butter and 8 fl oz water in a pan and tip all the flour in quickly. Beat well with a wooden spatula until the mixture leaves the sides of the pan clean. Gradually beat in the eggs until the pastry is glossy, and add the diced cheese.

5. Carefully fold the *hot* sauce into the filling and spoon the mixture into the pastry shell. Top with choux pastry and bake at Gas Mark 7 (220°C, 425°F) for 40–45 minutes or until puffed up and cooked through. Serves 4–5 as a main course, 6–8 as a starter.

# HOT TROUT MOUSSE WITH WHISKY PRAWN SAUCE

The sauce can be made, and the preparation for the mousse completed, in the morning or even the day before.

---

SAUCE:
*8 oz prawns in their shells*
*¼ pint fish stock (made from trout bones)*
*½ pint double cream*
*1 teaspoon tomato purée*
*1 sachet saffron fronds or powdered saffron*
*1 teaspoon sweet paprika*
*2 tablespoons whisky*
*1 clove garlic, crushed*
*a little salt*
*milled pepper*
*2 egg yolks*

MOUSSE:
*10 oz trout flesh, weighed after skinning and boning (you will need to buy 2 × 8 oz trout)*
*2 large eggs*
*¼ teaspoon ground mace*
*good teaspoon salt*
*½ level teaspoon milled white pepper*
*½ pint double cream*

---

1. To make the sauce: head and shell the prawns, retaining all the debris. Put the tails

into the refrigerator until required. Place the debris into a pan together with all the ingredients except 1 tablespoon double cream and the egg yolks.

2. Simmer for 30 minutes. Strain well and simmer again until you have ½ pint of sauce. Check the seasoning.

3. Just before serving, bring the sauce to boiling point. Mix the egg yolks and remaining cream together with 1 tablespoon water and whisk into the sauce.

4. Add the peeled prawns (the sauce will heat them through without toughening them). Do not return the pan to the heat or the sauce will split – it will still be edible, but unsightly, undesirable and unnecessary!

5. To make the mousse: have the fish, eggs and cream well chilled. Also chill the bowl of your food processor, and a second bowl or basin. Cut the fish into 1 inch pieces, removing any stray bones as you do so. Butter well an oblong seamless loaf tin, terrine or a 2 pint soufflé dish.

6. Preheat the oven to Gas Mark 6 (200°C, 400°F). Stand a container (a bain marie) of water in the oven. Make a fine purée of the fish and eggs, adding the seasonings. Scrape this into the second bowl. Beat in the cream, gradually, until it is all incorporated. The resultant mixture should be fairly stiff and heavy.

7. Spoon it into the mould and level the top. Stand the mould in the bain marie and cook for 45 minutes to an hour, or until the mixture is firm to the touch. Unmould on to a warm serving dish and serve immediately with the hot sauce. Serves 6.

# SCALLOPS À L'INDIENNE

Fresh scallops are often sold without their shells, which are half their attraction. However, if you give your fishmonger good notice he will ensure these are supplied. If fresh scallops are unavailable you can use frozen ones. My recipe is for a light, mild, creamy curry sauce with a rice accompaniment. If you like it hotter, just add more curry paste. See photograph on page 119.

*Hot trout mousse with whisky prawn sauce*

RICE:
*2 pints fish or chicken stock (use cube)*
*8 oz long grain rice*
*1 clove garlic, crushed*
*1 oz butter*
*1 level teaspoon mild curry powder*

FILLING:
*6 fat scallops*
*½ pint dry white wine*
*1 shallot, chopped*
*1 heaped teaspoon mild curry paste*
*1 level teaspoon grated orange rind*
*1 small sherry glass of whisky*
*½ pint double cream*
*salt, if required*
*squeeze of lemon juice*
*1 heaped teaspoon soft butter, mashed*
*with 1 level teaspoon white flour*

1. Bring the stock to the boil, 'rain' in the rice, add the crushed garlic. Boil for 12 minutes, strain well (reserving the stock), stir in the butter and curry powder. Keep warm, covered, in a low oven, Gas Mark 2 (150°C, 300°F), while you prepare the scallops.

2. Cut each scallop in half equator-wise. Bring the wine to the boil with the shallot. Simmer for 15 minutes. Add the scallops. Cover with a circle of buttered paper and a lid and simmer, *without bubbling, for no more than 2 minutes.* Remove the scallops to a covered dish and keep warm. (Note: if the water is bubbling and the scallops boil they will shrink and toughen.)

3. Strain the stock into a small pan. Boil rapidly to reduce by half. Whisk in the curry paste, orange rind, whisky and cream. Bring back to the boil and boil at a good roll for 2 minutes or so.

4. Add a little salt if necessary and a good squeeze of lemon juice. The sauce should be no thicker than single or pouring cream: its consistency can be adjusted to thicken slightly by whisking in *little bits* of butter and flour paste (*beurre manié*) and leaving to bubble gently for a minute or two.

5. Spoon the warm rice into warmed scallop shells. Arrange two or three slices of scallop on top. Spoon over plenty of the sauce and serve immediately, accompanied by a green side salad. Serves 4.

# DOVER SOLE AND QUEEN SCALLOP SALAD IN PIMENTO MAYONNAISE

See photograph on page 33.

*1 × 1½–2lb Dover sole, filleted*
*and skinned*
*1 small piece of onion*
*1 small piece of bay leaf*
*½ pint dry white wine*
*8 oz queen scallops or 6 larger ones*

SAUCE:
*2 red peppers*
*½ pint home-made mayonnaise*
*¼ pint single cream*
*salt and freshly milled pepper*
*8 lettuce leaves, finely shredded*
*whole radicchio leaves*

1. Wash all the fish under cold running water. Put the onion, bay leaf, ¼ pint water and the white wine in a shallow pan and simmer for 10 minutes. Cut each fish fillet diagonally into four long strips. Poach for 2 minutes, no more: the fish should be firm and tender but not overcooked.

2. Simmer the queen scallops for the same length of time. If larger scallops are used, cut them into quarters before simmering. Cool.

3. Strain the liquid into a smaller pan and reduce to about 2 tablespoons by boiling rapidly. Strain into a bowl and leave to cool until ready for use.

4. Preheat the oven to Gas Mark 9 (240°C, 475°F). Cut the peppers in half, removing any stalk and seeds. Stand them on a baking tray and heat them in the oven until the skins blister (about 10 minutes). Peel this off with a sharp knife and press the flesh through a hair sieve (there isn't enough to use a food processor).

5. Mix the pepper flesh with the mayonnaise, stir in the cream and white wine reduction, and season with salt and pepper.

6. Divide the shredded lettuce and radicchio evenly between six smallish bowls; divide the fish likewise and pour over the pimento mayonnaise. Serves 6.

# LOBSTER BELLEVUE

*1 heaped teaspoon paprika*
*1 tablespoon oil*
*1 tablespoon white or red wine vinegar*
*1 small onion, peeled and quartered*
*12 black peppercorns*
*1 (1½–2 lb) live lobster*

GARNISH:
*stiff home-made mayonnaise*
*hard-boiled egg, quartered*
*tomato segments, skinned and seeded*
*cucumber slices*
*a few prawns*
*small sprigs of watercress*

1. To boil a lobster: select a pan large enough and deep enough to contain the lobster. Pour in 6 pints water, add salt and bring to the boil. Add all ingredients except the lobster and bring to the boil. Reduce the heat and simmer for 10 minutes.

2. Bring this liquid (called a court bouillon) back to the boil and pop in the lobster. Bring back to boiling point and simmer for 15 minutes. Leave the lobster to cool in the liquid for 2 hours.

3. Remove the lobster from the pan and leave to cool covered with a damp clean cloth.

4. To split or open a cooked lobster: break off the claws where they join the body. Bend back and crack the small pincer at the 'hinge'.

5. With a hammer or rolling pin crack, but do not crush, the main claw sufficiently to allow the removal of the white meat with a lobster pick, fork or bodkin (a small knitting needle is also good for this job). Crack each knuckle likewise.

6. Open out the tail and lay the lobster flat, the head to the right. You will notice a line running the length of the fish with a 'cross' about 2 inches down from the eyes.

7. Plunge the point of a good heavy cook's knife right through this cross down to the board. The knife should be vertical at this stage. Now bring the knife down, cutting firmly through the line of the head and ending with the head split in half.

8. Turn the lobster round completely.

Open the tail out flat again. Insert the knife at the same point and, in exactly the same way, cut through the line and on to the end of the tail.

9. Open out the two halves. Remove the 'string' or dark thread (intestine) which should be obvious in the centre of one or other halves of the tail (sometimes it is empty and almost transparent and difficult to see – but you'll find it!). Right at the head end you will see the 'sack' – it has a slightly papery appearance. Remove this from both halves with a teaspoon and discard. Leave everything else, including the eggs or coral, the greenish part which some consider to be a delicacy, and any pink and white creamy-looking substance. Leave all the smaller claws as they are.

10. Remove the crescent of pink and white meat from each tail. Turn this flat-side down on to the board and cut each into 5 or 6 pieces to put back on to the filled or stuffed tail.

11. The lobster is ready for serving. Simply replace the cut tail meat, put a lemon wedge in the body cavity, lay the cracked claw alongside and serve on a large plate with a bowl of mayonnaise.

12. For a special occasion you may want to gild the lily. Fill the entire length of each half shell with a fine, small-diced Russian Salad (page 31), or Potato Salad (page 31).

13. Invert each cut lobster tail on to the *opposite* shell so that the curved coral pink lobster meat is uppermost on the bed of salad. Remove the meat from each cracked claw, keeping it whole if you can. Arrange this on top of the main part of the body, near the head.

14. Pipe swirls and rosettes of very stiff mayonnaise down the shell. Decorate with quarters of hard-boiled egg, skinned and seeded tomato segments, cucumber twists, a prawn or two and small sprigs of watercress. I often remove the solid coral and press this through a hair sieve, sprinkling a little over the decorated lobster and mixing the remainder into a good tablespoon or two of the mayonnaise.

Note: bottled mayonnaise is rarely stiff enough to pipe, so if used omit this operation and serve it separately in a sauceboat.

# Pasta, Eggs and Rice

## LASAGNE WITH TUNA FISH

This is sufficient to fill a dish approximately 10 × 5 inches which will give 6 good servings. You will need enough pasta sheets to make three layers in your particular dish.

*sheets of lasagne*
*8 oz mushrooms*
*juice of 1 small lemon*
*4 oz Parmesan cheese, freshly grated*
*2 × 8 oz tins tuna fish, drained and*
*flaked (reserving the oil)*
*4 oz Mozzarella or other melting*
*cheese, cut into cubes*
*2 large tomatoes, skinned, seeded*
*and chopped*

LIGHT BÉCHAMEL SAUCE:
*1 pint milk*
*bay leaf*
*sprig of thyme*
*few pieces of onion*
*3 oz good butter*
*2 oz white flour*
*½ pint single cream*
*salt and pepper*

**1.** Cook the pasta sheets in plenty of boiling water a few at a time, lifting them out while they are still *al dente* into a bowl of cold water. Rinse and pat dry.

**2.** To make the sauce: infuse the milk over the lowest heat with the bay leaf, small sprig of thyme and a few pieces of onion. This should take about 30 minutes. If the milk boils just turn off the heat and leave the pan at the side of the cooker.

**3.** Melt the butter in a second pan, stir in the flour, strain over the infused milk, bring back to the boil and simmer for 10 minutes.

**4.** Stir in the cream and 2 oz of the grated Parmesan cheese; if lumpy – which it shouldn't be – strain again. The sauce is ready for use when seasoned up a bit with salt and pepper and perhaps a squeeze or two of lemon juice to bring the subtle flavours to life.

**5.** To prepare the mushrooms: wipe and slice them thinly, stalks and all. Put them into a non-stick pan with the lemon juice, and toss over a good heat until they just fall. Strain.

**6.** Butter an ovenproof dish. Pour in a thin film of the sauce and a little Parmesan. Lay in the first layer of pasta sheets. Pour over a little more sauce, sprinkle on the remaining Parmesan cheese and the sliced mushrooms. Lay the second layer of pasta sheets in the dish. Flake over the tuna fish, season lightly with salt and milled pepper, and a few driblets of the fish oil. Top with the final layer of pasta, pour over all the remaining sauce, dot with bits of Mozzarella cheese and distribute the chopped tomatoes over the surface.

**7.** Bake at Gas Mark 8 (230°C, 450°F) for 30 minutes, or until hot, bubbling, and the cheese melted and golden brown. Serve cut into wedges, with a tossed green salad on a side plate. Serves 6.

*Lasagne with tuna fish*

# GNOCCHI ALLA ROMANA

This was the very first dish I ever made when I was a student at Lausanne's famous hotel school.

Straight from Rome, gnocchi is a sort of Yorkshire pudding made with semolina. Filling and tasty, it can be served without sauce or with delicious home-made Tomato Sauce (see page 162).

---

*1¾ pints rich milk*
*salt*
*7 oz semolina*
*4 oz freshly grated Parmesan*
*3 oz butter*
*2 egg yolks*
*½ teaspoon grated nutmeg*

---

1. Bring the milk, with 1 teaspoon of salt, to the boil and then lower the heat. 'Rain' in the semolina, stirring and beating all the time with a balloon whisk. Cook this mixture over a low heat for 15 minutes, when it will be very thick.

2. Add half the grated cheese, 1 oz butter and the two egg yolks, beating each in well as you work. Dampen a work surface and tip the mixture out on to it. Wet your right hand and press the mixture into a squarish shape, about ½ inch thick (less if anything). Leave to cool completely (about 1½ hours).

3. Using a plain scone cutter or drinking glass 2 inches in diameter cut the mixture into discs, dipping the implement into cold water between each cut. Butter an ovenproof dish. Cut the leftovers of the gnocchi mixture into 1 inch bits and lay them in the bottom of the dish. Dot with bits of the remaining butter and dredge with a little cheese.

4. Arrange the discs, overlapping somewhat, on top of this, dot each disc with butter and scatter over the rest of the cheese and the nutmeg. Bake in a preheated oven at Gas Mark 8 (230°C, 450°F) for 15–20 minutes or until a golden brown crust has formed.

5. Serve with a fresh tomato sauce (though they don't do this in Rome) and salad. Serves 4–5 as a main dish.

*Gnocchi alla romana with fresh tomato sauce*

## PASTA SHELLS WITH PRAWNS

I have been serving pasta this way for decades; I have no idea where or when the idea came to me, but it is good, economical and can't go wrong.

---

*1 packet small pasta shells*
*1 lb fresh or frozen prawns*
*(shelled weight)*
*2 avocados*
*juice of 1 small lemon*
*salt and pepper*
*tabasco*
*1 tablespoon finely chopped parsley*
*and/or chives*

DRESSING:
*2 cloves garlic, crushed*
*1 level teaspoon salt*
*1 level teaspoon freshly ground*
*white peppercorns*
*1 modest heaped teaspoon*
*English mustard*
*¼ pint rich olive oil*
*juice of 1 lemon*

---

**1.** Boil the pasta shells in an abundance of water leaving them *al dente*. Rinse under cold running water and drain well, shaking the water out of the cavities.

**2.** Mix the dressing ingredients.

**3.** Mix the pasta shells and prawns in a large bowl, pour over the dressing and toss well. Cover with plastic film, and leave to chill in the refrigerator for two or three hours.

**4.** To prepare the avocado: cut the fruit in half, twist to separate the two parts and lift out the stone. Peel the fruit, cut into long slices and put into lemon juice immediately to prevent discoloration. Just before you are ready to use them, season the slices lightly with salt and milled pepper and a dash or two of tabasco if you like things hot!

**5.** Assemble the dish by arranging the slices of avocado in a star shape over the prawns and pasta, incorporating any juices into the salad. Sprinkle liberally with the chopped parsley or chives. Serves 6, or more if used as part of a cold buffet or as a first course.

## DANISH EGG CAKES

*4 eggs, seasoned and beaten*
*1 oz butter*

ANY ONE OR ALL OF THESE
TOPPINGS:
*tomatoes, skinned, seeded and chopped*
*onion rings, crisply fried*
*bacon, crisply fried*
*mushrooms, fried in butter*
*shrimps*
*asparagus*
*fish, cooked and flaked*

---

**1.** Preheat the grill.

**2.** Melt 1 oz butter in a frying pan. When it is hot pour in the egg mix and immediately disperse your chosen topping(s), either cold or ready prepared, whichever is appropriate.

**3.** Lower the heat and leave until the egg is almost set. Slide the pan under the hot grill to puff up the egg cake and heat the topping.

**4.** Serve flat. Serves 2.

## SPAGHETTI WITH GREEN VEGETABLES, HERBS AND SEAFOOD

*8 oz spaghetti broken into 6 inch lengths*
*salt*
*1 small cauliflower*
*2 tablespoons lemon juice*
*1 pint chicken stock (use a stock cube)*
*8 oz Kenya beans*
*4 oz mange-tout peas*
*8 oz courgettes, thinly sliced*
*3 tablespoons olive oil, plus extra for*
*reheating spaghetti*
*1 oz butter, plus extra for*
*reheating spaghetti and serving*
*1 large clove garlic, finely chopped*
*4 oz frozen petit pois (defrosted)*
*12 oz fresh or frozen shelled prawns or*
*shrimps or any other shellfish*
*pepper*
*2 tablespoons finely chopped chives,*
*basil and parsley, mixed*
*freshly grated Parmesan cheese*

*Pasta shells with prawns*

**1.** Cook the spaghetti in plenty of boiling salted water. Rinse under cold water and drain well.

**2.** Break the cauliflower into tiny florets and poach for 3–4 minutes in the lemon juice and stock. Remove with a draining spoon.

**3.** String the beans and mange-tout peas. Poach the trimmed beans in the same stock for the same length of time, and then the mange-tout peas, for one minute.

**4.** Heat the oil and butter in a large frying pan. Add the garlic and courgettes and fry these without colouring for 2 minutes only. Add the peas and mix well. Add the cauliflower, mange-tout peas and beans, mix well and warm through completely, over a low heat, turning them all the time. Add the prawns at the last minute.

**5.** In a second large pan heat the spaghetti through in a little oil and butter. Season lightly with salt and pepper. Turn on to a large serving platter. Spoon over the vegetables, avoiding the juices. Dab with 2 or 3 knobs of butter, sprinkle liberally with the herbs and serve with freshly grated Parmesan cheese. Serves 4 as a main course.

# SMOKED SALMON OMELETTE

An elegant brunch for one.

---

*2 oz good butter*
*2 slices white bread, cut into tiny cubes*
*2 oz smoked salmon, cut into cubes*
*2 tablespoons cream*
*3 eggs, beaten and seasoned*
*knob of butter for frying the omelette*
*little extra smoked salmon for garnish*

---

**1.** Make the croûtons the day before. Melt the butter until foaming, add the bread, toss and stir pieces continuously until crisp right through and golden brown. Drain on kitchen paper and store in an airtight container.

**2.** In a small pan, toss the smoked salmon in the cream until warm through.

**3.** Warm the croûtons in a low oven.

**4.** Beat and season the eggs. Make the omelette. Just before gathering it up, spoon in the smoked salmon and a spoonful of the warm croûtons.

**5.** Finish gathering it up and turn the omelette on to a warm plate. Make an incision down the back and fill this with more croûtons and strips of extra salmon if the housekeeping permits.

# SAFFRON RICE

---

*12 oz long grain rice*
*salt*
*2 oz butter*
*2 thimbles or sachets powdered saffron*
*1 level teaspoon ground coriander*
*3–4 strips orange rind*

---

**1.** Cook the rice in lightly salted boiling water for 12–15 minutes. Drain through a sieve or colander and rinse under hot water to remove surplus starch. Drain again.

**2.** Slowly melt the butter in a large, non-stick frying pan, without browning it. Spoon in the rice a little at a time, turning it in the butter with a slotted spoon. Dredge over the saffron and coriander and add the orange rind, mixing well in until the colour is a lovely saffron yellow and the rice piping hot. Add extra seasoning to taste.

**3.** Leave in the peel so that orange oil permeates the rice when it is hot. Pick it out just before serving. Serve with Conyngs in Greke Wine (see page 82). Serves 6.

*Smoked salmon omelette*

# Vegetables

## BAKED COURGETTES WITH PEPPERS, ANCHOVIES, MOZZARELLA CHEESE AND ALMONDS

This dish can be served as an accompaniment to roast meats, or chilled and used as a first course. If you choose to do the latter, substitute cottage cheese as Mozzarella toughens when cold.

---

*1 each red, yellow, green peppers (or 3 red)*
*3 tablespoons rich olive oil*
*1 onion, chopped*
*2 cloves garlic, crushed*
*8 × 4 inch courgettes topped and tailed*
*salt and milled pepper*
*lemon juice*
*2 oz whole blanched almonds (optional)*
*6 oz Mozzarella cheese – or cottage cheese*
*(see note above)*
*1 × 2 oz tin anchovy fillets*

---

1. Heat the oven to Gas Mark 9 (240°C, 475°F).

2. Roast the peppers until the skins blister – they may well char a little, but this doesn't matter. Peel after they have cooled somewhat: seed and chop into $\frac{1}{4}$ inch dice.

3. Heat the oil a little, add the onion and, over low heat, cook until soft but not brown.

4. Add the chopped peppers and garlic and cook gently for 10 minutes.

5. Meanwhile, bring a large pan of salted water to the boil and cook the courgettes for 7–8 minutes. Drain and, when cool enough to handle, cut them in half. Scoop out $\frac{1}{2}$ inch of the flesh, using a melon baller or teaspoon. Chop this flesh, add it to the peppers and cook the mixture for a further 2–3 minutes.

6. Arrange the courgettes in a buttered baking dish. Season them with salt, pepper and good squeeze of lemon juice. Put 2 or 3 almonds in each shell. Fill with the pepper mixture. Top with pieces of Mozzarella cheese and a strip of anchovy fillet. Bake at Gas Mark 6 (200°C, 400°F) for 30 minutes, until browned, hot and bubbling. Serves 8.

## COURGETTES WITH PEAS AND HERBS

See photograph on page 236.

---

*4 medium-sized (5 inch) courgettes*
*juice of $\frac{1}{2}$ lemon*
*1 oz butter*
*8 oz packet frozen petit pois (defrosted)*
*1 tablespoon freshly chopped herbs*
*(basil in the summer or oregano) or $\frac{1}{2}$*
*teaspoon dried oregano in the winter*
*1 level teaspoon caster sugar*
*salt and milled pepper*

---

1. Top, tail and wash the courgettes. Cut into tiny $\frac{1}{4}$ inch cubes. Toss in the lemon juice to prevent discoloration.

2. In a shallow, heavy-bottomed pan, melt the butter without browning. Add the peas and courgettes and all the remaining ingredients. Using a slotted spoon, turn and stir gently all the time. Bring them to piping hot.

3. Turn into a warm tureen. Serves 4.

*Baked courgettes with peppers, anchovies, Mozzarella cheese and almonds*

# SWEET GLAZED CARROTS WITH MACE, GINGERMINT AND PARSLEY

*1½ lb carrots*
*chicken stock*
*2 oz butter*
*ground mace*
*juice of ½ lemon*
*2 teaspoons sugar*
*1 tablespoon chopped gingermint*
*1 tablespoon freshly chopped parsley*

**1.** Peel the carrots. If young ones, leave whole; if older, cut into even-sized sticks about 2 × ½ inch. Put them into a pan with just enough stock to cover them, the butter, ½ teaspoon mace, lemon juice and sugar.

**2.** Cook until just tender. Drain, retaining the stock.

**3.** Boil this down until it is of a syrupy consistency – about ¼ pint – and toss the carrots in this. Put to keep warm, tossing the two green herbs in just before serving, and adding a good dredge of mace. Serves 4.

# AUBERGINE, TOMATO AND BASIL MOULD

*4 medium but even-sized aubergines*
*(about 5 inches long)*
*olive oil for frying*
*1 small carton plain yoghurt*
*extra freshly chopped basil or parsley*
*for garnish*
*salt and milled pepper*

TOMATO SAUCE:
*2 (14 oz) tins Italian plum tomatoes*
*1 chicken stock cube*
*1 clove garlic, crushed*
*1 dash tabasco sauce*
*1 good sprig or 1 teaspoon dried basil*
*1 teaspoon sugar*

**1.** Put all the ingredients for the sauce into a 3 pint heavy-bottomed pan. Bring to the boil and simmer until a cohered pulp is arrived at (a scant ¾ pint when sieved). Press through wire sieve. Cool. Reserve a third for serving.

**2.** Meanwhile, wipe the aubergines and top and tail them. Cut into ¼ inch thick discs, spread the discs on a clean surface and sprinkle lightly with salt. Leave for 30 minutes, then rinse under cold water and dry with paper towels.

**3.** Heat a little olive oil in a large frying pan. Brown the aubergines quickly on both sides, adding more oil as and when necessary.

**4.** Layer the fried discs in a 2½ pint ovenproof mould (or seamless cake tin), spreading each layer with tomato sauce and a little yoghurt. Add an extra sprinkling of fresh basil, if you like, and seasoning.

**5.** Cover and bake at Gas Mark 5 (190°C, 375°F) for 35–40 minutes.

**6.** Turn out of the mould and coat with the remaining sauce, hot. If serving cold leave to cool before turning out. Serves 6–8 as an hors d'oeuvre: 4–5 as a first course or vegetable.

# POTATO LATKES

See photograph on page 109.

*5 large potatoes to yield 1½ lb grated*
*potato*
*1 teaspoon bicarbonate of soda*
*3 oz plain white flour*
*1 large onion, grated*
*1 clove garlic, crushed*
*2 eggs, beaten*
*¼ pint single cream*
*salt and milled pepper to taste*
*oil for frying*

**1.** Grate the potatoes on the coarse side of a grater or in a food processor using the coarse grating disc.

**2.** Drop them, as you go along, into a large bowl of cold water, into which you have put the bicarbonate. This helps keep them a good colour.

**3.** Leave them to soak for an hour. Drain well, and pat excess moisture away. Mix with

*Sweet glazed carrots with mace, gingermint and parsley*

the flour, onion, beaten eggs and cream. Season well.

**4.** Heat $\frac{1}{4}$ inch oil in a heavy-bottomed frying pan, until lightly smoking. Drop teaspoons of the mixture into the oil and fry a few at a time on both sides until cooked and golden brown.

**5.** Drain on crumpled kitchen paper. Serve hot. Makes 24–30.

# PINK FIR APPLE POTATOES

Pink Fir Apple potatoes are now grown in England. They may have a strange appearance but their superb flavour and waxy texture make them exciting enough to serve as a starter! They also make a perfect accompaniment to almost any dish where 'plain boiled' potatoes are called for, and are excellent in potato salad. They are ideal when served with Stilton and Walnut Sauce (see page 163).

Just wash or scrub them lightly before boiling or steaming.

# PETIT DAUPHINOIS

I recommend this to anyone as an excellent alternative to its big brother, Gratin Dauphinois, where cost is to be counted and the vast quantity of cream is unacceptable. It is not the same dish. In fact it is very different and all the better for this difference. The long slow cooking process is the real secret of its success.

---

*butter*
*1 clove or more garlic*
*potatoes*
*salt and pepper*
*scalded milk*

---

*Pink Fir Apple potatoes with Stilton and walnut sauce*

**1.** Select an ovenproof dish some 3 inches deep. Butter this liberally and rub the inside with the cut face of a clove of garlic. Crush some garlic and sprinkle a little in the bottom of the dish.

**2.** Wash, peel and slice enough potatoes to fill the dish and put them into a large bowl of cold water. The slices should be as thin as a one penny piece. Drain and pat the potatoes dry with kitchen paper.

**3.** Arrange the potatoes in layers in the dish, very lightly salting and peppering each layer, and adding a further small amount of crushed garlic and tiny dabs of butter to alternate layers. Finally, pour over sufficient scalded milk to cover the potatoes completely, allowing a little time when pouring for the milk to run through to the bottom of the dish.

**4.** Cover the dish with foil or a lid and cook at Gas Mark 2/3 (150/170°C, 300/325°F) for 4 hours.

**5.** After 2 hours remove the foil or lid so that a golden crust can form. All the milk should be cooked in. The finished dish will be a deliciously cohered mass, to accompany almost anything.

# CREAM CHEESE STUFFED POTATOES

These can be prepared in advance.

---

*3 medium-sized potatoes*
*6 oz full fat cream cheese*
*1 oz butter, softened*
*half a bunch of spring onions, chopped*
*salt and pepper*

---

**1.** Bake the potatoes in their jackets in the usual way, having rubbed the skins with butter, oil or bacon fat to make them crisp.

**2.** Cream the cheese and butter. Cut the potatoes in half, scoop out the flesh and push through a ricer or mash well. (Do not use a food processor as this will glutinize it!)

**3.** Beat in the cheese mixture and half the spring onions. Season well. Pile into the empty shells. Reheat in the oven Gas Mark 6 (200°C, 400°F).

**4.** Sprinkle with the remaining spring onions. Serve piping hot. Serves 6.

# WHIPPED POTATOES

*3 lb potatoes, peeled*
*¼ pint double cream*
*2 oz unsalted butter*
*salt*
*½ level teaspoon ground nutmeg or mace*

1. Steam or boil the potatoes without salting them. Drain well, and if the potatoes have been boiled drain and then 'dry' them over a low heat to rid them of excess water.

2. Press them through a potato ricer or mash in the usual way. (Those of you with food processors will no doubt have discovered to your cost that potatoes cannot be puréed on these machines – they go glutinous.)

3. Warm the cream, butter, salt and nutmeg in a non-stick pan. Gradually incorporate the mashed potato, beating with a spatula until light and foamy. To keep hot, transfer the potatoes to an ovenproof dish. Cover first with a piece of wetted greaseproof paper which will prevent a crust forming, then a lid, and stand the dish in the oven at Gas Mark ½ (130°C, 250°F). They will be absolutely all right for up to an hour kept like this. Serves 4–6.

# BRANDIED CHEESE POTATOES

Once in a while a cook will come up with a new idea which really is stunning and yet not costly. These potatoes can be prepared a day in advance and are ideal for serving with grilled meat. They would also make a good supper dish.

*4 medium-sized waxy potatoes baked*
*in their jackets*
*2 oz butter*
*1 good tablespoon bland mayonnaise*
*2 tablespoons brandy*
*3–4 oz grated Dutch cheese*
*salt and a little milled pepper*

1. Cut a lid from each potato, scoop out the flesh and mash with the remaining ingre-dients. Don't be tempted to do this in a food processor or the potato mixture will be glutinous. The texture should be somewhat rough hewn.

2. Put the mixture back into the potato shells, dredge with further cheese if desired and reheat the potatoes at Gas Mark 7, (220°C, 425°F) or until hot and golden brown. Serves 4.

# NEW POTATOES IN CREAM

1. Allow 3–4 oz baby new potatoes for each serving. Wash these well and cook in lightly salted water until just tender. Drain. Return the potatoes to the pan and toss over a low heat until dry. Pour over enough cream to just coat the potatoes. Continue tossing them until the cream thickens and adheres.

2. Season with plenty of nutmeg or freshly chopped herbs. Serve hot or cold.

# PURÉE OF HARICOT BEANS WITH SPRING ONIONS

This purée is cheap to make and is ideal with a piece of boiled gammon or bacon. See photograph on page 151.

*2 × 8 oz tins haricot or butter beans,*
*drained, rinsed and drained again*
*2 oz butter*
*¼ pint single cream*
*1 tablespoon chopped parsley*
*salt and pepper*
*1 bunch spring onions, finely chopped*
*parsley to garnish*

1. Make a purée of the beans.

2. Heat the butter with the cream in a non-stick pan. Gradually incorporate the purée and parsley. Season to taste.

3. If the purée is too stiff add a little more cream or chicken stock.

4. Mix in the spring onions at the last minute. Garnish with parsley. Serves 4–6.

## FENNEL WITH CREAM AND PARMESAN CHEESE

*4 good-sized heads of fennel*
*chicken stock (use a cube)*
*salt*
*juice of ½ lemon*
*½ pint double cream*
*3 oz freshly grated Parmesan or Gouda*
*cheese*

1. In the morning, or the day before, cut the fennel into quarters. Cook in lightly salted chicken stock, just to cover, and lemon juice, until almost tender. Drain well and leave to cool.

2. Arrange in a buttered ovenproof dish. Bring the cream to the boil with three-quarters of the cheese. Pour this over the fennel and sprinkle with the remaining cheese.

3. Bake in a preheated oven, Gas Mark 6 (200°C, 400°F), until hot, brown and bubbling. Serves 8.

## MANGE-TOUT PEAS

See photograph on page 56.

*1 lb mange-tout peas*
*salt*
*½ lemon*
*2 tablespoons single cream*
*mace*
*unsalted butter*
*chopped chives*

1. Top, tail and string the mange-tout peas. Soak them in an abundance of cold water to remove any dirt on the skins.

2. Have ready a large pan of lightly salted boiling water, adding 2–3 strips of lemon peel or the juice and skin of ½ lemon. Put the drained mange-tout peas into the pan, cover with a lid, bring the water back to the boil and cook for one minute only.

3. Either drain the peas in a colander, return them to the hot pan and bathe them in 2 tablespoons of hot cream and a good dredging of mace, *or* dot them with plenty of unsalted butter (it tastes creamier) and sprinkle liberally with snipped chives which will complement rather than confuse the delicate flavour.

4. To prepare in advance: when cooked, drain the mange-tout peas and cool or 'refresh', as the French say, under running cold water. This blanching and refreshing retains the nice green colour of the vegetables.

5. Drain them well again and store in a plastic container in the refrigerator until ready to serve. Slowly melt 2 oz of butter in a large pan – don't allow it to brown – turn the peas in this over a low heat until hot right through. They must not fry. Sprinkle with chopped chives and serve. Serves 4.

## 'SHAKEN PEAS' IN CREAM WITH CUCUMBER AND LETTUCE

*12 oz petit pois, defrosted*
*1 small cucumber, peeled, seeded and*
*cut into sticks or crescents*
*2 tablespoons thick cream*
*1 oz butter*
*salt*
*1 small lettuce, shredded*
*1 bunch of chives or young spring*
*onions, chopped*
*1 tablespoon freshly chopped mint*

1. In a large, lidded pan toss or shake the peas and cucumber with the cream, butter and salt over a good heat until lightly cooked but still crisp.

2. Just before serving, mix in the lettuce, chives and mint. Toss until heated through (this should take about 1 minute). These might appear to be a little wet, but this is how things should be as long as the vegetables are crisp. Serves 6.

# BEETROOT AND ALMOND PURÉE

*1 lb boiled beetroot, peeled*
*4 oz ground almonds*
*2 oz butter*
*salt and nutmeg*
*1 teaspoon grated orange rind*
*⅛ pint single cream*

GARNISH:
*blanched almonds*
*raisins*

**1.** In a food processor or blender make a fine purée of all the ingredients except the cream.

**2.** Heat the small amount of cream in a non-stick pan. Gradually add the purée, allowing it to come to the boil after each addition.

**3.** Spoon into a warm tureen and garnish with almonds and raisins. Serves 5–6.

# CARROT PURÉE

The purée can be made the day before. See photograph on page 236.

*3 lb carrots, cleaned, peeled and cut into pieces*
*chicken stock (use a stock cube)*
*2 oz butter*
*1 level teaspoon caster sugar*
*1 level teaspoon grated orange zest*
*1 level teaspoon ground mace*
*⅛ pint double cream*

**1.** Cook the carrots in enough well-seasoned chicken stock to cover them, until quite tender. Drain well (retaining the liquid for a soup on some other occasion). Dry over a low heat.

**2.** Purée in the blender adding the butter, sugar, zest and mace and more salt if necessary.

**3.** To serve: heat ⅛ pint double cream in a non-stick pan, add the purée gradually, stirring over a low heat until it is piping hot.

# BEETROOT AND ORANGE PURÉE

*1 lb raw beetroot*
*chicken stock (use a stock cube)*
*1 teaspoon grated orange rind*
*2 oz butter*
*pinch of salt*
*¼ teaspoon powdered mace*
*or black pepper*

**1.** Wash the beetroot well and leave whole. Cook in lightly salted water until almost tender.

**2.** Drain, trim and peel. Cut in smaller pieces and cook again in chicken stock, just to cover, with the orange rind, until quite cooked. Drain the beetroot well and pass through a blender or food processor.

**3.** Dry the purée over a low heat. Beat in a good piece of butter and season well with salt, and mace or black pepper.

**4.** For an attractive garnish you can use thin slices of beetroot cut from a small root. Makes 8 small servings.

# RUNNER BEAN PURÉE WITH BASIL

*1 lb runner, French or stick beans*
*chicken stock (use a stock cube)*
*1 tablespoon fresh basil, finely chopped*
*1 tablespoon freshly picked, washed, and chopped parsley*
*1 oz butter*
*1 tablespoon double cream*

**1.** Top, tail and string the beans if necessary. Cook until tender in chicken stock. Blend to a fine purée. As beans hold liquid it is a good idea to squeeze some of this away by twisting the purée in a tea towel.

**2.** Add the herbs, the butter and the cream, and stir over a low heat until very hot. Serves 4–5.

Clockwise from top left: *Beetroot and almond purée; Runner bean purée with basil; Carrot purée; Purée of haricot beans with spring onions; Sweetcorn and lentil purée*

# SWEETCORN AND LENTIL PURÉE

*3 cobs of ripe corn, cooked and hulled*
*6 oz yellow lentils, soaked and cooked in*
*chicken stock*
*1 clove garlic, crushed*
*squeeze of lemon juice*
*2 oz butter*
*salt and milled white pepper*
*⅛ pint cream*

1. Make a purée of all the ingredients except the cream.
2. Heat the cream in a non-stick pan. Gradually add the purée, allowing it to come to the boil after each addition. Serves 5–6.

# CUCUMBERS WITH LEMON AND GARLIC SAUCE

I have unashamedly lifted right up-market the popular 'Ragoo of Cowcumbers', so popular in the eighteenth century, and which original recipe I unearthed over twenty years ago.

Flexible, in that it can be served hot or cold, as a first course or as an accompanying vegetable, this dish will win with all cucumber lovers (and growers).

But be warned: the sauce, which I think delicious, is pretty powerful on the garlic!

*3 'straight' cucumbers*
*skin of 1 lemon*

SAUCE:
*6 oz butter*
*3 egg yolks*
*juice of 1 large lemon*
*salt and milled white pepper*
*2 large cloves garlic, crushed*
*¼ pint double cream*

1. Peel and then seed the cucumbers by cutting them in half and scraping out the seeds with a teaspoon or melon baller. Cut into even-sized sticks about 1½ × ½ inch (or trim them into small barrel shapes if you have the patience).
2. Boil for just 2 minutes in lightly salted water, to which you have added the lemon skin cut up.
3. Drain well. Keep warm wrapped in a clean towel to absorb any excess moisture, for which cucumbers are notorious.
4. To make the sauce: melt the butter in a small pan. Leave to settle. Whisk the yolks, 1 tablespoon water, lemon juice, salt and pepper in a round-bottomed bowl arranged over a pan of simmering water.
5. When the mixture ribbons, which won't take more than about a minute, remove the basin from the heat, stand it on a damp cloth to prevent it from skidding and whisk in the butter very gradually, starting with 1 teaspoon and gradually adding more as the emulsion builds up.
6. Add the garlic. Warm the cream in a small pan, whisk into the sauce, pour over the waiting cucumber and serve. Serves 6.

# CAULIFLOWER POLONAISE WITH SHRIMPS

See photograph on page 154.

*1 cauliflower, broken into florets*
*juice of 1 lemon*
*2 oz butter, melted to 'nut-brown' or*
*French dressing*

GARNISH:
*4 hard-boiled eggs, cut into smallish pieces,*
*but not chopped too finely*
*4 oz coarse white breadcrumbs, fried until*
*crisp in 2 oz good butter*
*6 oz fresh or frozen prawns or shrimps*
*1 heaped tablespoon parsley, fairly*
*coarsely chopped*

1. Cook the cauliflower in plenty of boiling lightly salted water, to which you have added the juice of a lemon, not only for added flavour but to keep the cauliflower white. This dish is nicer if the cauliflower still has some bite in it when cooked.

*Cucumbers with lemon and garlic sauce*

2. Pour the butter or splash a little French dressing over the hot cauliflower. Re-form into a 'whole' shape, scatter the garnish around and over. Serves 4–5.

# CAULIFLOWER CHEESE

*2 small cauliflowers, white with tight, well-formed florets*
*salt*
*skin and juice of 1 lemon*
*(keep 1 teaspoon juice for the sauce)*

LIGHT CHEESE SAUCE:
*¾ pint single cream*
*4 oz Gruyère, grated*
*3 oz Parmesan, grated*
*1 teaspoon lemon juice*
*1 teaspoon whisky*

1. Leave the green leaves which are a good colour. Cut the cauliflowers into 6 pieces, or break in their naturally formed florets.
2. Boil for 5 minutes (for crisp cauliflower), in an abundance of lightly salted water to which you have added the skin and juice of the lemon.
3. To make the sauce: bring the ingredients (except 2 oz Parmesan) to the boil in a non-stick pan. Simmer, stirring, for about 10 minutes.
4. Serve in a sauceboat. Pass extra Parmesan for sprinkling. Serves 8.

# STUFFED TOMATOES

*1 tablespoon olive oil*
*4 oz bacon, cut into small dice*
*4 oz onion, finely chopped*
*4 oz white mushrooms, finely chopped*
*1 tablespoon ginger- or applemint, chopped*
*2 tablespoons parsley, finely chopped*
*1 level teaspoon dried ground thyme, or 1 level dessertspoon freshly chopped thyme*
*1 clove garlic, crushed*
*salt and pepper*
*4 oz white breadcrumbs, fried till golden brown in 2 oz butter*
*8 large tomatoes*
*tabasco sauce*
*squeeze of lemon juice*

1. Heat the oil, fry the bacon until almost crisp, add the onion and fry until soft. Add the mushrooms and soften these too. Mix in all the herbs and garlic. Season well and mix in the crumbs.
2. Cut the *bottoms* off the tomatoes about 1 inch down the fruit. Empty with a teaspoon and discard the pulp. Season the insides with salt and pepper, the odd dash of tabasco, and a little squeeze of lemon juice. (It's these touches that count so much in cookery.) Fill the tomatoes with the stuffing. Balance the caps on top.
3. Bake in a well-buttered dish at Gas Mark 6 (200°C, 400°F) for 20 minutes, or until really hot right through, but not collapsed! Serves 8.

*Cauliflower polonaise with shrimps*

# Savoury Butters and Sauces

## FILLET STEAKS WITH TOMATO, CURRY AND ORANGE BUTTER

*4 (6–8 oz) fillet steaks*

MARINADE:
*½ pint red wine*
*1 tablespoon olive oil*
*1 teaspoon grated orange zest*
*1 small onion, finely chopped*
*1 clove garlic, crushed*
*1 teaspoon mild curry powder*
*salt and milled pepper*

SAVOURY BUTTER:
*8 oz butter, softened*
*1 level teaspoon salt*
*2 tablespoons (2 oz) tomato purée*
*1 teaspoon finely grated orange zest*
*1 heaped teaspoon mild Madras curry*
*powder or paste*

GARNISH:
*½ skinned and seeded tomato*
*for each steak*

1. With a wetted rolling pin gently beat each steak. Tie round its girth with string to hold the shape of the steak while being cooked.

2. Mix the ingredients for the marinade together and marinate the steaks in a glass or enamel dish covered with plastic film for 6–8 hours, turning them at hourly intervals.

3. To make the savoury butter: blend all the ingredients. Chill. Form into balls with a melon baller and store in the freezer until required.

4. Remove the steaks from the marinade and pat dry with kitchen paper. Grill or pan-fry them. If grilling, then baste, after well sealing them on both sides under a searing heat, with a spoonful of the marinade.

5. Heat the tomatoes under the grill, taking care they don't collapse. Top each steak with half a tomato filled with balls of the chilled butter. Serves 4.

## LEMON GARLIC BUTTER

To serve with grilled fish or vegetables.

*8 oz butter, softened*
*1 level teaspoon salt*
*2 cloves garlic, crushed*
*milled white pepper*
*finely grated zest and juice of 1*
*large lemon*

Blend all the ingredients together. Form into your chosen shape. Store the butter in the freezer until required.

Clockwise from top: *Cucumber dill butter; Lemon garlic butter; Tomato, curry and orange butter; Foie gras and artichoke butter*

# CUCUMBER DILL BUTTER

To serve with grilled fish or chicken. See photograph on page 157.

---

*6 oz butter*
*salt and pepper*
*1 tablespoon chopped fresh dill*
*juice and peel of ½ lemon*
*½ cucumber, peeled, seeded and*
*cut into minuscule dice*

---

Cream together the butter, seasoning, dill and lemon juice and rind. Fold in the cucumber. Form into a flat ½ inch block. Mark into squares and freeze. Cut the block into squares and store in freezer bags until needed.

# GARLIC MAYONNAISE

This is one of the most enjoyable ways of eating jacket potatoes. Spoon the mayonnaise into the potatoes before serving.

---

*4 egg yolks*
*1 level teaspoon mustard*
*salt*
*8 cloves garlic, crushed*
*½ pint olive oil or, for a lighter*
*sauce, ½ arachide to olive oil*
*2 tablespoons white wine vinegar*

---

**1.** Using a balloon whisk, mix the yolks, mustard and salt until thick and sticky.

**2.** Add the garlic and continue beating as you add the oil drop by drop. As soon as the mayonnaise starts to get really thick add a drop of the vinegar.

**3.** Continue like this until all the oil is incorporated.

**4.** The vinegar is used to control the consistency of the emulsion. If you find the mayonnaise too sharp then substitute cold water for vinegar. If you prefer to make your mayonnaise in a blender, then do so, adding the crushed garlic about halfway through. There is enough mayonnaise here for 8 servings.

# FOIE GRAS AND ARTICHOKE BUTTER

Serve on top of grilled steak, chicken breasts or veal chops. See photograph on page 157.

---

*6 oz butter, softened*
*4 oz mousse de foie gras (Swiss Parfait)*
*1 level teaspoon salt*
*freshly milled white pepper*
*1 small tin artichoke bases, drained*
*and cut into small dice*
*lemon juice*
*artichoke bases for garnish*

---

**1.** Blend together the butter and mousse de foie gras, season lightly. Toss the diced artichoke bases in lemon, season lightly. Mix carefully into the blended butter.

**2.** Form into an oblong approximately 6 × 3 × 1 inch and chill well. Cut into 6 squares. Place each square on top of an artichoke base and in turn stand this on top of the grilled steak.

# BASIC HOLLANDAISE SAUCE

---

*6 oz unsalted butter*
*2 tablespoons white wine vinegar*
*1 small piece onion*
*6 peppercorns*
*1 small piece bay leaf*
*3 egg yolks*
*lemon juice*
*salt and freshly ground white pepper*

---

**1.** Put the butter into a small pan and stand it somewhere where the butter will melt and get quite warm. Put the wine vinegar, 3 tablespoons water, the onion, peppercorns and bay leaf into a small pan and boil rapidly without a lid until the mixture is reduced down to 1 tablespoon.

**2.** Now add two more tablespoons of water (you require the original quantity of liquid to extract the aromas in the first stage; you then need to replace some of the liquid which has evaporated during the reduction).

3. Select a bowl which has a rounded base and which will sit in the top of a pan of boiling water. Before positioning the bowl, put the egg yolks in and strain the liquid on to them, stirring well with a tiny balloon whisk or spatula.

4. Arrange the bowl over the boiling water and whisk gently, but completely, taking care to see that the egg doesn't set on the sides of the bowl.

5. Continue whisking until the mixture is thick and the whisk leaves a definite trail, but stop before the eggs scramble! (Have a big bowl of cold water to hand as a safety precaution. Dip the base of the bowl into the water to remove the residual heat quickly, thus avoiding any possibility of the egg over-cooking.)

6. Now stand the bowl on a folded damp cloth (this helps keep the bowl steady as you whisk). Whisk in a few drops only of the melted butter, incorporating it well, and, as the sauce thickens, add the butter more quickly until it is all incorporated (do not use the milky sediment which will have settled to the bottom of the pan while the butter has been slowly melting).

7. Adjust the seasoning, adding a little lemon juice and salt and pepper if you think it is needed. Squeeze little pieces of butter over the surface to prevent a crust forming. The butter can be whisked briskly into the sauce just before serving. Stand the sauce in a warm place until you are ready to use it. As this is a warm sauce, it must not be kept where it will get too hot or it will separate, so keep an eye on it. A good place to put it is on top of a plate which is standing on top of a pan of hot, but not simmering, water.

8. Serve with any boiled or steamed vegetables, poached fish, hot fish mousses and soufflés, hot asparagus and hot artichokes.

**Sauce Mousseline:** to the Basic Hollandaise Sauce add ⅓ pint cream, half whipped. Serve with any dish where hollandaise sauce could be served.

**Maltese Sauce:** use the Basic Hollandaise Sauce but substitute orange juice for lemon juice, and add 1 teaspoon carefully grated orange rind and a hint of mace to the finished sauce.

**Sauce Foyot:** to the Basic Hollandaise Sauce add 1 teaspoon finely chopped or crushed garlic, 1 tablespoon chopped tarragon, 1 tablespoon chopped parsley.

**Choron Sauce:** to the Basic Hollandaise Sauce add 1 dessertspoon mild tomato purée and 1 dessertspoon chopped fresh tarragon.

**Sauce Béarnaise:** to make Sauce Béarnaise, follow the recipe for Basic Hollandaise Sauce but make the following changes. Substitute tarragon vinegar for wine vinegar. At the 'reduction' stage, crumble into the liquid half a chicken stock cube (use Knorr or Maggi which are less potent than other brands). This is almost as good as the meat glaze called for in the traditional French recipe for béarnaise. Finish the sauce with 1 dessertspoon chopped tarragon and/or parsley. Don't add salt until the end as the stock cube may well suffice. Serve the sauce with grilled fillet steak, Pan-fried Châteaubriand (see page 93), baby lamb cutlets, or with grilled or deep-fried fish.

# PESTO

It was in Genoa that the simplest of Italian 'sauces', pesto, originated. Once tasted, always hankered after.

*4 oz fresh picked basil leaves*
*8 tablespoons rich olive oil*
*3 large cloves garlic, crushed*
*2 oz pine kernels*
*2 oz freshly grated Parmesan cheese*
*1 oz freshly grated Pecorino cheese*
*2 oz soft, not melted, butter*

1. In a blender, make a smooth paste of all the ingredients except the cheeses and butter.

2. Scrape the contents of the blender into a bowl and stir in the cheese by hand, then add the butter.

3. Spoon the pesto over hot pasta – spaghetti, tagliatelle, spaghettini, pappardelle. With 6 oz dry pasta per person, serves 4 as a main course.

# AVOCADO AND WATERCRESS MAYONNAISE

Served with eggs, this sauce gives a new dimension to that ubiquitous first course, the egg mayonnaise. The sauce is also excellent with cold poached salmon or chicken.

---

*6 oz home-made mayonnaise*
*3 Hass avocados (or 2 larger ones),*
*peeled and pitted*
*2 bunches of crisp, fresh watercress, picked*
*over*
*1 bunch of chives, roughly chopped*
*2 good sprigs of fresh basil (optional)*
*juice of 1 lemon*
*salt and milled pepper*

---

1. Blend the ingredients in a food processor and press through a fine sieve.
2. The sauce should have the consistency of heavy pouring cream but, if it is too stiff, thin it down with cold water. Serves 6.

# CUMBERLAND SAUCE

This sauce is especially good with all kinds of roast game as well as with raised pies and any cold meats.

---

*3 oranges*
*3 lemons*
*1 lb redcurrant jelly*
*¼ pint ruby port (tawny port will not*
*give such a good colour)*
*1 level dessertspoon dry mustard*
*1 small onion, very finely chopped*
*a little salt*
*tip of a teaspoon powdered mace*
*1 sherry glass cider vinegar (not* malt
*vinegar)*

---

1. Using a potato peeler or zester, remove the rind from all 6 pieces of fruit. Care must be taken to ensure that no white pith is taken off with the rind, as this is the bitter part of citrus fruits. Collect the strips of rind into manageable piles and with a very sharp, thin-spined knife shred the rind as finely as

*Avocado and*
*watercress*
*mayonnaise*

you possibly can – try to shred it as fine as a pin, for this will guarantee your sauce is good looking and elegant. Be patient!
2. Put the shredded rind into a pan and pour over enough water to cover it. Bring the contents of the pan to the boil and immediately pour through a strainer. Cool the peel under running cold water for a minute or so, then put on one side.
3. Squeeze and strain the juice of two oranges and two lemons. Bring this to the boil with all the remaining ingredients and simmer for 15 minutes over a low heat, stirring to ensure that the jelly melts evenly and doesn't catch.
4. Add the shredded rind and boil for a further 5–10 minutes until the sauce starts to thicken. Cool, then refrigerate until thick. Serve chilled and do not strain. It will keep for up to two weeks in the refrigerator. Makes 1 pint. Enough for 8.

# BEEF AND RED PEPPER SAUCE

For Bolognese addicts this will be a winner. I have omitted flour – well, almost – and used a purée of peppers to make the whole thing cohesive. Good for dieters, too. Serve it with pasta, adding extra peppers cut into julienne strips if liked. These should be softened in a little olive oil or butter before mixing in with the pasta.

---

*4 tablespoons olive oil*
*1 medium-sized onion, finely chopped*
*1 lb best steak, trimmed and minced*
*1 × 4 oz tin tomato purée*
*½ bottle red wine*
*1 teaspoon paprika*
*1 × 2 oz tin anchovy fillets*
*1 teaspoon flour*
*3 red peppers*
*2 dashes of tabasco*
*1 teaspoon brown sugar*
*salt and pepper*

---

1. On top of the stove, heat 2 tablespoons oil until hazy. Soften the onion, then add the mince a little at a time letting it take what colour it will.

2. Add the purée, wine, paprika, anchovy fillets and flour and transfer into an oven-proof dish. Cook at Gas Mark 6 (200°C, 400°F) for 30 minutes.

3. Meanwhile, seed the red peppers, chop them roughly and, over a low heat, soften them completely in the remaining 2 table-spoons oil, adding the tabasco and a tea-spoon of brown sugar.

4. Make a fine purée in a blender or food processor. Check the seasoning and stir the purée into the cooking meat sauce. Cook for a further 30 minutes. Serves 8–10.

## SAUCE RAVIGOTE

This sauce, more elaborate than a French dressing, is delicious with cold asparagus.

---

*½ pint rich French dressing
2 hard-boiled eggs, whites only, finely chopped
2 tablespoons capers, finely chopped
2 tablespoons finely chopped chives or 1 small bunch spring onions, finely chopped
1 tablespoon finely chopped parsley
1 tablespoon finely chopped tarragon or chervil*

---

Mix all the ingredients together.

## FRESH TOMATO SAUCE

---

*1 lb tomatoes, skinned, seeded and chopped
1 dessertspoon dry sherry
¼ pint tomato juice
1 level teaspoon caster sugar
1 large sprig dill or mint
1 dessertspoon lemon juice
salt
milled white pepper*

---

Put all the ingredients into an enamel pan and simmer until reduced to a fine pulp. Press through a fine sieve, reheat and serve.

## SPECIAL GRAVY

This basic gravy can be used for any roast meat or poultry; it can be made days in advance and is therefore a great time-saver.

---

*1½ oz butter
1 oz flour
¾ pint chicken stock (use a cube)
¼ pint sherry
2 tomatoes, cut up
1 level teaspoon made English mustard
1 heaped teaspoon redcurrant jelly
1 tablespoon lemon juice
1 level teaspoon turmeric
salt and milled pepper*

---

1. Melt the butter, stir in flour and cook over a low heat until it has browned. Stir all the time.

2. Add the stock gradually. Bring to the boil and add the remaining ingredients, except the salt and pepper.

3. Simmer the sauce for 20 minutes and reduce to about ¾ pint. Strain and put on one side, or cool and refrigerate if made the day before.

4. Decant away as much of the fat in the particular roasting tin as you can. Over a low heat, using a straight-edged wooden spatula, scrape the pan juices together.

5. Pour the basic sauce into the roasting pan. Bring to the boil, stirring all the time. Check the seasoning and simmer for about 5 minutes. Strain the sauce into a warm sauce or gravy boat. Serves 6–8.

## SPECIAL APPLE SAUCE

---

*8–10 oz stiff apple purée (use 1 lb Cox's apples)
grated rind and juice of 1 orange
4 oz ground almonds
good sherry glass of demerara rum
¼ teaspoon ground cinnamon
salt and milled pepper*

---

1. Simmer the peeled, cored and sliced apples in the orange juice with the grated rind

over a low heat until soft. Stir in the other ingredients and simmer for 5 minutes.

2. Put through a blender or rub through a hair sieve. Reheat and serve.

3. If the sauce is too thick – it should be the consistency of custard – add a little extra orange juice.

# CRANBERRY PURÉE

*1 punnet Ocean Spray cranberries*
*juice of 1 lemon*
*2 tablespoons water*
*1 oz or more sugar*

Put the ingredients into a pan and simmer until soft. Press through a sieve. Cool, then chill well.

# RICH BOLOGNESE SAUCE

Italian Bolognese Sauce is somewhat lighter than my version. On occasion I have made the sauce using all red wine and not the stated half wine, half stock; I use the richer sauce when I make a meat lasagne. The quantities given make 2 pints.

*1 lb best rump or stewing steak*
*2 oz onion, finely chopped*
*3 tablespoons olive oil*
*3 oz tomato purée*
*1 oz flour*
*½ pint red wine*
*1 large clove garlic, crushed*
*½ pint stock, made with a stock cube*
*salt and freshly ground black pepper*

1. Strip the steak of fat and sinew (I always use rump, which is more expensive but has an excellent flavour). Put the meat through a mincer twice.

2. In a heavy-bottomed pan fry the finely chopped onion in the oil until golden brown. Gradually add the minced meat, stirring well over a good heat until the meat browns. Now reduce the heat and add the tomato purée, taking care to work it in well and see that it does not burn. Sprinkle the flour over and mix in well.

3. Now – and here is the secret of a good brown sauce – over a low heat gradually allow a crust to form on the bottom of the pan. This should take about 10 minutes, but watch it carefully. Remove the meat mixture.

4. Turn up the heat again and pour in the red wine. With a wooden spatula work all the crust into the liquid. When the bottom of the pan is quite clear put the meat mixture back into the wine sauce, add the garlic and the stock and simmer for 30 minutes. Check seasoning. Serve with the pasta of your choice.

# STILTON AND WALNUT SAUCE

This sauce is ideal for serving with top quality baby new potatoes or with the Pink Fir Apple Potatoes (see page 147). They make an excellent first course when served this way, the exotic sauce lifting them into the sublime.

*½ pint single cream*
*8 oz Stilton cheese, mashed*
*lemon juice*
*dash of tabasco*
*4 oz (or more) walnuts, roughly crushed,*
*heated in the oven and lightly dredged*
*with salt*

1. Put the cream, cheese and about 1 teaspoon of lemon juice into a small non-stick pan. Heat slowly, stirring all the time, until the cheese has completely melted and is quite hot. Add the odd spot of tabasco. The sauce must not actually bubble or it will 'oil out'.

2. Stir in the walnuts and serve. This is sufficient for 4–5 servings.

# Puddings and Cakes

I have often been quoted as saying that life without puddings would be unbearable and I really would be miserable if I thought there was nothing rich and sickly to come after my main course. I don't doubt that fresh fruit and cheese is good for one – but it's no good for my soul.

This is an area of cooking where restaurateurs could learn a lot from the British housewife, for it is here, in the field of baking, cake and sweet making, that she excels. I am at my happiest dining in a home where the woman enjoys cooking for I know that at the end of an excellent meal a choice of puddings will be offered – all served with plenty of cool, thick cream. Cream is, to me, the unbeatable partner for puddings, giving a lift to subtle flavours and acting as a foil to those that are particularly rich and sweet.

All puddings, even the simplest, demand and deserve the best ingredients: unsalted butter (essential for good flavour); real vanilla sugar (keep a vanilla pod in your sugar jar); egg yolks for thickening home-made custards; fresh lemon juice, butter and a little icing sugar to make rich, crumbly melt-in-the-mouth pastry. You *will* notice the difference if you use freshly ground almonds, a dash of liqueur and, whenever possible, *real* essences and extracts. Next time you are in France spend your last francs at Fauchon in Paris, or in one or other of the excellent shops in the major channel ports. You'll save much more on a bottle of Cointreau, eau de vie or crème de cassis than you will on bottles of wine.

*Chocolate caramel cake; Chocolate trifle; Exotic fruit salad with Turkish delight*

## STRAWBERRIES CARDINAL

This classic dish is so easy to make and very rewarding to eat. Its success lies in the quality of the strawberries and raspberries and the one simple technique of cutting the strawberries in half so that the cut face absorbs the delicious raspberry purée.

Having created such an elegant dish – and simplicity is elegance – I think it almost criminal to blanket the fruits with cream – but of course the choice is up to you.

---

*2 lb strawberries for 8 good servings*

PURÉE:
*¾ lb raspberries*
*2 tablespoons lemon juice*
*8 oz caster sugar (or less)*

---

1. Pick over the strawberries. Unless they are very sandy, do not wash them. With a stainless steel knife (carbon steel will taint the fruit) cut them in half – if they are huge, quarter them.

2. To make up the purée: pick over the raspberries. Put into a stainless or enamel-lined pan. Mix the juice and sugar. Over a minimal heat soften the fruit, letting it gradually come to the boil. Stir from time to time.

3. Simmer for 2–3 minutes (longer will remove the 'fresh' flavour of the raspberries). Cool. Rub through a fine-meshed sieve. (Do not blend or you will end with a cloudy purée and will still have the seeds to get rid of!)

4. Cool, then chill. An hour before serving, gently turn the cut strawberries into the purée, using a large slotted spoon and a large bowl.

5. Pile them into polished glass dishes or one large glass bowl. This is one of the few occasions when glass – and cut glass in particular – complements food.

## PINEAPPLE SALAD WITH RASPBERRY PURÉE

---

*2 pineapples*
*caster sugar*
*juice of 1 lemon*
*kirsch, whisky or gin*
*(optional)*

RASPBERRY PURÉE:
*2 × 8 oz packs frozen raspberries*
*juice of 1 lemon*
*4 oz caster sugar (less if the raspberries are frozen in sugar)*

---

1. Peel the pineapples. Cut into half lengthways, then into half again, also lengthways. Remove any woody core.

2. Now cut the pineapple into thin slices and arrange on a serving platter. Dredge lightly with caster sugar and splash with lemon juice. Splash with kirsch, whisky or gin, if liked. Chill, covered with clingfilm.

3. To make raspberry purée: put all the ingredients in a pan, bring to the boil slowly and stir from time to time. Leave to cool. Press through a fine sieve. Chill well. Spoon over the pineapple just before serving.

*Strawberries cardinal*

# EXOTIC FRUIT SALAD

At one time I suppose any imported fruits, or at least fruits not normally grown in England, would have been classed as luxury fruits.

Today it is such exotics as guavas, passion fruits, kiwis, mangoes, lychees and nectarines which come under this heading. But I feel some of the more aromatic melons, such as pineapple melons, fresh dates and the pineapple itself ought perhaps to stay within the boundaries of luxury fruits. My fresh fruit salad can be a combination of almost any exotic fruits, many of which should be available to people living near a major town or city.

My reason for including the pineapple and perhaps ogen or Spanish cantaloup melon is to help out in those areas where only one or two of the rarer fruits are available.

You are hardly likely to embark on making such a salad for a small number, though a simple coupling of kiwi fruit with mango or fresh apricots is exotic enough, particularly if dressed with an orange-scented syrup. My recipe here is for a dozen or so guests and would be a real summer treat for them, a dish that looks almost as exotic as it tastes.

I PINT SYRUP:
*10 oz caster sugar*
*2 large strips lemon rind (cut with*
*a potato peeler)*
*juice of 2 lemons*
*2 large strips orange rind (cut with*
*a potato peeler), plus some for a garnish*
*1 level teaspoon ground ginger*
*½ teaspoon cinnamon or*
*1 stick cinnamon*

FRUIT (SMALL BUT RIPE):
*1 pineapple*
*1 mango*
*2 nectarines*
*1 pineapple or ogen melon*
*3 kiwi fruits*
*2 peaches*
*6 apricots*
*6 lychees*
*3 passion fruits*

*Exotic fruit salad: nectarines, passion fruit, mangoes, lychees, kiwi fruits, pineapple*

1. Bring all the ingredients for the syrup plus ¾ pint cold water to boiling point. Reduce the heat, simmer until all is clear.

2. Cool and chill. Decant into a large basin through a muslin or paper-lined sieve.

3. Cut the pineapple in half. Knife peel and core it. Cut in slices, then into even-sized fan-shaped pieces. Peel the mango with a potato peeler. Carve the flesh away from the stone as neatly as possible, then cut into tidy pieces. Cut the nectarines in half, pit them but do not skin them. Cut into crescents. Cut the melon in half, seed and scoop the flesh out with a melon baller.

4. Peel the kiwis and cut into thinnish 'discs' about ⅛ inch thick. Skin the peaches, having first dipped them quickly into a pan of boiling water.

5. Cut the peaches in half – take out the stone. Cut into crescents, then in half again. Pit the apricots and leave in halves. Skin the lychees, and halve.

6. As each fruit is prepared it should be put directly into the chilled syrup to avoid staining – turning each addition to coat the cut fruits. Always use a stainless steel knife.

7. Chill all this well for 2–4 hours before serving. Cut the passion fruit in half, scoop out the pulp and mix with the other fruit. Decorate with strips of orange rind.

# CHARENTAIS MELON WITH MANGO AND KIWI

*1 charentais melon*
*2 tablespoons lemon juice or Poire William*
*1 small mango*
*1 kiwi fruit*

1. Cut the melon in half. Scoop out the seeds. Pour into each half a little lemon juice or liqueur.

2. Peel the mango and cut out wedges of the flesh. Cut each wedge into smaller segments.

3. Peel the kiwi. Cut into discs, then into smaller pieces. Toss the two fruits together in a basin with the remaining lemon juice or liqueur. Pile into the melon halves. Cover with plastic film and chill for 4 hours. Serves 2.

# COMPÔTE OF KUMQUATS

For those of you who have never seen one of these very pretty fruits, they are actually a native of China called *chin kan*, which means gold orange. Akin to those little orange balls we see on miniature trees around Christmas time (but don't try eating *those*) they are a citrus fruit about 1 inch in diameter, except they're oval. Made into a delicate compôte they taste similar to good marmalade.

Eaten raw they have a 'bite' which adds piquancy to any fruit salad.

*1 lb kumquats*
*6 oz caster sugar*
*2 tablespoons triple strength orange flower water*

1. Arrange the washed fruits, whole, in one even layer in a heavy-bottomed pan. Sprinkle over the sugar. Splash over the flower water, and just enough water to barely cover the fruits.

2. Cover with a lid and simmer until just tender (about 1 minute). Leave to cool in the syrup. Chill and serve ice cold. If using in a fruit salad, quarter the fruits, as a whole raw kumquat in the mouth can be a bit of a shock to those not used to such happenings.

# NECTARINES IN CREAM

Simple sweets are invariably effective. Here is a nectarine sweet to add to your collection.

*6 good nectarines*
*6 rounded tablespoons caster sugar*
*2 × 6 oz cartons double cream*
*vanilla pod*

1. Peel, pit and quarter the nectarines. Place them rather close together in a shallow baking dish.

2. Sprinkle the caster sugar over the fruit, and pour over the two cartons of double cream. Lay a vanilla pod among the fruit, and place in the oven at Gas Mark 5 (190°C, 375°F) for 30 minutes or until they are tender. (Vanilla pods are obtainable at health food shops, and are an essential part of this dish.) Serve ice-cold.

3. One variation on this theme is to make a pie by adding a sweet pastry crust. Yet another is to serve the nectarines with balls of chocolate ice-cream.

Note: the vanilla pod can be washed under the cold tap and used again.

# RØD GRØD MED FLØDE

This delicious Danish red fruit purée can be made with gooseberries, adding a couple of elderberry flower heads to give a subtle scent. In this case a drop or two of green colouring should be added.

*2 lb red berries (any combination of raspberries, blackberries, red- or black-currants, cherries and strawberries)*
*6 oz caster sugar*
*2 tablespoons lemon juice*
*potato flour*
*red food colouring*
*caster sugar*

1. In a stainless steel or enamel pan gradually bring to the boil the fruit, sugar, lemon juice and a little water. Simmer until completely fallen. Strain. Make the syrup up to ¾ pint with water. Bring back to the boil.

2. Slake 2 heaped teaspoons of potato flour in a teacup of cold water. As the syrup is boiling, stir in the mixture a little at a time, allowing the potato flour to thicken the syrup between each addition. Add only enough red colour to make the syrup bright.

3. Stop stirring in the potato flour as soon as the mixture is thick enough. Stir in the strained fruit. Dredge the surface with caster sugar to stop a skin from forming. Cool, then chill.

Note: potato flour is essential here, as it thickens without clouding. Serves 6.

# ORANGE SYLLABUB

*rind and juice of 1 orange*
*2 oz caster sugar*
*¼ pint dry madeira or sherry*
*½ pint double cream*
*candied fruits for decoration*

1. Put the orange rind, juice, sugar and wine into a bowl. Cover and leave for a few hours.

2. Stir in the cream, gradually beating it until it ribbons and peaks.

3. Spoon into tall glasses and put to chill. Decorate at will. Serves 4.

# GOOSEBERRY FOOL WITH ROSE FLOWER WATER

*1 lb young green gooseberries*
*2 oz unsalted butter*
*4 oz (or less) sugar*
*1 tablespoon triple strength rose flower water*
*½ pint double cream*

1. Top, tail and wash the gooseberries. Melt the butter without letting it take on any colour. Add the gooseberries, put on a lid and cook over a low heat for 10 minutes, or until soft.

2. Remove from the heat and sweeten to taste. Add the rose flower water and mix in. Leave to cool.

3. Put the fruit through the fine grid of a mouli (a blender makes the purée too foamy).

Whip the cream and fold into the cooled purée.

4. Spoon into individual glasses. Chill, covered with clingfilm. Serves 6.

# PINEAPPLE AND STRAWBERRY SALAD WITH DRAMBUIE

*1 lb strawberries*
*1 small pineapple*
*2 oz caster sugar*
*juice of 1 lemon*
*4 fl oz Drambuie*

1. Quarter the strawberries. Peel and core the pineapple. Cut into ½ inch thick strips and then into ½ inch bits. Dredge with caster sugar.

2. Toss the pineapple and strawberries in the juice and liqueur. Chill well. Serves 6–8.

# ORANGES IN RED WINE

*8 navel oranges*
*4 oz brown sugar*
*½ pint red wine, Burgundy-type*
*level teaspoon ground ginger*

1. Make a chiffonade (very finely shredded julienne strips) from the rind of 2 of the oranges. Peel all of them, using a sharp knife.

2. Segment all the oranges. Dissolve the sugar in the wine, bring to the boil, add the chiffonade of rind and the ginger. Simmer for 5 minutes. Allow the wine syrup to cool completely.

3. Pour over the orange segments. Chill well. Serve with thick pouring cream.

# PEPPERED PEARS IN RED WINE

I picked up this interesting way of poaching pears from Augustin Paege's charming Box Tree restaurant in New York. Try it, it's good.

*8 pears*
*4 oz caster sugar*
*zest of 1 orange*
*1 pint red Burgundy, see method*
*2 inch piece cinnamon*
*heaped teaspoon black peppercorns*

1. Select an enamel-lined or stainless steel pan just large enough to hold the pears standing upright. Bring to the boil the sugar, zest, wine, cinnamon and peppercorns, reduce the heat and simmer carefully for 5 minutes.

2. Meanwhile, peel the pears and core them from the base. Leave the stalks on. Put the pears into the hot syrup and poach until tender, about 20 minutes, covered with a lid. You may have to add a little more wine as they should be covered to the base of the stalk, in which case add a little more sugar too. You will eventually arrive with a pan and quantities which 'fit'.

3. Allow the mixture to cool before removing the pears with a slotted spoon and placing on a dish.

4. Strain the syrup and reduce to a thick consistency by boiling rapidly. Cool again, then spoon over the pears before chilling well, covered with plastic film. While I prefer to serve the pears as they are, you can serve them with thick, unsweetened pouring cream or with soured cream. Serves 4.

*Peppered pears in red wine*

## CHOCOLATE CHIP SPONGE PUDDING WITH RASPBERRY COULIS AND SOURED CREAM

This dark toned but light and fluffy sponge pudding is not to be restricted to the colder months any more than a hot soufflé. In fact, it is lighter textured than many a soufflé I've had! I make this pudding in the summer, and instead of chocolate chips I scatter in a small punnet of fresh raspberries, which creates great excitement among my guests!

RASPBERRY COULIS:
*8 oz fresh or frozen raspberries*
*2 oz (or slightly less) caster sugar*
*juice of 1 lemon*

PUDDING:
*4 oz unsalted butter*
*4 oz caster sugar*
*2 teaspoons vanilla essence*
*2 large eggs, beaten*
*4 oz plain white flour*
*2 oz cocoa powder*
*2 heaped teaspoons baking powder*
*2 oz bitter chocolate, broken and crushed into ¼ inch chips*

SERVING:
*⅓ pint soured cream*

1. To make the raspberry coulis: toss all the ingredients together in a pan over a low heat until the juices from the raspberries draw. Press and rub through a fine sieve. Chill well.

2. Butter generously a 1½ pint pudding basin or mould. Cream the butter and sugar until light and fluffy. Add the vanilla essence and gradually beat in the eggs; if they show signs of splitting or curdling, add a small spoonful of the flour, which should be sifted together twice with the cocoa powder and baking powder.

3. Thoroughly cut and fold in the remaining flour and cocoa mixture using a little cold water to arrive at a loose dropping consistency. (This means that the mixture drops away from the spoon or spatula as soon as it is held up from the bowl.) Stir the chocolate chips into the mixture.

4. Spoon it into a buttered basin and cover with buttered foil. Make a pleat and tie down with string. Steam over water boiling at a steady roll for 1½–2 hours.

5. Turn out on to a serving dish and serve immediately accompanied by a bowl of soured cream and with the chilled (or hot, if preferred) raspberry coulis. Serves 5–6.

## ZABAGLIONE

A lighter version of this delicious hot Italian custard can be made by substituting a cream sherry or Sauternes for the rich dark marsala. I serve mine with small slices of Madeira Cake (page 223).

*8 egg yolks*
*2–3 oz caster sugar*
*¾ pint marsala*

*Chocolate chip sponge pudding with raspberry coulis and soured cream*

1. Select a round-bottomed fireproof bowl which will sit comfortably over a pan of boiling water, leaving a couple of inches of rim proud of the pan. Arrange the bowl over the water which must be boiling and in contact with the bottom of the bowl. Protect your hand from steam with an oven glove or cloth.

2. Gently whisk the egg yolks, caster sugar and marsala with a balloon whisk until the mixture is as thick as double cream. Make sure you 'cover' the sides and the bottom of the bowl all the time. (If you whisk too hard you incorporate too much air which may give a false impression of thickness and is why zabaglione often appears to have collapsed.)

3. Stand the bowl in a sink of cold water to remove any residual heat, adding a dash of marsala to cool things down. Pour into glasses and serve. Serves up to 8, depending on the glasses.

Note: the zabaglione can safely be made before you change for dinner. In which case, leave it standing in its bowl, over warm, but not boiling, water. It can also be served cold, and can be put, still cold, into an ice-cream machine to make a delicious ice-cream.

## LEMON SPONGE PUDDING

*4 oz unsalted butter*
*4 oz caster sugar*
*2 large eggs, beaten*
*grated rind of 2 lemons*
*5 oz self-raising flour*
*1 level teaspoon baking powder*
*juice of 2 lemons*
*1 slice lemon*
*1 tablespoon lemon cheese or lemon curd*

SAUCE:
*4 oz lemon cheese or lemon curd*
*¼ pint single cream*

1. Cream the butter and sugar until light and fluffy. Gradually beat in the eggs, then add the lemon rind.

2. Sieve the flour and baking powder, and gradually fold into the creamed mixture incorporating well, using the lemon juice to

*Lemon sponge pudding*

mix to a soft dropping consistency, plus a little cold water if necessary. (This will depend on the size of the eggs used.)

3. Generously butter a 2½–3 pint basin. Place the slice of lemon in the base. Spoon over the lemon cheese, then the mixture. Cover with buttered foil, making a good pleat across the top. Tie down well with string, making a loose handle over the top of the basin for ease of lifting out of the steamer. Steam at a good roll for 1½ hours.

4. To make the sauce: mix the two ingredients together and heat through over a low heat until hot, but not boiling. Pour into a warm sauceboat and serve. Serves 6–8.

## OMELETTE SOUFFLÉE AUX ABRICOTS

*12 apricot caps*
*8 oz apricot jam, sieved*
*4 egg yolks*
*1½ oz icing sugar*
*1 teaspoon grated orange zest*
*2 tablespoons Grand Marnier*
*4 egg whites*
*1 oz unsalted butter*
*extra icing sugar for glazing*

1. Have ready a 10–11 inch frying pan which should fit into your oven; some icing sugar in a sieve standing on a plate at the side of the stove; a warm ovenproof serving dish; the grill preheated and searing hot; the oven preheated to Gas Mark 7 (220°C, 425°F).

2. Heat the apricots in the sieved jam and have at the ready. Cream the yolks and icing sugar until fluffy: mix in the zest and liqueur (this can be done in advance).

3. Beat the whites to a stiff peak and mix them lightly but thoroughly into the creamed yolks.

4. Melt the butter in the frying pan, swirling it round until an almond-scented haze is given off. Pour the mixture into the pan – it will probably fill it completely. Over a good heat, let the mixture set on the bottom for a minute. Transfer the pan to the oven for 10–12 minutes when the omelette will be puffed up and almost set.

**5.** Make an incision right across the omelette, cutting almost through. Spoon a good half of the hot apricot mixture on to one half of the omelette. With a large spatula, fold this over on top of the other half and tip the omelette on to the warm serving dish. Dredge liberally with icing sugar – wipe the edges of the dish – and pour *round*, not over, the remaining apricot mixture.

**6.** Pop the dish under the hot grill until the sugar caramelizes (it will scorch in parts, but don't worry). Serve immediately – it is bliss. Serves 4.

# RUM-FLAMED BANANAS WITH CHOCOLATE AND ALMONDS

*2–3 bananas, skinned and halved*
*lengthways*
*juice of ½ lemon*
*1½ oz butter*
*1½ oz caster sugar*
*¼ teaspoon grated orange zest*
*juice of ½ orange*
*2 fl oz Jamaica or Bacardi rum*

GARNISH:
*1 oz toasted flaked almonds*
*2 oz coarsely grated or chopped dark*
*chocolate (kept cool and crisp)*
*¼ pint double cream for pouring*

**1.** Brush or bathe the bananas with the lemon juice to keep them white. Melt the butter with the sugar and orange zest and juice and simmer the mixture to a syrupy consistency.

**2.** Add the bananas (quarter them for ease of handling if you feel you must). Cook until just tender, basting.

**3.** Warm the rum, pour it over the bananas, tip the pan to the flame and ignite. Sprinkle over the chocolate and almonds while still flaming.

**4.** Serve immediately with the pouring cream. Serves 2–3.

# COFFEE, WALNUT AND DATE PUDDING

*4 oz unsalted butter*
*4 oz caster sugar*
*2 eggs, beaten*
*1 level teaspoon instant coffee,*
*dissolved in 1 tablespoon boiling water*
*and cooled*
*4 oz self-raising flour, sieved*
*2 oz walnuts, roughly chopped*
*4 oz dates, roughly chopped and soaked*
*in 2 tablespoons rum*

APRICOT SAUCE:
*2 oz caster sugar*
*1 teaspoon vanilla essence (or use*
*vanilla sugar if you have it to hand!)*
*8 oz apricot jam*

**1.** Generously butter a 2 pint pudding basin or mould. Put a small circle of buttered paper in the bottom.

**2.** Cream the butter and sugar until light and fluffy. Beat in the eggs a little at a time and add the coffee essence. Fold in the sieved flour, then the nuts and dates and the modest amount of rum.

**3.** Spoon the mixture into the basin. Level the top. Cover with buttered foil, making a 1 inch pleat and tying down well.

**4.** Steam for 2 hours over gently boiling water. Top up the pan at frequent intervals with more water. When cooked, run a palette knife round the sides of the basin and invert on to a warm serving dish. Remove the disc of paper. Serve with apricot sauce (see below), thick cream or custard.

**5.** To make the sauce: bring the sugar, vanilla essence and 4 fl oz water to the boil and simmer until clear and syrupy.

**6.** In a second smaller pan, put in the jam and half the syrup. Then, stirring all the time, bring to the boil over a low heat. Press through a hair sieve; adjust the consistency using more of the syrup. Serve hot or cold.

**7.** If the sauce is to be served cold it will require more syrup, added when the purée is quite cold. Lemon juice, rum, kirsch or any other liqueur can be added for extra flavouring. Serves 5–6.

*Rum-flamed bananas with chocolate and almonds*

# CRÊPES FLAMBÉES AU MARASCHINO

Pancakes have always been a favourite with me especially when packed with a purée of seasonal fruits. A luxurious dimension can be achieved if, after the all-essential dredging with a goodly coating of icing sugar, a handsome glass or two of warm liqueur is poured over and set alight, melting and caramelizing the sugar. Try kirsch, maraschino, Pear William or framboise. Here I have chosen apple-stuffed pancakes flamed in maraschino, a fine conclusion to any meal.

PANCAKE BATTER:
*4 oz soft white flour*
*1 oz caster sugar*
*2 whole eggs*
*4 egg yolks*
*up to $\frac{3}{4}$ pint milk*
*grated zest of $\frac{1}{2}$ lemon (1 teaspoon)*
*3 oz unsalted Dutch butter,*
*melted but cool*

APPLE FILLING:
*2 lb Cox's or Starking apples*
*juice of 1 lemon*
*juice of 1 orange*
*strips of rind of both*
*1 oz unsalted butter*
*2 oz caster sugar (or to taste)*

APRICOT PURÉE:
*$\frac{1}{2}$ lb apricot jam, sieved*

TOPPING:
*icing sugar*
*2–3 fl oz maraschino*
*$\frac{1}{2}$ pint thick pouring cream*

**1.** To make the batter: sift the flour and sugar into a mixing bowl. Whisk together the eggs and yolks with $\frac{1}{2}$ pint milk. Make a well in the flour mixture. Gradually incorporate the eggs and milk and beat well.

**2.** Strain into a clean bowl to eliminate lumps. Add the lemon zest. Add more milk until the batter is the consistency of thin cream. (Flours vary in strength, so an exact quantity of liquid cannot be given.)

**3.** Stir in the melted butter. You will not need to grease your pan if you follow this method. You will also get lacier pancakes.

*Crêpes flambées au maraschino*

**4.** Make up wafer-thin crêpes in a spanking hot pan. This quantity will make at least 20 (6 inch) crêpes. (As this batter is deliciously soft you may find larger crêpes difficult to cope with.)

**5.** To make the apple filling: peel and core the apples and slice thinly. Simmer in a heavy-bottomed pan over a low heat with rest of ingredients until a purée is formed. Remove the strips of rind. Mash the purée roughly. It should be soft but not too wet.

**6.** To make up: arrange all the crêpes on a clean worktop lightly dredged with caster sugar. Spread apricot purée on a quarter of each, and apple purée on second quarter. Fold clean side over, then fold in half. Arrange *monter à cheval* – slightly overlapping each other – in a lightly buttered flameproof dish. (Everything up to this point can be done in advance.)

**7.** To serve and flambé: preheat the grill to a vivid heat. (Then, once you have assembled everything in advance, preheat the oven to Gas Mark 5 (190°C, 375°F) and warm the crêpes through for 15 minutes.)

**8.** Using a fine wire sieve, dredge the crêpes well with a good coating of icing sugar. Wipe the edges of the dish.

**9.** Slide the dish under the grill to caramelize the sugar quickly.

**10.** Warm the maraschino thoroughly and pour over and round the crêpes. The liqueur can be warmed over a low flame in a silver sauceboat, a small pan, even the glass jug of a coffee percolator, but I find one of those huge soup ladles handy.

**11.** Ignite, basting them with the blazing liqueur (for the faint-hearted, one of those long-handled stuffing spoons is handy). Serve on hot plates with the thick pouring cream. Serves 5–6, allowing 2–3 tiny crêpes each.

# RICH DARK CHOCOLATE SAUCE

There is no way you will arrive at this type of chocolate-lovers' sauce if you don't use a good brand of chocolate: I suggest Cadbury's Bournville, Terry's Bitter, Peter's or Menier . . . and perhaps in that order.

You'll notice the English come out tops in my kitchen!

*6 oz chocolate broken into pieces*
*4 oz caster sugar*

**1.** Put the chocolate in a basin over simmering water and let it melt. Stir in ⅓ pint water, add the sugar, and continue to let this heat until all is dissolved and smooth. Allow to cool and then refrigerate.

**2.** This should be a thinnish sauce – about as thin as single cream – but this will depend on the type of chocolate you have used. If it is too thick, melt it down again over hot water and add a little more water. If you stir in water when it's cold it will go creamy and not be the dark glossy sauce you are looking for.

# CHOCOLATE SPONGE PUDDING WITH APPLES

*2 small firm apples*
*1 oz butter*
*1 tablespoon lemon juice*
*4 oz unsalted butter*
*4 oz caster sugar*
*2 medium-sized eggs, beaten*
*1 oz ground almonds*
*4 oz self-raising flour, sieved with*
*2 oz cocoa*
*3 tablespoons cream sherry or milk*

HOT CHOCOLATE SAUCE:
*4 oz plain chocolate*
*1½ oz caster sugar*
*2 oz unsalted butter, cut into small cubes*
*squeeze of lemon juice*

**1.** Peel and core the apples and cut into small pieces. Melt the butter with the lemon juice in a small pan and cook the apples in this until tender. Mash roughly with a fork. Leave to cool.

**2.** Cream the butter and sugar until fluffy. Gradually beat in the eggs. Beat in the ground almonds, then fold in the flour and cocoa adding enough sherry or milk to give a soft dropping consistency.

*Chocolate sponge pudding with apples*

**3.** Generously butter a 2 pint basin or 6 individual dariole tins. Put the apples into the bottom. Spoon in the mixture. Cover with buttered foil and tie down. Steam for 2 hours, or 1½ hours for the individual tins.

**4.** Serve with hot chocolate sauce (see below), home-made custard, raspberry sauce (see Guards' Pudding, page 186) or ice-cream.

**5.** To make the chocolate sauce: break the chocolate into pieces and put into a bowl arranged over a pan of boiling water. Add ¼ pint boiling water and the caster sugar. Stir until a creamy consistency is reached. Remove from the heat.

**6.** Just before serving, whisk in the cubes of butter and a couple of drops of lemon juice. Pour into a warm sauceboat. Serves 6.

# LIGHT STEAMED RAISIN RING PUDDING

*4 oz unsalted butter*
*4 oz caster sugar*
*2 large eggs, beaten*
*juice of 1 orange*
*grated rind of the orange*
*1 level teaspoon ginger*
*4–6 oz seedless raisins, soaked*
*overnight in a little rum if liked*
*4 oz self-raising flour*
*1 oz cornflour*
*1 level teaspoon baking powder*

**1.** Cream the butter and sugar until light and fluffy. Gradually beat in the eggs, orange juice and rind, ginger and raisins.

**2.** Sieve the flour and cornflour with the modest amount of baking powder. Gradually incorporate this into the creamed mixture, adding a little more orange juice or cold water to arrive at a soft dropping consistency.

**3.** Generously butter an 8 inch ring mould, spoon the mixture into this, levelling it with the back of a wetted spoon. Cover with buttered foil. Steam for 1½ hours, keeping the water at a good rolling boil.

**4.** If your steamer will not hold the ring mould, use an ordinary pan with an old plate

*Light steamed raisin ring pudding*

in the bottom and enough water to come halfway up the sides of the mould: if you employ this method, make sure you have a good 'seal' using both foil and pan lid. If you make this recipe in a basin, increase the steaming time by 20 minutes. Serves 6–8.

# BLACK TREACLE DUFF

For those who find black treacle too powerful – but I doubt if they will if they are lovers of suet duffs – then brown treacle (which is often rather difficult to get) or golden syrup can well be substituted.

---

*8 oz self-raising flour*
*2 oz suet*
*2 oz hard, cold butter, grated*
*1 heaped teaspoon grated lemon rind*
*1 whole egg*
*juice of 1 lemon*
*6 oz black treacle or syrup*

---

**1.** Using butter, thoroughly grease a 3 pint pudding basin (make sure it fits the steamer). Toss the flour with the suet, grated butter and lemon rind. Beat the egg and add to the lemon juice with enough water to make up ⅓ pint. Mix in at one fell swoop and gather the mixture into a soft dough.

**2.** Divide the dough into 4 portions, each a little larger than the other. Press (don't roll) the dough into 4 circles which will fit the basin in layers.

**3.** Put the first small circle into the base of the basin. Spoon over a tablespoon of treacle. Fit the rest of the circles, alternating with a good spoonful of treacle, ending with a top of suet dough.

**4.** Cover the basin with well-buttered foil, allowing a good 1 inch pleat across the top. Tie down well, making a handle across the top of the basin for ease of lifting.

**5.** Steam at a good rolling boil for 2½ hours, topping the pan up with boiling water as and when necessary.

**6.** Turn the pudding on to a warm serving dish and serve with custard. I always pass lemon segments as well to contrast with the sweetness of the treacle. Serves 5–6.

# GUARDS' PUDDING

---

*6 oz brown breadcrumbs*
*6 oz suet*
*1 level teaspoon bicarbonate of soda*
*4 oz demerara sugar*
*3 good tablespoons raspberry jam*
*(about 6 oz)*
*juice and rind of 1 large lemon*
*1 large egg, beaten*

CUSTARD:
*4 whole eggs*
*2 oz caster sugar*
*1 teaspoon cornflour*
*1 pint milk*
*1 teaspoon vanilla essence*

RASPBERRY SAUCE:
*8 oz raspberries, fresh or frozen*
*juice of 1 lemon*
*3 oz caster sugar*
*2 tablespoons gin or water*

---

**1.** Combine all the dry ingredients. Mix in the jam, lemon juice and rind, and finally the beaten egg.

**2.** Generously butter a 2–2½ pint pudding basin. Place a buttered circle of paper in the bottom. Spoon in the mixture which will be fairly stiff. Steam for 2½ hours over boiling water, remembering to top up the pan with more water from time to time.

**3.** To serve: unmould, remove the paper and serve with custard or with raspberry sauce.

**4.** To make the custard: cream together the eggs, sugar and cornflour. Bring the milk to the boil, add the vanilla essence and pour over the egg mixture, whisking briskly all the time. If the sauce does not thicken immediately, return the mixture to the pan and, over a minimum heat, stirring all the time, bring the sauce just to boiling point, when it will thicken.

**5.** Have your sink half filled with cold water into which you can plunge the bottom of the pan to remove any residual heat which may be sufficient to curdle the custard.

**6.** To make the raspberry sauce: bring all the ingredients to the boil over a very low heat. Simmer gently for 5 minutes and then press the contents through a fine sieve,

*Guards' pudding with raspberry sauce and custard*

applying only a minimum of pressure to the fruit so that the sauce remains clear. (If you wish, you can serve the sauce without sieving it.) Serves 5–6.

# TARTE TATIN (CARAMEL UPSIDE-DOWN APPLE PIE)

*5 large dessert apples*
*squeeze of lemon juice*
*4 oz unsalted butter, softened*
*6 oz caster sugar*

*PASTRY:*
*6 oz self-raising flour*
*4 oz unsalted butter*
*2 teaspoons icing sugar*
*pinch of salt*
*1 egg beaten with 1 tablespoon cold water*
*cream or sour cream for serving*

1. Make up the pastry and leave in a cool place to rest for half an hour. Then roll it out in one piece to make a lid to fit your dish.

2. Take a tin or metal seamless dish 8–9 inches in diameter. Peel, core and slice the apples into water with a squeeze of lemon juice added to prevent discoloration. Spread the softened butter over the entire base of the tin. Cover with a layer of sugar, using it all.

3. Drain and pat dry the apples and arrange over the butter and sugar.

4. Cover with lid of pastry as you would do for an ordinary pie, but omitting the pastry edges. Bake in a preheated oven Gas Mark 7 (220°C, 425°F) for 45 minutes. If, after 20 minutes the pastry is nearly burning, lower the temperature a notch, but remember the pastry ought to be very brown and crisp. Place a serving dish over the finished tarte and invert the two. The finished result should be a sticky caramel apple mixture on top of the crisp pastry. Serve with chilled cream or sour cream. Serves 6–8.

Note: if you have a thin-bottomed tin and an Aga, success should be immediate. If not, you might discover that the marriage of your particular mould and your particular oven doesn't produce a rich, dark, sticky caramel. In this case, make a fudge with the butter and sugar in a pan on top of the stove, taking the mixture to almost caramel stage before pouring it into a tin and topping with the sliced apples and pastry lid.

# GINGER TREACLE PUDDING

*6 oz fresh brown breadcrumbs*
*6 oz suet*
*2 oz brown or wholemeal flour*
*1 teaspoon ground ginger*
*1 level teaspoon bicarbonate of soda*
*2 eggs, beaten*
*7 oz golden syrup*
*extra syrup and/or thick cream for serving*

1. Mix all the dry ingredients together. Add the beaten eggs and golden syrup, which should be slightly warm for ease of handling (this is done by standing the tin in hot water for about 15 minutes).

2. Butter and line a basin or mould. Fill this 3 parts full and fit a foil lid with a pleat in it. Steam for 2½ hours.

3. Serve with custard, or extra warm syrup and/or thick cream. Serves 5–6.

*Tarte tatin*

# Cold Puddings

## BLACKBERRY AND APPLE CRUMB PUDDING

CRUMBS:
*3 oz unsalted butter*
*6 oz Jewish egg loaf or other good*
*white bread with the crust left on,*
*crumbled*
*1 oz caster sugar*

APPLE FILLING:
*2 lb apples*
*juice and zest of 1 lemon*
*2 oz sugar (optional)*

BLACKBERRY FILLING:
*1½ lb fresh or frozen blackberries*
*2 oz sugar*
*½ teaspoon vanilla essence*
*½ sachet gelatine*

GARNISH:
*½ pint double cream, lightly*
*sweetened*
*2 oz toasted almonds*

**1.** Melt the butter without browning in a large skillet or frying pan. Stir in the crumbs and sugar over a low heat and allow the crumbs to fry until fully crisp and a good deep golden brown. You will need to stir them constantly to ensure this, so patience is vital!

**2.** Cool and crush with a rolling pin so that a good rough texture is achieved. DO NOT be tempted to use a blender.

**3.** To make apple filling: peel and core the apples and cut into even slices. Remove lemon zest with a potato peeler and squeeze out the juice. Simmer apples, juice, sugar and zest in ⅛ pint water, with lid on, until tender. Break into a rough pulp and cool.

**4.** To make blackberry filling: put blackberries, sugar and essence into a lidded pan. Shake over a low heat until the juices draw. Bring to boil, simmer until fruit is tender, 3 minutes. Remove from the heat. Sprinkle over gelatine and stir in. Cool.

**5.** Whip ½ pint of lightly sweetened double cream to a soft peak.

**6.** To make up the pudding: in a glass bowl spread the blackberry mixture, apple purée, crumbs and a final layer of cream. Top the mixture with 2 oz toasted almonds. I make mine up about an hour before serving and serve it at room temperature to ensure that things don't go soggy. Serves up to 8.

## CHOCOLATE RUM FUDGE
### (uncooked method)

*8 oz Bournville chocolate, in pieces*
*8 oz unsalted butter, cut into cubes*
*⅛ pint Jamaica rum*
*2 teaspoons vanilla essence*
*2 lb icing sugar, sieved*

**1.** Melt the chocolate with the butter in a bowl over a pan of hot water, stirring from time to time. Remove the bowl from the heat. Stir in the rum and vanilla. *Gradually* beat in the sieved icing sugar, incorporating thoroughly.

**2.** Turn into a non-stick shallow baking tin, and press to approximately ¾ inch thick.

*Blackberry and apple crumb pudding*

Mark into ¾ inch squares. Chill well, then cut into squares. Dredge with a mixture of equal parts cocoa and sieved icing sugar (1 dessert-spoon of each should suffice).

# FLOATING ISLANDS

The recipe for this delicate rose-scented pudding is straight from our 'Age of Elegance' and differs in a subtle way from its French counterpart Îles Flottantes.

---

*4 egg whites*
*2 oz icing sugar, sieved on to paper*

SAUCE:
*4 egg yolks*
*¼ teaspoon cornflour*
*1 oz caster sugar*
*½ pint single cream*
*1 tablespoon triple strength rose*
*flower water*

GARNISH:
*a few crystallized rose petals*
*and/or 1 oz toasted flaked almonds*

---

1. To make the sauce: cream the yolks, cornflour and sugar in a fireproof bowl which will fit comfortably over a pan of boiling water.

2. In a small non-stick pan bring the cream to the boil and pour it over the yolks, whisking briskly with a small balloon whisk. Fit the bowl over the pan of boiling water; now whisk *gently* until the sauce is as thick as good pouring cream (thicker than single cream but not as thick as double).

3. As soon as the sauce is thick enough, stand the bowl in cold water to remove any residual heat which may curdle the sauce, stirring or whisking all the while. Leave to cool before adding the rose flower water. Dredge the surface of the sauce with a little caster sugar to prevent a skin forming. Chill well.

4. To make the 'islands': whisk the four egg whites to stiff peaks. Whisk in the sieved icing sugar.

5. Fill a shallow pan (frying pan) with water and bring almost to a gentle boil (one

*Floating islands*

stage on from simmering, one less than a rolling boil!).

**6.** Using a tablespoon rinsed in cold water between each addition, spoon four islands into the water (you are making 8 in all). Cook for 3–4 minutes before turning them with a slotted spoon to cook for a further 3–4 minutes on the other side. (Do not be tempted to turn them too soon, before the egg has set.)

**7.** Drain on a clean towel. Repeat with the remaining mixture, making four more islands. Leave to cool.

**8.** Arrange in a shallow serving dish. Spoon the sauce over and around. Garnish with crushed crystallized rose petals and/or toasted flaked almonds. If a skin has formed on the sauce, sieve before using. Serves 4.

# PEARS IN SAUTERNES WITH ORANGE RUM SABAYON SAUCE

PEARS:
*rind of 2 oranges*
*1 pint Sauternes-type wine (I use*
*Spanish)*
*1 pint orange juice*
*8 even-sized ripe pears*
*2 oz caster sugar*

SAUCE:
*6 egg yolks*
*2 oz caster sugar*
*½ pint poaching liquor (see method)*
*4 tablespoons Jamaica rum (or extra*
*orange juice)*
*1 oz unsalted butter, softened*

**1.** Cut the orange rind into fine julienne strips (the proper term for this is a chiffonade).

**2.** Bring the wine and orange juice to simmering point together with the chiffonade of orange rind.

**3.** Meanwhile, cut out the base of each pear and, using a potato peeler, remove all the peel. Try, if possible, to retain the stalk.

**4.** Poach the pears in the pan of wine, with the lid on, until tender – this will take about 20 minutes.

**5.** Remove them carefully to a serving dish. Strain the juice into a jug, retaining ½ pint. This liquor is used for the sabayon sauce.

**6.** Boil the remaining poaching juice, caster sugar and orange rind until syrupy. Cool, then spoon this syrup over the pears. Chill well.

**7.** To make the sauce: in a Pyrex basin, cream the yolks and sugar until light and fluffy. Using a small balloon whisk, whisk in the ½ pint liquor. Arrange the basin over a pan of boiling water and whisk steadily and consistently until the mixture thickens or ribbons.

**8.** Using a cloth to protect the hands, remove the basin from the heat and immediately whisk in the rum (which will also remove any residual heat which might curdle the sauce). Stand the bowl in a sink containing 2–3 inches of cold water and continue whisking for a minute, adding bits of the softened butter as you do this.

**9.** When cool, cover with plastic wrap and chill.

**10.** Whisk the sauce again before serving. Serves 6–8.

# ORANGE CRACKLING CREAM

*9 oz caster sugar*
*8 oranges*
*½ pint double cream*
*2 oz flaked almonds, browned in*
*the oven*
*¼ pint orange juice*

**1.** Make the crackling first. Melt 4 oz sugar in ¼ pint water over a low heat and then boil until the syrup becomes a dark toffee brown. Pour on to a greased enamel plate to harden.

**2.** With a very sharp small knife, cut all the peel off the oranges, leaving no white pith. Save any juice.

**3.** Slice the oranges into thin rounds and arrange in a shallow dish. Dissolve the remaining sugar in the ¼ pint orange juice and

*Pears in Sauternes with orange rum sabayon sauce*

boil for 5 minutes. When cool, pour over the oranges.

4. Crush the crackling to a coarse gravel texture and, just before serving, sprinkle over the oranges. Whip the cream and smooth over the oranges with a palette knife. Finally, decorate with toasted almonds. Serves 4.

# ALMOND AND APRICOT VACHERIN

CAKE BASES:
*5 egg whites*
*10 oz caster sugar*
*6 oz crushed toasted almonds*

ALMOND CUSTARD ICE-CREAM:
*8 egg yolks*
*3 oz caster sugar*
*1 pint single cream or half cream and half milk*
*1 teaspoon almond extract or 2 tablespoons kirsch or other liqueur*

FILLING:
*12 fresh apricots, pitted and soaked in 2 tablespoons Amaretto, crème de banane, kirsch, brandy or other liqueur*
*½ pint double cream, whipped to piping consistency*
*icing sugar*

1. To make the cake bases: stiffly beat the egg whites, as for meringues, incorporating half the sugar as you beat and the second half towards the end of the beating when the mixture must stand in peaks. Using a slotted spoon, fold in the crushed almonds. Divide the mixture evenly between two 8 inch sandwich tins lined with silicone paper. Bake at Gas Mark 5 (190°C, 375°F), for 35–40 minutes. Leave to cool a little before turning on to a wire cooling tray and removing the papers. These can be made days in advance and stored in an airtight tin or frozen.

2. To make the almond custard ice-cream: beat the egg yolks and sugar until fluffy and all the granules are dissolved. Bring cream and extract to the boil and pour it over the egg mixture, whisking briskly all the time.

3. Arrange the bowl over a pan of boiling

*Almond and apricot vacherin*

water and, stirring gently all the time, thicken the custard until it is the consistency of double cream and coats the back of a wooden spoon well – if you draw your finger across the back it should leave a definite trail.

4. Leave the custard to cool completely; then chill it, either following the instructions for your ice-cream machine or in a suitable container which will fit into the ice-making compartment of your refrigerator or deep freeze. If the latter method is used, stir the mixture every 30 minutes or so to prevent ice crystals from forming.

5. To form the ice-cream layer: line an 8 inch sandwich tin with plastic film. Press the ice-cream into this to make a thick round 'cake'. Freeze.

6. To assemble the vacherin: invert one of the meringue bases on to a platter. Remove the ice-cream from its mould and take off the plastic film. Place the ice-cream on top of the meringue base. Pipe a collar of whipped cream round the edge of the ice-cream. Fill with apricot halves and splash with a suitable liqueur. Rest the second meringue on top of this and dredge liberally with icing sugar. Serves 7–8.

# ORANGE FLOWER WATER CUSTARDS

*6 egg yolks*
*1½–2 oz vanilla sugar*
*1 level teaspoon cornflour*
*¾ pint single cream*
*½ sachet gelatine crystals*
*1 tablespoon orange flower water*

1. Cream the egg yolks, sugar and cornflour. Bring the cream to boiling point then pour over the mixture, whisking briskly.

2. Arrange the bowl over a pan of boiling water and whisk the mixture until it ribbons. Scatter the gelatine over and whisk in. Finally, whisk in the flower water.

3. Cool, then pour the custard into custard cups. Cover each with clingfilm and chill well.

4. Serve them alone or with a compôte of fruit or fresh berries. Serves 6.

## FLUMMERY

*1 pint double cream*
*1 sachet gelatine dissolved in a little water*
*2 oz caster sugar*
*1 tablespoon rose flower water*
*grated rind and juice of 1 lemon*

GARNISH:
*fresh raspberries*

**1.** Put all the ingredients into a double boiler or into a basin which will fit into the top of a pan of boiling water. Stir gently but continuously until the sugar and gelatine are completely dissolved.

**2.** Pour into custard cups and allow to cool before putting into the refrigerator to set. Top with a good cushion of fresh raspberries. Serves 5–6.

## WALTON'S EIGHTEENTH-CENTURY LEMON CHEESECAKE

*1 sweet pastry case*

LEMON CHEESE:
*4 oz butter*
*4 oz sugar*
*4 egg yolks*
*zest and juice of 4 lemons*

FILLING:
*6 oz sugar*
*6 oz butter*
*4 oz fine white breadcrumbs*
*3 large eggs*
*zest and juice of 4 lemons*

**1.** Make the sweet pastry case: bake blind in a tin 8 inches in diameter, 1½ inches deep.

**2.** To make lemon cheese: whisk together the butter, sugar, egg yolks and lemon zest and juice in a bowl over boiling water until thick. Alternatively, a good commercial brand can be used.

**3.** To make the filling: beat together sugar and butter until white. Add breadcrumbs, eggs, and lemon zest and juice.

**4.** Make up the tart: smooth a good layer of lemon cheese over the base of the flan and then fill to the top with the lemon filling.

**5.** Bake at Gas Mark 6 (200°C, 400°F) for approximately 30 minutes. Ideally the cheesecake is best served whilst still a little warm with icing sugar dredged over it. Serves 6–8.

## CRUMB APRICOT CREAM

*1 oz unsalted butter for frying*
*3 slices white bread, crusts removed*
*and made into rough crumbs*
*2 teaspoons vanilla essence*
*1 pint single cream*
*1 teaspoon finely grated orange rind*
*4 large eggs*
*1 oz (or more) caster sugar*
*a good half jar apricot jam mixed with*
*the juice of ½ orange*
*1 × 12 oz tin apricot halves*
*3 tablespoons Cointreau or Grand*
*Marnier (2 miniature bottles)*

GARNISH:
*½ pint whipped cream*
*extra apricots, tinned or fresh*

**1.** Melt the butter in a heavy-bottomed frying pan. Add the breadcrumbs and, stirring all the time, let them acquire a good golden colour and become quite crisp. Splash over 1 teaspoon vanilla essence during the frying process. Leave to cool completely.

**2.** Meanwhile, bring the single cream, together with the remaining vanilla essence and grated orange rind, to the boil slowly so that the flavours infuse. Beat the eggs with the sugar. Pour over the boiling cream, whisking all the time.

**3.** Spread the jam and orange juice mixture into the bottom of an ovenproof dish about 3–4 inches deep.

**4.** Distribute the apricot halves evenly over the jam.

**5.** Add the liqueur to the custard mixture

*Walton's eighteenth-century lemon cheesecake*

and pour into the dish. Stand the dish in another ovenproof dish containing hot water.

**6.** Bake at Gas Mark 4 (180°C, 350°F) for 30–40 minutes or until the custard is set. Leave to cool completely.

**7.** Spread the cold crisp crumbs over the top. Pipe round a collar of whipped cream and decorate with extra apricots if you are feeling in a lavish mood. Serves 6–8.

# OTHELLO LAYER CAKE

### CAKE BASES:
*6 whole eggs*
*8 oz vanilla sugar (for best results keep a vanilla pod in the sugar jar) or*
*8 oz caster sugar and 2 teaspoons vanilla essence*
*6 oz self-raising flour*

### CREAM FILLING:
*1 oz caster sugar*
*½ teaspoon cornflour*
*3 egg yolks*
*9 fl oz carton double cream*

### JAM FILLING:
*4 oz good quality apricot jam*
*caster sugar*

### CHOCOLATE ICING:
*4 oz the very best plain chocolate*
*1 teaspoon flavourless oil or liquid paraffin*
*4 oz caster sugar dissolved in 2 tablespoons water*

### TO DECORATE:
*whipped cream*
*glacé apricots or other fruits, chocolate flakes or squares*

**1.** Line two baking sheets with buttered greaseproof or silicone paper. With a pencil, describe 2 circles, using a 7–8 inch flan ring as your guide.

**2.** Beat the eggs, vanilla sugar or sugar and vanilla essence together until white and thick. If you can see the trail left by the beater when it is drawn slowly through the mixture, then it is thick enough. Fold in the sifted flour gradually, using a slotted spoon.

**3.** Divide the mixture equally into four portions, and spread out two on each sheet with a palette knife. Bake the thin 'pancakes' in a preheated oven, Gas Mark 6 (200°C, 400°F) for 10–12 minutes. Turn on to a cooling tray and remove the papers. Allow to cool and, using a flan ring or plate as a template, trim the layers.

**4.** To make cream filling: cream together sugar, flour, yolks and, for added luxury, a little rum or brandy, add the cream which has been heated to boiling point, then put in a double boiler or stand the basin over a pan of boiling water. Stirring continuously, let the sauce cook for a minute. Allow to cool, sprinkling the surface with a little caster sugar to prevent a skin forming. If the finished 'cream' or 'custard' appears oily, beat in a spoonful or two of hot water.

**5.** To make jam filling: put 4 oz apricot jam into a basin over hot water until it becomes soft, press through a wire sieve and allow to cool. Sprinkle the surface of the purée with caster sugar to prevent a skin forming.

**6.** To make up the cake: spread the jam on to the first base, covering this with the second base on to which you can then spread the cream filling, covering it with the third base. Spread this with jam and any remaining cream filling and top with the fourth base.

**7.** To make the icing: melt chocolate and oil in a basin over hot water. Boil the sugar syrup to 'small thread' on a sugar thermometer. If you don't possess one, boil the syrup until it looks thick. Do not stir the mixture or the sugar will crystallize.

**8.** Allow to cool a little then pour into the chocolate, beating until a coating consistency is achieved. If you end up with a solid-looking fudge in your pan, don't panic – all is not lost. Restore to consistency by adding hot water a tablespoon at a time, beating well. Note: you will have to work fairly quickly with this icing. A palette knife and jug of boiling water into which you can frequently dip the knife will facilitate this operation.

**9.** Spread the fourth base with the chocolate icing. Pipe whipped cream around the sides, and decorate.

*Othello layer cake*

# PRALINE AMARETTO SOUFFLÉ

This recipe for a cold soufflé will serve 12 portions, using a collared 4 pint soufflé dish. The soufflé-cum-mousse can be made in any serving dish, or as individual sweets.

PRALINE:
*6 oz caster sugar*
*6 oz flaked almonds*

MOUSSE:
*2½ sachets gelatine crystals*
*8 large eggs, separated*
*2 oz caster sugar*
*12 fl oz milk*
*6 fl oz single cream*
*6 fl oz Amaretto di Saronno*
*18 fl oz double cream*

GARNISH:
*almonds*

1. To make the praline: put the sugar and ¼ pint water into a wide, heavy-based pan (not non-stick, as the temperature required is too high for this type of surface).

2. Bring to the boil and boil hard until it sounds sticky, or treacly, but not yet turning colour.

3. Tip in the almonds, stir well in, lower the heat and continue cooking until they turn a good toffee colour. Stir to ensure even browning.

4. Do not touch with bare fingers. Turn the caramel (praline) on to a tray lined with buttered foil. Leave to cool. Crush to an even-textured 'crumb' – coarser or finer as you like. I like mine to be like demerara sugar, not as fine as caster sugar.

5. Put the gelatine crystals, covered with cold water (about 6 tablespoons) into a small basin standing it in a pan of simmering water to melt totally.

6. Cream the egg yolks with the sugar. Bring the milk and single cream to the boil, and pour over the egg yolks, whisking all the time until the mixture coats the back of a wooden spoon.

7. Strain in the melted gelatine and whisk or stir in very thoroughly for a couple of minutes. Stir in the Amaretto di Saronno.

8. Stand the bowl in a sink of cold water to cool, stirring from time to time. As soon as it starts to thicken stir in 4 heaped tablespoons praline (about three-quarters of the total amount).

9. Whip 12 fl oz double cream until it stands in soft peaks. Mix well into the praline mixture. Beat the egg whites until they stand in firm peaks. Cut and fold these into the mixture.

10. Pour into the dish. Put to set. Garnish with the extra whipped cream and almonds and dust well with the remaining crushed praline. Serves 12.

# CRANBERRY ALMOND TART

*5 oz plain white flour*
*1 tablespoon icing sugar*
*3 oz hard butter, cut into dice*
*1 tablespoon lemon juice*
*1 egg yolk*
*12 oz cranberries (fresh, frozen or tinned)*
*juice of 1 orange*
*2 oz caster sugar*
*1 fl oz whisky or rum*

TOPPING:
*3 oz unsalted butter (softened)*
*5 oz caster sugar*
*2 eggs, beaten*
*1 heaped teaspoon grated orange rind*
*5 oz ground almonds, sieved with 1 oz plain white flour*
*whipped cream for serving*

1. Sieve the flour and sugar together. Rub in the butter until sandy textured and bind with a mixture of the lemon juice, 1 tablespoon water and the egg yolk. Gather into a ball, but be careful not to overwork it. Leave to relax for 30 minutes or more.

2. Roll out the pastry and use it to line an 8–9 inch diameter × 1½ inch deep loose-bottomed flan tin. Chill again. Line the pastry with buttered foil, fill with dried beans and bake blind at Gas Mark 6 (200°C, 400°F) for about 15 minutes.

*Praline Amaretto soufflé*

3. Wash the cranberries well. Simmer over the lowest heat with orange juice until they 'pop' and are soft. Add the sugar and alcohol at this stage to prevent the skins from toughening. Mash to a purée. Spread over the bottom of the cooked flan case (still in the metal tin) avoiding any excess juice.

4. To make the topping: cream the butter and sugar well. Incorporate the eggs gradually and add the orange rind. Fold in the almonds and flour and spread over the cranberry base.

5. Bake at Gas Mark 4 (180°C, 350°F) in the centre of the oven for 45 minutes. The pastry should be lovely and crisp. Serve hot or cool (not refrigerated), with whipped cream. Serves 8–10.

# EIGHTEENTH-CENTURY RATAFIA TRIFLE

2 packets sponge biscuits
½ lb apricot jam
⅛ pint (or 2 miniatures) Amaretto di Saronno

CUSTARD:
4 eggs
2 oz (or less) caster sugar
1 teaspoon cornflour
1 pint milk

TOPPING:
½ pint whipped cream
1 packet ratafia biscuits
1 packet chocolate-coated or silvered almonds
2 oz blanched whole almonds

1. Split the sponge biscuits in half. Spread liberally with apricot jam. Cut into inch-wide pieces and arrange in a deep trifle bowl. Splash with liqueur.

2. To make the custard: beat the eggs, sugar and cornflour together until light and fluffy.

3. Bring the milk to the boil and pour over the egg mixture whisking well as you do this. Return the mixture to the pan and, over a low heat, stir until thickened. (Add an ice cube to remove any residual heat.) Leave to cool.

4. Ladle over the trifle sponges, cover with clingfilm, refrigerate for half a day or overnight to mature.

5. Decorate with swirls of whipped cream, ratafia biscuits and almonds. Serves 8–10.

# CHOCOLATE PYE

One of the recipes I count as a Smith discovery. It appears in all my books (but changed somewhat in each one, so don't feel cheated!).

PASTRY:
8 oz plain white flour
5 oz unsalted butter
2 oz icing sugar
1 egg yolk

FILLING:
10 oz Bournville chocolate, broken into bits
4 tablespoons amontillado sherry
1 teaspoon vanilla essence
1 level teaspoon gelatine crystals
5 eggs, separated

GARNISH:
whipped cream (about ½ pint)
toasted walnuts or almonds, chocolate flakes or squares, crystallized rose petals or violets (all optional)
gilded or silver almonds (when feeling lavish)

1. Make up the pastry in the usual way, with 3 tablespoons cold water, and use to line one large (9 inch) loose-bottomed tart tin or a dozen smaller ones. Bake blind at Gas Mark 6 (200°C, 400°F). This will take about 10–12 minutes. Turn off the heat and leave the pastry shell(s) to dry out completely. Cool on a wire rack.

2. Arrange a bowl over a pan of boiling water. Melt the chocolate with the sherry and vanilla essence.

3. Soften the gelatine in 2 tablespoons cold water until it is fluffy. Stir this into the hot chocolate mixture until fully dissolved. Re-

*Chocolate pye*

move the bowl from the heat and beat in the egg yolks one by one, incorporating thoroughly. Leave to cool but not set.

4. Beat the egg whites until they stand in stiff peaks. Mix a heaped tablespoon of egg white into the chocolate to slacken the mixture, then cut and fold in the remainder. Put into the pastry case(s) and leave to set. Don't refrigerate these 'pyes' or the pastry will go soggy.

5. Decorate with whipped cream and anything you fancy. Serves 8–10.

# CHOCOLATE ALMOND TART

These ingredients are sufficient to make a 10 inch diameter, 2 inch deep tart.

---

PASTRY:
*3 oz unsalted butter*
*5 oz plain flour*
*1 oz caster sugar*
*1 egg yolk*

FILLING:
*3 oz self-raising flour*
*2 tablespoons cocoa*
*4 oz unsalted butter*
*4 oz caster sugar*
*2 medium-sized eggs, lightly beaten*
*1 teaspoon vanilla essence*
*4 oz ground almonds, rubbed through a sieve*
*finely grated rind of 1 lemon*
*2 tablespoons lemon juice*
*4 heaped tablespoons seedless raspberry jam*

DECORATION:
*icing sugar*

---

1. Butter a loose-bottomed tart tin or flan ring well. (If you are a crinkle dish addict, then this pastry must first be baked blind or you'll have a soggy base.) Rub the butter into the flour. Toss in the sugar, beat the yolk and 2 tablespoons of water together and add to the mixture using a fork. Work everything into a loose dough and form into a round pad.

2. Leave the pastry to rest for 30 minutes.

*Chocolate almond tart*

Roll out evenly and line the tin. Put to rest again or bake blind if using a crinkle dish.

3. Sieve the flour and cocoa together. Cream the butter and sugar until light and fluffy. Gradually add the beaten eggs and essence. Fold in the flour and cocoa, ground almonds and lemon rind. Mix to a dropping consistency with the lemon juice.

4. Spread the jam liberally in the base of the pastry shell. Spoon in the mixture and level the top somewhat. Bake at Gas Mark 7 (220°C, 425°F) for 15 minutes, then Gas Mark 4 (180°C, 350°F) for a further 15 minutes or until the tart is cooked.

5. Serve warm or cold. Dredge the top with icing sugar just before serving. Serves 8–10 depending on your appetite.

# SOUTHERN PECAN PIE

I have made the pie with walnuts and honey instead of corn syrup and pecans with excellent results.

---

PASTRY:
*2 oz unsalted butter*
*2 oz lard*
*6 oz plain flour*
*1 teaspoon icing sugar*
*1 egg yolk*
*1 tablespoon lemon juice*

FILLING:
*3 whole eggs, beaten*
*12 oz maple syrup, light clear honey or ordinary syrup*
*½ teaspoon salt*
*2 teaspoons vanilla extract*
*6 oz caster sugar*
*4 oz butter, melted*
*8 oz (shelled weight) pecans or walnuts*
*vanilla ice-cream for serving*

---

1. To make the pastry: rub butter and lard into the flour. Sift in the sugar. Beat together egg, lemon juice and 1 tablespoon water. Mix to a soft dough.

2. Line a 9 inch diameter, 1–1½ inch deep, loose-bottomed pie tin with the pastry. Chill well.

**3.** To make the filling: beat the eggs, syrup, salt, vanilla extract, sugar and butter. Fold in the nuts.

**4.** Turn the mixture into pastry shell. Bake at Gas Mark 6 (200°C, 400°F) for 40 minutes or until set. Serve warm or cold with vanilla ice-cream. Serves 8–10.

# CHOCOLATE TRIFLE

Many folk make this trifle with all chocolate-flavoured ingredients, such as chocolate sponge and chocolate butter cream inside the sponge as well . . . this I find too much as it actually kills the flavour of the chocolate.

I don't even sweeten the cream, as I like the foil of the clean unsweetened cream against the richest of chocolate sauces and the slight tangyness of the jam (try using a plain fruit purée, remembering that apricots and raspberries are excellent with chocolate).

In this recipe I have used pears. I think you'll enjoy it. I have also added a few bitter chocolate-coated almonds to the top (these you can buy at any good confectioners).

Use these amounts for an 8 inch diameter, 4 inch deep bowl (which will serve a dozen portions). See photograph on page 164.

---

*2 packets commercial trifle sponges*
*12 oz apricot jam (low sugar)*
*1 pint double cream*
*6 small pears, cut in half and poached*
*in a light syrup, cooled and drained*
*a few ratafia biscuits*
*Poire Guillaume (optional)*

CHOCOLATE SAUCE:
*3 oz good plain chocolate*
*3 tablespoons Jamaica or demerara rum*
*5 egg yolks*
*1 oz caster sugar mixed with 2 heaped*
*dessertspoons cocoa*
*¾ pint single cream*
*1 teaspoon vanilla essence*

DECORATION:
*ratafia biscuits*
*chocolate squares or buttons*
*bitter chocolate-coated almonds*
*(optional)*
*crystallized fruit (optional)*

---

**1.** To make the chocolate sauce: in a basin over hot water melt the chocolate with the rum and 3 tablespoons water. Cream the egg yolks, adding the sugar and cocoa mixture as you go along. Beat until fluffy.

**2.** Bring the cream to the boil with the essence. Pour over the egg mixture, whisking all the time. Incorporate thoroughly. Then pour on to the chocolate mixture, incorporating this thoroughly, too. Leave to cool, but do not chill.

**3.** To assemble the trifle: split the sponges in half and spread *liberally* with a low-sugar apricot jam. Cut into halves diagonally.

**4.** Half whip the cream. Arrange the trifle sponges, pears and the odd ratafia biscuit in a glass bowl, spooning over half of the cream and all of the chocolate sauce as you go.

**5.** Fully whip the remaining cream until it stands in stiff peaks. Fill into a piping bag fitted with a star tube and decorate the top of the trifle at will with swirls of cream, ratafias, chocolate squares or buttons, bitter chocolate-coated almonds and crystallized fruits. Just how rich you make this is up to you and will depend on your eye (and the state of the housekeeping), but a trifle should be rich and the opposite to what the name implies!

**6.** For very special occasions, I dribble some appropriate liqueur over the trifle sponges and add a drop or two to the cream as I whip it: Poire Guillaume – Pear William – is excellent for this as it is dry in flavour and adds a marvellously unexpected contrast to the rich trifle. Serves 12.

# DANISH SWEET LEMON SOUP

Sweet soups *are* good and are easy to prepare – do give them a try. They are particularly nice at a garden lunch after a light main course. This one is very delicious and nourishing: my children when youngsters used to like it served as they do in Denmark, with raw porridge oats sprinkled on top.

---

*2 oz caster sugar*
*4 egg yolks*
*finely grated rind and juice of 3 lemons*
*1 pint buttermilk*

---

*Port and claret jelly*

Whisk the sugar and yolks until white, then add the juice and rind of the lemons, and finally stir in the buttermilk. Chill well. Serves 4.

# SHOOFLY PIE

Whether Shoofly Pie is from the stoves of America's Deep South, where it is said flies descended on this sweet, sticky pie and had to be shooed away, or from the Pennsylvania Dutch, is open to conjecture. Whatever its origin, it's good. My youngest sister makes the pie with chopped figs or dates soaked in rum.

---

*4 oz muscatel raisins*
*2 oz soft brown sugar*
*¼ teaspoon bicarbonate of soda*
*4 dessertspoons rum, whisky or water*

TOPPING:
*4 oz plain white flour*
*½ teaspoon cinnamon*
*¼ teaspoon nutmeg*
*¼ teaspoon ground ginger*
*2 oz butter*
*4 oz shortcrust pastry*
*2 oz brown sugar*
*double cream, soured cream or*
*ice-cream for serving*

---

**1.** Soak the raisins, brown sugar and bicarbonate of soda in the alcohol overnight to plump up the fruit.

**2.** Sieve the flour and spices for the topping. Rub in the butter.

**3.** Line a loose-bottomed 7 inch fluted pie tin with pastry. Spoon over the soaked raisins. Spread over the topping and sprinkle on the brown sugar. Bake at Gas Mark 7 (220°C, 425°F) for 15 minutes, then lower to Gas Mark 5 (190°C, 375°F) for 20 minutes. Serve warm or cold with thick cream, soured cream or ice-cream. Serves 5–6.

# PORT AND CLARET JELLY

See photograph on page 209.

---

*zest of 2 oranges*
*1 oz caster sugar*
*1 packet blackcurrant jelly*
*½ pint ruby port*
*½ pint claret-type wine*
*whipped cream (optional decoration)*

---

**1.** Take the zest off the oranges with a potato peeler – this eliminates getting much of the bitter white pith on the flavoursome orange peel. Finely shred this zest and place in a bowl, together with the sugar and jelly cubes.

**2.** Bring the two wines to just under boiling point and pour into the bowl, stirring until all the jelly is dissolved. Allow to cool, then pour into 8 small, stemmed sherry glasses or a wetted mould and leave to set.

**3.** Decorate with lots of unsweetened whipped cream if liked. Serves 8, or 6 if made in a mould.

# Ice-creams

## THREE-NUT ICE-CREAM

See photograph on page 212.

*4 oz caster sugar*
*4 oz flaked almonds*
*2 pints basic custard ice-cream,*
*freshly made (see next recipe)*
*4 oz walnut halves*
*4 oz hazelnuts*
*crystallized chestnuts (optional)*

**1.** Put 2 oz caster sugar with 2 tablespoons cold water into a heavy-bottomed pan and bring to the boil. Boil fairly rapidly until a caramel starts to form. Lower the heat and tip in the flaked almonds. Stir them round with a fork and leave the mixture to cook until the nuts are brown.

**2.** Turn them on to a piece of lightly oiled foil or a non-stick baking tray. Leave to cool. Crush to a fine powder either with a rolling pin or in a blender or food processor.

**3.** Add to the basic custard ice-cream as it is beginning to set.

**4.** Repeat this process with the remaining 2 oz sugar and the walnut halves, taking care not to burn the walnuts as, being dark in colour, it is difficult to see when they are crisp. Roughly crush these and add to the ice-cream. *Never touch the caramel mixture with your bare fingers.*

**5.** Toast the hazelnuts in a hot oven, Gas Mark 9 (240°C, 475°F), and rub off the skins with a damp cloth. Cool and crush roughly. Add to the basic custard ice-cream.

**6.** A few of the walnuts and hazelnuts can be reserved for garnishing the portions when serving, if liked. Likewise, the ice-cream can be garnished by adding the odd crystallized chestnut or two to each serving, as in the photograph on page 212. Serves 10–12 (about twenty balls).

## BASIC CUSTARD ICE-CREAM

This is a very rich ice-cream; for a somewhat plainer, but equally delicious form, substitute milk for cream.

*8 egg yolks*
*3 oz caster sugar*
*1 pint single cream*
*vanilla pod*

**1.** Beat the egg yolks and sugar until they are creamy and thick and all the sugar has dissolved. Bring the cream to the boil, together with the vanilla pod. Remove the pod and pour the cream on to the eggs and sugar, whisking well all the time.

**2.** Arrange this bowl over a pan of boiling water and, stirring all the time, thicken the 'custard' until it coats the back of a wooden spoon well.

**3.** Leave the custard to cool completely, then churn and chill; either follow the instructions for your particular machine, or place in a suitable container in the ice-making compartment of your refrigerator, or in the freezer. Stir the mixture at 30-minute inter-

vals until half frozen to ensure a creamy texture. Serves 5–6.

# BROWN BREAD ICE-CREAM

*2 tablespoons madeira*
*1 pint basic custard ice-cream (see page 211)*
*3 oz wholemeal breadcrumbs*
*2 oz unsalted butter*
*3 oz caster sugar*

**1.** Add the madeira to the basic ice-cream at the custard stage.

**2.** Fry the breadcrumbs in the butter until crisp. Add the sugar and let this caramelize. Cool completely. Crush with a rolling pin. Add to the basic ice-cream as it is beginning to set. Freeze, stirring at 30-minute intervals during the process. Serves 4.

# CRANBERRY ORANGE ICE-CREAM

*1 lb cranberries*
*1 lb caster sugar*
*3 fl oz orange juice*
*1 teaspoon finely grated orange rind*
*3 medium-sized egg whites*

GARNISH:
*orange segments*

**1.** Put the cranberries into a pan with 8 oz caster sugar, the orange juice and rind. Bring to the boil, lower the heat and simmer until the berries pop. Cool.

**2.** Put the berries and juice through a blender and then press through a hair sieve for a fine purée. Chill for an hour.

**3.** Beat the egg whites until they stand in soft peaks, adding the remaining sugar as you go along. Continue beating until you have a meringue-type mixture. Incorporate the cranberry purée thoroughly. Spoon into a

Back row: *Brown bread ice-cream; Cranberry ice-cream;* front row: *(Chocolate peach balls); Three-nut ice-cream; Creamy damson ice-cream* freezer box and freeze until firm. If the ice-cream is too solid when you wish to serve it, move the container to the refrigerator an hour before serving. Garnish with orange segments. Serves 4–5.

# GRAPEFRUIT, LEMON AND MELON SUNDAE

*1 lemon*
*1 oz sugar*
*1 pint lemon sorbet*
*1 ogen melon*
*2 large grapefruit*
*6 tablespoons Galliano or Green Chartreuse*

**1.** Remove the rind from the lemon with a canelle knife, cutting carefully round in one continuous spiral if possible. Even though you are going to cut the rind into pieces this is still the most economical way. Bring the small amount of sugar and $\frac{1}{4}$ pt water to the boil in a small pan. Simmer the lemon rind, cut into inch-size pieces, until tender, 2–3 minutes. Cool in the syrup.

**2.** Using a melon baller, scoop out the sorbet on to a metal tray lined with silicone paper (or a plastic tray without paper) in one layer. Make enough balls to half fill six 10–12 oz glass dishes. Return them to the freezer until you are ready to make up the dessert; they can be made in advance.

**3.** Scoop out the melon into the cool lemon-flavoured syrup and put to chill. Remove the zest and rind from the grapefruit; segment these with a knife into a basin and chill. Put the sundae glasses on a tray in the refrigerator and refrigerate the liqueur.

**4.** Have a sieve ready over a basin. Drain the melon balls and grapefruit segments. Quickly layer the melon, grapefruit and lemon sorbet balls into serving glasses, slotting in and amongst pieces of the lemon zest. Pour over each a tablespoon of liqueur. Serves 6.

# CRANBERRY ICE-CREAM

*1 × 6 oz punnet Ocean Spray cranberries*
*1 oz (or more) caster sugar*
*1 pint basic custard ice-cream (see page 211) or*
*the equivalent commercial vanilla-flavoured ice-cream*

**1.** Toss the cranberries over a low heat until they pop and are soft. Add sugar to taste. (If you cook cranberries with the sugar the skins tend to toughen.) Cool.

**2.** Beat the frozen ice-cream until it is of a consistency where you can fold in the cranberries. For garnish, buy an extra punnet and serve the softened cranberries as a sauce. Serves 4.

# CREAMY DAMSON ICE-CREAM

*2 lb damsons*
*8 oz caster sugar*
*2 tablespoons port (optional)*
*1 pint double cream*

**1.** Simmer the fruit with the sugar and 2 tablespoons port or water until soft. Press through a hair sieve, discarding the skins and stones. Leave the purée to cool.

**2.** Whip the cream until it stands in fairly obvious but still soft peaks. Combine the fruit and cream. Spoon the mixture into ice trays or a freezer box and freeze for 2 hours. Remove the container, scrape the mixture into a cold bowl and whisk well until smooth and airy. Return the ice-cream to the freezer for a further 2 hours. Serves 5–6.

# PINEAPPLE ICE-CREAM

Nothing is more delicious than a pile of pineapple ice-cream served in the shell. The ice-cream is quite easily made in a shallow dish placed in the ice-making compartment of your refrigerator. For a special party, serve kirsch (well chilled) to drink with the dessert.

---

*½ pint single cream*
*2 whole eggs, beaten*
*2 egg yolks*
*4 oz caster sugar*
*½ pint double cream, half whipped*
*8 oz pineapple flesh, liquidized*

---

**1.** Boil the single cream and whisk it into the well-beaten whole eggs and egg yolks. Add the sugar and reheat gently until this extra-sweet custard thickens. Set aside to become absolutely cold. Add the double cream and stir well.

**2.** Lastly, add the pineapple flesh and fold all together before pouring into your dish for the ice-making compartment. Stir occasionally to ensure even freezing. Serves 4.

# AVOCADO ICE-CREAM

Contrary to what people may imagine, this is a sweet not a savoury ice.

---

*2 ripe avocados (Hass are excellent in flavour but you may prefer the greener colour of one of the other varieties)*
*juice and grated rind of 1 lime or*
*1 small lemon*
*2 oz caster sugar*
*1 pint basic ice-cream, freshly made (see page 211)*

---

Peel and pit the avocados and mash with the juice, rind and sugar. Chill well before blending the mixture into the basic ice-cream as it is beginning to set. Freeze. Serves 6.

# Cakes and Fancy Breads

## MULTI-COLOURED SWAP SHOP CAKE

A marble cake with a difference, as mine has a seam of moist redcurrant jelly running through the marbling. This adds an interesting dimension to its overall appearance.

*12 oz unsalted butter*
*12 oz caster sugar*
*6 eggs*
*12 oz self-raising flour*
*2 teaspoons baking powder*
*2 oz ground almonds*
*2–3 drops cochineal*
*2 teaspoons essence de framboise*
*(optional)*
*1 tablespoon cocoa powder*
*grated rind of 1 lemon*
*1–2 drops yellow colouring*
*1 teaspoon essence de pistache*
*1–2 drops green colouring*
*2 teaspoons redcurrant jelly*

**1.** Butter and line a 12 × 4 × 4 inch oblong cake tin. Cream the butter and sugar thoroughly. Beat the eggs and fold into the creamed mixture gradually, adding a little of the flour if it shows signs of curdling.

**2.** Sift together the flour and baking powder. Fold thoroughly into the mixture, adding the ground almonds as you go along. Add 2–3 tablespoons of milk or water in order to arrive at a loose dropping consist-ency. Divide the mixture into three or four equal parts, depending on whether you want three or four colours.

**3.** Add to the first part the 2–3 drops of cochineal, and 2 teaspoons essence de framboise. To the second beat in the tablespoon of cocoa powder. To the third add the grated lemon rind and 1–2 drops yellow colouring. To the fourth add the teaspoon of essence de pistache and 1–2 drops green colouring.

**4.** To make the cake: spoon small amounts of different colours along the bottom of the tin. Give the tin a sharp bang on the worktop to settle things in. Add tiny bits of the jelly right down the centre. Continue adding the mixture until it is used up, but do not put jelly on the top.

**5.** Bake at Gas Mark 5 (190°C, 375°F) for half an hour, then Gas Mark 4 (180°C, 350°F) for a further 35–40 minutes or until cooked. Test with a clean knitting needle or skewer, which should come out clean when inserted in the centre of the cake. The cake will also sound quiet if you listen with your ear to it. Dredge the surface of the cake with icing sugar when cold.

## SPONGE CAKE

Many people make this type of cake without butter; I find the odd ounce of unsalted butter makes it just that little bit more moist.

*Multi-coloured Swap Shop cake*

*4 oz whole eggs*
*4 oz caster sugar*
*1 teaspoon finely grated lemon rind*
*(optional)*
*4 oz self-raising flour, sieved*
*1 oz unsalted butter, melted but cold*

**1.** Beat the eggs and sugar together with the lemon rind until quite stiff and thick. Fold and cut in the sieved flour, mixing lightly but thoroughly. Pour in the butter, again mixing well.

**2.** Butter well and dredge with caster sugar a lightweight 8 inch diameter metal cake tin. Spoon in the mixture and bake at Gas Mark 5 (190°C, 375°F) for 20–25 minutes. Serve with jam, cream cheese, whipped or clotted cream.

# CHESTNUT CREAM CHEESE AND VANILLA ROLL

*3 eggs*
*3 oz vanilla sugar*
*1 teaspoon vanilla extract or essence*
*where vanilla sugar isn't used*
*3 oz self-raising flour sifted on to paper*
*1 scant oz unsalted butter, melted but cool*

CREAM CHEESE AND CHESTNUT FILLING:
*1 × 550 g (19 oz) tin*
*Faugier Marrons au Syrop*
*8 oz pack Philadelphia cream cheese*
*1 teaspoon icing sugar*
*1 teaspoon vanilla extract*
*(or essence)*
*6 fl oz double cream*

DECORATION:
*icing sugar*
*whipped cream*
*1–2 drops vanilla extract*

*Chestnut cream cheese and vanilla roll*

**1.** Butter a 14 × 9 inch tin with unsalted butter and line the base with greaseproof paper, also buttered.

**2.** Whisk the eggs, sugar and vanilla until thick and the whisk leaves a very distinct trail. Briskly whisk in the flour and incorporate the cool melted butter at the same time.

**3.** Pour into the lined tin. Spread the mixture paying particular attention to the corners. Bake at Gas Mark 5 (190°C, 375°F) for 12 minutes.

**4.** Have ready a clean tea towel, well wrung out in cold water. Invert the sponge on to this and remove the base paper. Leave to cool but not go cold, or it won't roll successfully.

**5.** To make the filling: roughly chop the marrons having drained them (reserve 4 or 5 for decoration if you like). Beat the cheese with the icing sugar and vanilla extract. Whip the cream until it stands in soft peaks and carefully fold into the cream cheese (don't try to do this together in a machine or you will end up with a curdled mess).

**6.** Spread the sponge liberally with the filling mixture and roll gently but firmly, using the towel to hold all together as you roll.

**7.** Leave to cool completely; dredge liberally with icing sugar and decorate at will with extra whipped cream. This should be whipped with half a teaspoon of icing sugar and a drop or two of vanilla extract. Marrons can also be used as decoration.

# GOBBET CAKES

So called by me as they illustrate perfectly that eighteenth-century word for a mouthful. Flavoured with lemon and ginger, these little cakes, served with coffee after dinner, would make a tasty and lightweight conclusion.

*4 oz unsalted butter*
*4 oz caster sugar*
*finely grated rind and juice of 1 lemon*
*3 oz self-raising flour*
*1 level teaspoon baking powder*
*2 eggs*
*slices of stem ginger (about 4 pieces)*

**1.** Cream the butter and sugar with the lemon rind. Sieve the flour and baking powder together. Beat the eggs and gradually fold into the creamed mixture. Add the sieved flour using a little lemon juice to arrive at a dropping consistency.

**2.** Butter your tartlet tins well. Use mini tartlet tins if you have them. The best kind are manufactured by Tala. Put teaspoons of the mixture into the tins with a slice of stem ginger on top. Bake at Gas Mark 5 (190°C, 375°F) for 12–15 minutes, or until done. Makes about four dozen baby buns.

# TANGY LEMON SPONGE CAKE

For the family this can be made as two separate sticky-topped cakes, in which case you will need 10 extra lemon slices; or as one deep rich layered cake as seen in the picture opposite which lifts it into a special category for party use.

This cake can be made by the all-in-one method in a food processor.

---

*1 × 12 oz jar lemon cheese*
*1 lemon cut into 10 slices*
*unsalted butter, equal to the weight of the eggs, and softened*
*grated rind of 1 large lemon*
*caster sugar, equal to the weight of the eggs*
*4 large eggs, beaten*
*7 oz self-raising flour*
*3 oz cornflour*
*1 teaspoon baking powder*
*lemon juice*

---

**1.** Butter, and line with buttered papers on the bases, two 7 inch sandwich tins. Spread the base of one with one-third jar of lemon cheese. Arrange the lemon slices, slightly overlapping, in a circle on this.

**2.** Cream the butter, lemon rind and sugar thoroughly. Beat in the eggs a little at a time. Sieve together twice the flour, cornflour and baking powder.

**3.** Mix the flours into the creamed mixture and, using a little lemon juice, beat until you have a softish dropping consistency. Divide the mixture between the two tins, levelling the tops.

**4.** Bake at Gas Mark 5 (190°C, 375°F) for 35–40 minutes or until the cakes are firm to the touch. Turn on to cooling racks. Leave to cool completely.

**5.** Divide each cake in half (or, if you have a good eye and stable hand, three layers makes for a gooier finish). Spread liberally with the remaining lemon cheese. Arrange in layers with, obviously, the one decorated with the lemon slices uppermost.

# WALNUT AND PINEAPPLE MERINGUE CAKE

Ideal for a special Sunday tea in the garden, or as a rich pudding after a dinner. Try sipping a glass of crème de cacao as you munch away. See photograph on page 222.

---

*7 large egg whites*
*15 oz caster sugar, sieved*
*9 oz walnuts, crushed*
*1 small pineapple*
*1 pint double cream*
*2 tablespoons kirsch (optional)*
*1 level tablespoon icing sugar*
*2 pieces of glacé pineapple for decoration (optional)*

---

**1.** Butter the sides and bases and line the bases only of three 8 inch victoria sponge tins (or make the cakes in batches to suit your supply of such tins: the mixture holds well enough for them to be cooked in batches).

**2.** Beat the egg whites until they stand in peaks. Beat in half the sugar, bringing the mixture back to stiff peak consistency.

**3.** Quickly whisk in the remaining sugar and cut and fold in the crushed nuts. Divide into three parts, pour into the prepared tins and bake at Gas Mark 5 (190°C, 375°F) for 20 minutes, baking the meringue bases either together or in separate batches.

**4.** If, after 20 minutes, there is evidence of scorching, reduce the oven temperature to Gas Mark 4 (180°C, 350°F) and add a further 10 minutes to the baking time. These cake

*Tangy lemon sponge cake*

bases are quite fragile, so turn them carefully on to a wire cooling tray, remove the papers and leave to cool.

**5.** To make up the cake: peel, core and chop the pineapple. Whip the cream with the kirsch and icing sugar until it stands in peaks.

**6.** Place one of the cakes on to a serving dish upside down. Pipe round a collar of cream: fill the centre with the pineapple. Arrange the second cake on top, the right way up. Spread with the remaining cream. Arrange the third cake on top. Dredge with icing sugar, a few blobs of cream and the glacé pineapple if used. Cut with a serrated knife. Serve the same day.

# RASPBERRY COCONUT SLICE

*6 oz unsalted butter*
*6 oz caster sugar*
*finely grated rind of 1 lemon*
*3 large eggs, lightly beaten*
*1 tablespoon self-raising flour*
*10 oz desiccated coconut*
*12 oz raspberry jam*

PASTRY:
*7 oz flour*
*4 oz lard*
*1 oz butter*

**1.** Make up the pastry. This will be sufficient to line a swiss roll tin of approximately 14 × 9 inches, and leave enough pastry to make lattice strips to decorate the top of the slice.

**2.** Cream the unsalted butter and sugar with the finely grated lemon rind. Beat in the eggs slowly and then the flour. Mix in the desiccated coconut.

**3.** Spread the jam evenly over the bottom of the pastry-lined tin. Spoon over the coconut mixture, spreading evenly. Arrange lattice strips of pastry over the top. Bake at Gas Mark 5 (190°C, 375°F) for 35–40 minutes. Leave to cool.

**4.** Cut into squares or fingers and store in layers in an airtight tin with greaseproof paper between the layers. Makes 16–20 squares.

*Walnut and pineapple meringue cake*

# MADEIRA CAKE

*6 oz butter*
*6 oz caster sugar*
*3 eggs beaten*
*4 oz self-raising flour*
*4 oz plain flour*
*rind and juice of 1 lemon*
*a little milk if necessary*
*1–2 slices candied citron peel*

**1.** Grease and line with greaseproof paper a round 7 inch cake tin.

**2.** Cream the butter and sugar until light and fluffy.

**3.** Add the eggs slowly, beating well all the time.

**4.** Sieve the flours together, fold half in, then add the lemon rind and juice. Fold in the remaining flour.

**5.** Add a little milk if necessary to give a dropping consistency.

**6.** Put the mixture into the prepared cake tin. Arrange the citron peel on top. Bake at Gas Mark 3 (170°C, 325°F) for 1–1¼ hours.

**7.** Turn on to a rack to cool.

# ORANGE AND GINGER PARKIN

*4 oz butter*
*1 lb golden syrup or old fashioned brown (not black) treacle*
*12 oz caster sugar*
*4 oz self-raising flour*
*good pinch of salt*
*1 lb medium oatmeal*
*1½ teaspoons ground ginger*
*2 eggs*
*1 tablespoon stem ginger, shredded crystallized orange (optional)*
*1 tablespoon candied orange peel*
*3 pieces stem ginger, cut into thinnest shreds (optional)*

**1.** Melt the butter and syrup in a non-stick pan over a low heat. It should be fully melted, but not hot. Mix all the dry ingredients together. Mix in the syrup and butter. Beat the eggs and add these and then add the remaining ingredients. Mix to a dropping consistency with milk.

**2.** Pour into a large well-buttered and -lined loaf tin, or an 8 inch diameter round tin with a loose base. Bake at Gas Mark 4 (180°C, 350°F) for 1–1¼ hours or until it is cooked.

**3.** The parkin should be left for two weeks or more, stored in an airtight tin to mature properly.

# ALMOND AND QUINCE SLICES

PÂTE FROLLE:
*6 oz flour*
*3 oz butter, unsalted (slightly chilled)*
*3 oz caster sugar*
*1 level teaspoon lemon rind*
*1 × size 4 egg*
*3 oz ground almonds, sieved*
*2–3 tablespoons quince or apricot jam*

FRANGIPANE:
*3 oz unsalted butter (soft)*
*5 oz caster sugar*
*2 × size 4 eggs (at room temperature)*
*5 oz ground almonds*
*1 oz plain white flour*
*1–2 oz blanched, flaked almonds*

FLAVOURING:
*1 tablespoon Jamaica rum*
*1 tablespoon triple strength orange flower water, plus 1 heaped teaspoon grated orange rind*
*1 tablespoon lemon juice plus 1 teaspoon lemon rind*

**1.** Sift the flour on to the work surface. Make a well in the centre and add butter (in small lumps), sugar, lemon rind and egg. Sprinkle almonds over the top. 'Peck' and combine to a smooth paste. Chill well before using to line a rectangular tin, 12 × 8 × ½ inch. Chill again before spreading on the quince or apricot jam.

**2.** To make the frangipane: cream the butter and sugar. Lightly beat the eggs, then beat into the creamed mixture by degrees.

Add flavouring, or leave it plain, and fold in the almonds and flour. Spread evenly over the jam base, and sprinkle thickly with blanched and flaked almonds.

**3.** Bake at Gas Mark 4 (180°C, 350°F) in the centre of the oven for 45 minutes. Cuts into about 16–18 pieces.

# ALMOND MACAROONS

*8 oz caster sugar*
*4 oz ground almonds, sieved*
*2 heaped teaspoons ground rice*
*2 egg whites*
*rice paper*
*split almonds for decoration*

**1.** Mix together sugar, ground almonds and ground rice. Stir in the *unbeaten* egg whites.

**2.** Line a baking sheet with rice paper, then either spoon or pipe dessertspoonfuls of the mixture on to the paper. Place a split almond in the centre of each macaroon. Bake at Gas Mark 2/3 (150/170°C, 300/325°F) for 20–25 minutes. Makes 18–20.

# AVOLA STICKS

Avola, in southern Sicily, produces the best almonds, hence the name of these biscuits.

*7 oz plain white flour*
*6 oz unsalted butter*
*7 oz ground almonds, sieved*
*8 oz caster sugar*
*2 × size 4 eggs, lightly beaten*

**1.** Rub the butter into the flour. Toss in the ground almonds and sugar, mixing thoroughly.

**2.** Mix in the eggs and gather to a soft paste.

**3.** Butter a baking sheet. Fit an 8 point 'rope' pipe or plain ½ inch pipe into a pastry bag. Pipe out 'sticks' about 3 inches long

Clockwise from top left: *Almond and quince slices; Almond petticoat tails; Almond macaroons; Avola sticks, with baby macaroons in the centre*

(quite hard work for a small hand, so drag in the men!).

**4.** Bake at Gas Mark 3 (170°C, 325°F) for 30 minutes. Cool on a wire rack. Makes 30–40 biscuits.

# ALMOND PETTICOAT TAILS

See photograph on page 225.

*4 oz plain flour*
*2 oz ground rice*
*2 oz caster sugar*
*4 oz unsalted butter*
*1 beaten egg white – see method*
*extra caster sugar*
*2 oz flaked or 'nibbed' almonds*

**1.** Sieve the flour, ground rice and sugar together on to a work surface.

**2.** Cut the butter into cubes and either rub or 'peck' in. Knead lightly, form into a ball, press and roll lightly into an 8 inch circle. Place on a buttered baking sheet.

**3.** Using a knife divide into 8 even segments without cutting right through. Brush with beaten egg white. Sprinkle with a little caster sugar and the flaked or 'nibbed' almonds. Press lightly with the palm of the hand.

**4.** Bake at Gas Mark 2 (150°C, 300°F) for 40–45 minutes. Cool for a little while before cutting right through the petticoat markings.

**5.** Store, as with other biscuits and maca-roons, in an airtight tin. If you want to freeze the shortbread, freeze it uncooked. Makes 8.

# SAND CAKE

To serve with Zabaglione (see page 174) instead of the more usual sponge fingers.

*6 oz self-raising flour*
*1 level teaspoon baking powder*
*2 oz ground rice*
*6 oz unsalted butter*
*4 oz caster sugar*
*1 teaspoon vanilla essence*
*3 eggs, beaten*
*1 tablespoon milk (optional)*

*Orange and almond liqueur cake*

**1.** Liberally butter and sugar a fluted mould or loose-bottomed deep cake tin 7 inches in diameter.

**2.** Sift the flour and baking powder together. Mix with the rice. Put on one side.

**3.** Cream the butter, sugar and vanilla essence until light and fluffy. Beat in the eggs slowly. Gradually beat in the flour mixture, adding a little milk or water until you have a soft dropping consistency. Turn into the mould or tin and bake at Gas Mark 4 (180°C, 350°F) for 1–1¼ hours. Yields 8 good slices.

# ORANGE AND ALMOND LIQUEUR CAKE

*8 oz self-raising flour*
*1 teaspoon baking powder*
*4 oz ground almonds*
*8 oz unsalted butter*
*8 oz caster sugar*
*2 heaped teaspoons finely grated orange rind*
*4 eggs, beaten*
*orange jelly marmalade*
*flaked almonds and candied orange slices for decoration (optional)*

FOR THE SPECIAL BUTTER CREAM:
*4 egg whites*
*8 oz icing sugar*
*2 drops red food colour*
*2 drops yellow food colour*
*8 oz unsalted butter, very soft*
*1 teaspoon grated orange rind*
*2 tablespoons orange liqueur*
*(Cointreau, Grand Marnier, or Curaçao)*

FOR THE ICING:
*6 oz icing sugar*
*2 tablespoons orange liqueur (as above)*

**1.** Butter and line the bases of two 8 inch victoria sponge tins. Sieve together on to a paper, twice, the flour, baking powder and ground almonds. Cream the butter, sugar and rind until light and fluffy. Beat in the eggs, then the flour mixture using a little cold water (about 2 tablespoons) to arrive at a soft dropping consistency.

**2.** Divide the mixture equally between the two tins: level the tops and bake at Gas Mark 5 (190°C, 375°F) for 35–40 minutes or until firm when pressed with the finger.

**3.** Turn the cakes on to a wire cooling rack and cool completely. Halve each cake.

**4.** To make up the butter cream: stiffly beat the egg whites, beat in half the icing sugar, adding the colouring at this stage. Fold in the remaining sugar. Cream the butter and rind very well. Gradually beat in the meringue mixture, orange rind and liqueur.

**5.** To make the icing: sieve the icing sugar into a bowl. Heat the liqueur over a low flame in a metal soup ladle (do not allow to ignite). Stir, then beat into the sugar.

**6.** Spread this over the baked base side of one of the cake bases using a palette knife dipped in boiling water to ease the process and to give a smooth finish. Set aside.

**7.** Spread one-third of the butter cream on the crumb face of one of the layers. Arrange a second cake on this: splash with a little liqueur and spread with some of the remaining butter cream. Spread the next cake with the jelly, fit it on top of the second layer and spread with some butter cream. Finally, top with the iced layer.

**8.** Spread butter cream round the sides of the cake. Press the flaked almonds into this.

**9.** Decorate at will with any remaining butter cream piped in blobs and stuck with candied orange.

**10.** Cut with a hot, wetted knife.

## CHOCOLATE AND ALMOND CAKE

*5 eggs, separated*
*8 oz caster sugar*
*8 oz unsalted butter*
*8 oz good quality plain chocolate*
*3 oz self-raising flour*
*4 oz ground almonds*

FOR THE ICING:
*2 tablespoons maraschino*
*6 oz icing sugar, sieved*
*2 oz cocoa powder, sieved*

**1.** Cream the egg yolks, butter and sugar together.

**2.** Break the chocolate into squares and melt in a basin over a pan of boiling water.

**3.** Sieve the flour and almonds together to get rid of any lumps. Stiffly beat the egg whites until they stand in peaks when pulled up by the whisk.

**4.** Pour the melted chocolate into the egg yolk mixture. Fold in the flour and almonds. Incorporate one-third of the egg whites thoroughly and then lightly but, again, thoroughly fold in the remainder. Pour the mixture into a well-buttered and papered $8\frac{1}{2} \times 3\frac{1}{2}$ inch round loose-bottomed cake tin. Bake at Gas Mark 5 (190°C, 375°F) for $1\frac{1}{4}$ hours. The cake is baked when the top is firm to the touch and when, if you listen to it, it is almost silent. Turn on to a rack to cool.

**5.** To make the icing: gently warm the alcohol, taking care it does not ignite. Mix the icing sugar and cocoa powder together. Incorporate the liquid to make a spreadable but stiffish icing. Use a hot wetted knife to spread a thick cushion of icing on top of the cake.

## BUTTERSCOTCH FUDGE CAKE

Commonly known in my family as 'naughty cake'. It's sticky and gooey and treacherous to fillings, but very moreish and you don't have to bake it!

*6 oz Dutch unsalted butter, melted*
*6 tablespoons golden syrup*
*4 oz glacé cherries, chopped*
*8 oz dried fruit mixed*
*6 oz mixed nuts, roughly chopped*
*8 oz wheatmeal biscuits*

DECORATION:
*whipped cream*
*glacé cherries*

**1.** To make the butterscotch sauce: stir together the butter and syrup in a heavy-based saucepan. Boil for 2–3 minutes, stirring constantly. Leave to cool for a few minutes.

**2.** Place all the fruit and nuts together in a large bowl. Crush half the biscuits and crumble the other half, then add to the fruit and nuts. Pour the butterscotch sauce over all the ingredients, and stir well to coat evenly.

**3.** Spoon the mixture into an 8 inch diameter well-buttered and -lined, loose-based cake tin. Leave to set in the refrigerator for 2–3 hours. When firm decorate with the whipped cream and cherries. Serves 12.

# CHOCOLATE AND GOOSEBERRY CAKE

*8 oz unsalted butter at room*
*temperature*
*4 oz caster sugar*
*4 large eggs*
*6 oz self-raising flour*
*1 teaspoon vanilla extract*
*1 teaspoon baking powder*
*2 oz cocoa powder*
*2 oz ground almonds (or an extra*
*2 oz self-raising flour)*
*gooseberry jam*

CHOCOLATE BUTTER CREAM:
*4 oz unsalted butter, softened*
*4 oz icing sugar*
*2 oz cocoa powder*
*1 teaspoon vanilla extract*

CHOCOLATE ICING:
*4 oz bar of dark chocolate*
*1 oz unsalted butter*
*1 tablespoon brandy*

CHOCOLATE LEAVES FOR
DECORATION:
*bay, rose or camellia leaves*
*8 oz bar of chocolate*

**1.** Cream the butter and sugar thoroughly. Beat the eggs and fold into the creamed mixture gradually, adding a little of the flour if it shows signs of curdling. Add the vanilla.

**2.** Sift together the self-raising flour, baking powder and cocoa powder. Fold thoroughly into the mixture, adding the ground almonds as you go along. Add 2–3 tablespoons of milk or water in order to arrive at a loose dropping consistency.

**3.** Line the base of two well-buttered 8 inch diameter sandwich tins with greaseproof paper. Divide the mixture between the tins and bake in a moderate oven, Gas Mark 5 (190°C, 375°F) for 35–40 minutes. Leave for 5 minutes before turning on to a wire cooling tray. Remove the paper.

**4.** To make the butter cream: blend all the ingredients together.

**5.** To make the icing: break the chocolate into bits. Soften together with the butter and brandy in a bowl over a pan of simmering water. Leave the mixture to cool before spreading it over the made-up cake.

**6.** To make up the cake: spread a good cushion of gooseberry jam over the bottom cake. Spread over the butter cream. Invert the top so that it is flat side up. Spread the icing over the top (this is a softish icing).

**7.** Make the chocolate leaves using a pastry brush, brush melted chocolate over the veined side of the leaves. Leave to set, then carefully peel away the fresh leaf.

# BLOND FRUIT CAKE

*6 oz muscatel raisins*
*4 oz glacé cherries*
*6 oz walnuts, roughly crushed*
*4 oz candied orange peel, finely chopped*
*2 tablespoons rum or whisky*
*12 oz unsalted butter*
*12 oz caster sugar*
*6 large eggs, beaten*
*12 oz self-raising flour*
*4 oz ground almonds*
*1 level teaspoon baking powder*

TOPPING:
*1 oz flaked almonds*
*strips of glacé fruits such as peach*
*or pear*
*sieved icing sugar*

**1.** Soak the fruits and nuts in rum.

**2.** Cream the butter and sugar thoroughly. Add the beaten eggs and incorporate well. Sieve the flour, ground almonds and baking powder together. Cut and fold into the creamed butter. Mix in the fruit and nuts.

**3.** Pour into a well-buttered tin about 12 × 4 inches, the base lined with a buttered

paper. Sprinkle over the extra almonds and peel if used.

**4.** Bake at Gas Mark 5 (190°C, 375°F) for 30 minutes, then reduce to Gas Mark 4 (180°C, 350°F) for 40–50 minutes. Dredge with sieved icing sugar before serving. Serves 12.

# ROMAN CHEESE-CAKE

This ancient recipe taken from my collection of antique cookbooks makes a handsome pudding. Serve with thick unsweetened cream.

---

PASTRY BASE (OPTIONAL):
*12 oz pastry, mixed weight, home-made (see method) or commercial brand*

FOR THE FILLING:
*4 oz unsalted butter*
*8 oz caster sugar*
*1 lb cream cheese*
*2 tablespoons any good-flavoured honey*
*4 fl oz single cream*
*1 teaspoon vanilla essence*
*5 eggs, separated*
*2 oz plain flour, sifted*
*4 oz flaked almonds*

FOR THE TOPPING:
*2 oz soft brown sugar*
*1 teaspoon cinnamon*
*2 oz flaked almonds*
*sieved icing sugar*

---

**1.** Line a 10 inch spring form tin with a thin sheet of shortcrust pastry (it will take about 12 oz commercial pastry, or 7 oz flour, 3 oz butter, 2 oz lard, 1 teaspoon icing sugar and 2 tablespoons cold water for mixing). Put the lined tin into the freezer or refrigerator while you make up the filling. (It is not necessary to line the spring form with shortcrust pastry for this recipe, it is optional.)

**2.** Cream the butter and caster sugar until light and fluffy. Add the cheese and beat well. Add the honey, cream, vanilla essence, egg yolks and flour. Mix well. Beat the egg whites stiffly and lightly fold into the mixture together with the flaked almonds.

*Roman cheesecake*

**3.** Pour into the pastry case or into a well buttered spring form and sprinkle evenly with the topping ingredients. Bake for 1 hour at Gas Mark 3 (170°C, 325°F). Then turn off the heat and allow to cool in the oven to prevent a rift forming. Dredge with sieved icing sugar before serving.

# RICH, RICH ECCLES CAKES

Eccles Cakes should always be served warm with clotted cream or rum butter. And that is advice from a Northerner! If you have great patience, as with mince pies, Eccles Cakes are extra special when made miniature, 2 inches in diameter when finished.

---

FILLING:
*4 oz seeded muscatel raisins, roughly chopped*
*4 oz currants*
*3 tablespoons rum or whisky*
*2 oz ground almonds*
*2 oz softened butter*
*2 oz demerara sugar*
*grated rind and juice of 1 lemon*
*½ teaspoon cinnamon*

SUGAR GLAZE:
*2 oz caster sugar*

PASTRY:
*1 lb flaky pastry (ideally, home-made)*

---

**1.** Soak the fruits in the alcohol overnight. Mix with the rest of the ingredients.

**2.** Make the sugar glaze by bringing to the boil 2 tablespoons water with the caster sugar. Leave to cool. (It should be clear and sticky, not wet.)

**3.** Roll out the pastry evenly into one vast sheet. Using a saucer as a template, cut out 4–5 inch circles. Just how many you will get depends on how well you roll the pastry.

**4.** Put spoonfuls of the mixture into the centre of each circle. Gather the pastry over the mixture and pinch together to seal the edges.

**5.** Invert the cakes on to a buttered baking sheet. Lightly press them flat, but don't squash them totally. Brush with a little of the sugar glaze.

**6.** Bake at Gas Mark 7 (220°C, 425°F) for 15 minutes. Reduce the temperature to Gas Mark 4 (180°C, 350°F) and bake for 20 minutes, or until crisp and browned.

**7.** Brush the cakes with more syrup when baked to glaze. Makes 10–14.

# BROWNIES

There are many different recipes for Brownies, some more 'cakey' than others. I prefer mine to be chewy, and this is what they are. They are also quite sweet and all the better for that, too.

---

*4 oz dark chocolate*
*4 oz butter*
*12 oz caster sugar*
*1 teaspoon vanilla essence*
*2 eggs, lightly beaten*
*4 oz self-raising flour sieved with ½ teaspoon salt*
*4–6 oz walnuts, roughly crushed*

---

**1.** Butter and line an 8 inch square tin. Soften the chocolate in a bowl over hot water. Beat in the butter away from the heat. Beat in the sugar and essence. Beat in the eggs a little at a time. Quickly stir in the flour and salt. Fold in the nuts.

**2.** Spoon and spread evenly into the cake tin. Bake at Gas Mark 4 (180°C, 350°F) for 35–40 minutes. Allow to cool slightly and cut into squares. Store in an airtight tin. The Brownies can be frozen. Makes about 16 squares.

# CHOCOLATE CARAMEL CAKE

This gâteau, or cake, is similar to a Doboz Torte where layers of sponge are sandwiched with chocolate butter cream, and a caramel topping covers all. I add an extra layer of caramel to give things a crunch and also include a layer of semi-sweet apricot jam or purée. See photograph on page 164.

SPONGE:
*3 large eggs*
*4 oz caster sugar*
*4 oz plain white flour*
*pinch of salt*

CARAMEL:
*6 oz caster sugar*

BUTTER CREAM:
*8 oz plain dark chocolate*
*8 oz unsalted butter*
*1 lb icing sugar*
*2 tablespoons apricot jam, sieved*

**1.** Make the sponge layers the day before. Prepare *five* flat trays lined with silicone paper or buttered greaseproof paper (tart tins and roasting tins upside down can be improvised). Draw a 7 inch circle on each.

**2.** Break the whole eggs into a large Pyrex bowl, add the sugar and whisk over simmering water until the mixture is thick and the whisk forms a definite trail when drawn through.

**3.** Sieve the flour with a pinch of salt on to a piece of paper. Then carefully fold and cut this into the eggs and sugar with a slotted spoon. Divide between the five papers and spread evenly with a palette knife to the edges of the drawn circles.

**4.** Bake in batches at Gas Mark 6 (200°C, 400°F) for 7–8 minutes, or until cooked and golden brown and perhaps slightly crisp at the edges. Turn on to a wire tray, remove the paper carefully, and leave to cool.

**5.** Using a paper template, trim the edges of the sponge circles to size.

**6.** To make the caramel: put the sugar into a heavy-bottomed pan, just cover with cold water, place the pan over a low heat and bring to the boil. Do not stir. Boil rapidly until a golden brown caramel develops.

**7.** While this is happening, stand two of the sponge bases on a wire cooling tray, nice side uppermost. When the caramel is ready, hold the pan with a cloth and pour half of the caramel over each base, starting in the centre and working round and out in a circular movement. *Do not touch the caramel with your fingers as it sticks and burns.* Before it sets hard on one of the cakes, mark serving portions with a knife blade by pressing it into

the half-set caramel (about 6–8 segments is right). Leave on one side: do not refrigerate or the caramel will soften.

**8.** To make the butter cream: break the chocolate into pieces and put in a bowl over a pan of simmering water. Cream the butter, then beat in the icing sugar and continue beating until smooth and fluffy. This can be done with a machine. Gradually add the melted chocolate, scraping every bit out of the bowl with a plastic or rubber spatula.

**9.** To assemble the cake: stand the plain caramel-covered base on a cake board or icing turntable. Spread some of the butter cream over the caramel. Place a plain sponge cake on top of this and spread with a good cushion of apricot jam or purée, then a cushion of the butter cream. The third piece of sponge is spread with butter cream only, as is the fourth. The fifth sponge, the top of the cake, is the segmented caramel-covered layer.

**10.** Spread the remaining butter cream round the sides and fork a pattern round it, or pipe columns of the butter cream up the sides. Pipe lines of butter cream across the top of the cake to mark the portions. Serves 6–8.

# CROISSANTS

You can buy excellent croissants these days so it seems hardly worthwhile making your own, but there are still those people, thank goodness, who set store by effort.

These crescent-shaped pastry-cum-bread buns vary in richness, from very flaky pastry-type affairs to a more bread-like consistency. I prefer the latter. It's the shape that gives the name. There was a time in eighteenth-century England when we actually had a similar beast to the croissant: they were called 'wigs'. My recipe is similar.

*¾ pint milk*
*½ oz brewers' yeast*
*18 oz fine plain white flour, sieved*
*½ oz salt*
*4 oz butter*
*beaten egg for glazing*

**1.** Warm 4 fl oz milk to blood heat (about 38°C, 100°F) and pour into bowl. Mix in the crumbled yeast and work to a soft dough with 4 oz flour. Leave to develop and rise to double its size in a lightly greased bowl covered with a cloth. This will take up to an hour.

2. When risen, add the rest of the milk and dredge in the remaining flour and salt. Knead as for ordinary bread with the heel of the hand, pushing away from you. You don't have to be quite so forceful as with bread – just knead until you have a firm but flexible dough.

3. Roll the dough into an oblong roughly 14 × 6 inches and ½ inch thick.

4. Spread the butter over the whole surface area of the rolled dough. Fold top to middle, bottom over the top, and turn so that the edges are in the same position as a closed book. Press all the edges together with the rolling pin. Leave in the refrigerator for an hour.

5. Roll again in a similar fashion, leaving the dough to rest for an hour after this. Repeat again: this time leave overnight in the refrigerator in a plastic bag lightly dredged with flour.

6. Roll out the pastry as before, this time approximately 12 inches long, 4–5 inches wide and ¼ inch thick. Cut into 4–5 inch squares. Cut these into two triangles from corner to corner. Roll up lightly (or somewhat loosely), from the long edge to the point. Seal this with a little beaten egg. Form into crescent shapes, nipping and sealing the edges together with a little beaten egg. Leave to rise again until doubled in size. Now pull the joined tips slightly apart, brush with beaten egg and bake at Gas Mark 8 (230°C, 450°F) for 20–25 minutes. Makes 6–8 croissants.

# BRIOCHES

Francophiles all adore these little (or large) yeast-like cakes. Taken with morning coffee or chocolate, their fluted sides make them even more appealing, though this is purely created by the tins in which they are baked.

Some say that brioches have their origins in Brie – hence the name – but this might well be disputed by the Swiss and Austrians who appear to have adopted them as their national bread.

They take a bit of effort and time, and the little ones are certainly more reliable to make than large ones and are well worth the effort. They freeze well, so if you do embark on making them, make a lot and freeze them in appropriate batches.

---

*8 oz plain white flour*
*½ oz brewers' yeast*
*1 level teaspoon salt*
*½ oz caster sugar*
*2–3 tablespoons milk*
*2 large eggs, beaten*
*3 oz unsalted butter, softened to a paste*
*extra beaten egg for glazing*

---

1. Sieve the flour. Put 2 oz into a bowl. Make a well and crumble in the yeast very finely. Add 2 tablespoons warm water and, using the finger tips, work into a smooth paste. Form this into a small ball.

2. Take a small pan or bowl of lukewarm water, drop this ball of dough into it to develop and rise in volume (about 8 to 10 minutes).

3. Meanwhile, mix the salt and sugar with the remaining flour. Add milk and eggs. It is quite a messy business to work this into a dough, but you must do so. When you have a workable mass which doesn't adhere to the fingers, add the butter and work this into the dough. Don't try adding any extra flour, just persevere.

4. Remove the risen yeast dough from the water, using the fingers spread out like a fan. Let it drain for a minute or so on a clean towel. Now knead lightly but thoroughly with the second paste. Put into a floured plastic bag, and leave to rise and develop for 3–4 hours in a warm part of the kitchen (not on top of the central heating).

5. Now knock the dough down, but not as laboriously as you would do for bread, and leave in a *cold* place or refrigerator on a floured tray, covered with a clean floured cloth, to firm up and take on a manageable consistency.

6. Knead lightly and form into small egg-sized balls. Cut off one-third of each ball and form into smaller balls with little points at one end.

7. Lightly butter your brioche tins. Put in

the larger of the two balls. Make a small incision and fit in the pointed end of the smaller of the balls. (This is to give them their mini cottage loaf shape when baked.)

8. Leave to prove again for 15 minutes in a warmer place than previously – the top of the boiler or back of the Aga.

9. Brush the top of each brioche with a little beaten egg. Bake in a preheated oven, Gas Mark 7 (220°C, 425°F) for 15 minutes. Turn out on to a wire tray to cool. Yields about 12/16 brioches, depending on the size of your tins.

# MUSCATEL BRAN CAKE

The secret of this wholesome cake is in the flavour of the muscatel raisins. These are readily available from most health food shops.

The cake is good when sliced and well buttered and served with a mild, crumbly cheese such as Wensleydale or Cheshire. Alternatively, it is delicious toasted for breakfast.

---

*8 oz Allbran*
*8 oz muscatel raisins (seedless)*
*8 oz Barbados sugar*
*4 oz walnuts, roughly chopped*
*2 teaspoons vanilla essence*
*¾ pint milk*
*8 oz wholemeal flour*
*3 teaspoons baking powder*

---

1. Put the Allbran, raisins, sugar, walnuts and vanilla essence into a bowl. Cover with the milk and mix well. Leave to soak for two hours.

2. Dredge the flour and baking powder together. Gradually fold into the mixture. Bake at Gas Mark 4 (180°C, 350°F) in an 8 inch square tin lined with buttered paper for 1¼–1½ hours.

# HERB AND CHEESE BREAD

---

*1 lb self-raising flour*
*1 level teaspoon salt*
*1 level teaspoon baking powder*
*6 oz butter or margarine*
*4 oz grated Edam cheese*
*1 level tablespoon mixed*
*dried herbs or 2 tablespoons*
*fresh herbs (thyme, chives,*
*parsley, mint)*
*2 beaten eggs*
*milk*

---

1. Sieve flour, salt and baking powder into a bowl. Rub in fat to fine crumbs.

2. Add cheese and herbs. Make a well and pour in the beaten eggs. Add a little milk until it becomes a soft dough. Divide into two 1 lb buttered loaf tins.

3. Bake the bread at Gas Mark 5 (190°C, 375°F) for 1½–2 hours. Serves 16.

# SESAME SEED ROLLS

These can be served hot or cold, and go well with all the soups. Allow two slices of white bread per serving. Remove the crusts and roll the slices flat with a heavy rolling pin.

Butter each rolled slice liberally, sprinkle with a level teaspoon of sesame seeds, a modest pinch of table salt, and a sprinkling of milled pepper. Roll them up from corner to corner and bake them in a hot oven, Gas Mark 8 (230°C, 450°F) until they are golden brown and crisp right through (about 30 minutes). You may have to turn them a time or two to ensure this.

You can vary the flavour of these rolls by spreading them with different savoury butters. Again serve hot or cold.

# Christmas

No matter how hard I try, I simply can't get away from tradition at Christmas time, however pagan based that tradition may be. I suppose I am a romantic at heart and cannot, for example, imagine Christmas Day on a sandy beach in the sun with not a strand of tinsel in sight.

For me, Christmas has to be comfortable; carols and log fires, hoar frosts and clear, starry nights. And what would that magical midnight hour be without a toast to start it all off?

Let other countries eat their elaborate Christmas dishes. But *I* must have my succulent roast turkey, creamy bread sauce, white-whipped potatoes, bacon rolls and chestnut stuffing – whatever the sweat and palaver involved. Even cabbage-sized Brussels sprouts are part of the main scheme of things.

And to complete my image of Christmas? A sticky, fruit-packed pudding, ablaze with liqueur and topped with rum butter and lashings of thick cream, followed by meltingly light mince pies, celery, walnuts, glacé fruits . . .

Some of you, of course, less bound up in tradition, will prefer to cook and present Christmas food in a different way.

This section, perhaps, is especially for them.

*Stuffed boned capon; Carrot purée; Courgettes with peas and herbs*

## STUFFED EGGS WITH RED SALMON CAVIAR

*8 hard-boiled eggs*
*2 teaspoons onion juice (see below)*
*2 oz smoked cods' or lumpfish roes*
*4 oz unsalted butter, softened*
*1 teaspoon lemon juice*
*8 oz full fat cream cheese*
*freshly milled pepper*
*salt, possibly*
*16 tiny buttered bread rounds*
*2 oz or more red salmon caviar*

1. I hard boil my eggs for 10 minutes from cold. Crack them and leave them under running cold water for 10–15 minutes. This will give you a yolk which is still soft in the centre. The sulphur and residual heat, which blackens or creates that undesirable but frequently present dark green ring, will be eliminated and the white will be delicate and soft as it should be.

2. To make onion juice: peel and halve a medium-sized onion, and grate this on the fine teeth of a grater, standing it on a small plate to catch the juice as it runs down.

3. Halve the eggs and put the yolks, roe, softened butter, onion juice and lemon juice into a blender and blend thoroughly. I then advise pressing the blended mixture through a hair sieve, to rid it of any possible lumps, before beating in the cream cheese. (Don't use the blender or food processor; you may find the mixture will curdle.) Season with pepper and possibly a little salt. However, do remember that the roe, cheese and caviar all contain salt.

4. Fill the mixture into a piping bag fitted with a large rose tube. Pipe into the half egg whites. Put these in a cool place. Allow time enough for the mixture to be cool but still soft when served.

5. Butter tiny circles of very fresh white or brown bread. Stand each half egg atop each bread and, depending on your generosity, top each egg with a little caviar or pass a jar of well-chilled caviar separately. Serves 8.

## SMOKED SALMON MOUSSE WITH RED CAVIAR

*1½ sachets gelatine crystals*
*12 oz Scotch smoked salmon (off-cuts will not really do)*
*2 oz jar red caviar or salmon roe*
*20 fl oz (2 large cartons) double cream*
*salt*
*¼ teaspoon milled white peppercorns*
*juice of ½ lemon*

FISH STOCK:
*bones of 2 Dover sole, washed and broken*
*good sprig of parsley*
*squeeze of lemon juice*
*pinch of dried thyme*
*½ pint dry white wine*
*12 black peppercorns*

1. Bring all the ingredients for the stock, plus 2 pints cold water, to the boil. Reduce the heat and simmer for 30–40 minutes.

2. Skim off any scum, strain into a clean pan. Reduce to ½ pint by boiling and pour the stock into a bowl. Sprinkle over the gelatine crystals and stir until entirely dissolved. Allow to cool completely, but not set.

3. Make a fine purée of the smoked salmon, using a little of the liquid fish jelly to help you do this. Turn this mixture into a bowl and add the remaining cool fish jelly. Fold in 1½ oz of the caviar – keeping the rest for the garnish.

4. Whip 18 fl oz cream, adding a little salt, the pepper and the lemon juice, until it stands in firm peaks. Cut and fold the two mixtures together.

5. Use double thickness oiled greaseproof paper collars, stapled at the top and secured round the middle with an elastic band, to wrap round either a soufflé dish or individual ramekins. Pour in mixture and chill for about 4 hours until set. Garnish with a teaspoon of red caviar and the remaining cream, lightly salted and whipped. Serves 8.

*Smoked salmon mousse with red caviar*

# ROAST NORFOLK TURKEY

*1 large onion, peeled and sliced*
*2 carrots, peeled and sliced*
*1 clove garlic, crushed*
*12 oz butter*
*1 level teaspoon each of rubbed thyme,*
*bay and rosemary*
*salt and milled pepper*
*2 × 7–8 lb turkeys, stuffed with your*
*chosen stuffing (see page 242)*
*½ lb streaky bacon*

**1.** Put the sliced vegetables and garlic into a roasting tin to make a bed on which to sit the stuffed turkeys.

**2.** Make a paste using the butter, herbs, salt and pepper and rub it all over the birds. Arrange strips of bacon over the breasts and cover with foil.

**3.** Roast the birds in a preheated oven at Gas Mark 6 (200°C, 400°F) for 1 hour, then lower the temperature to Gas Mark 4 (180°C, 350°F) for a further 1–1½ hours. Baste at half-hourly intervals. Remove the foil and bacon for the last half-hour of the roasting time. Serves 12–14.

# SHERRIED TURKEY GRAVY

*2 tablespoons olive oil*
*turkey giblets, cut into manageable*
*pieces*
*2 pints cold chicken stock (use stock*
*cubes)*
*1 dessertspoon tomato purée*
*1 oz white flour*
*¼ pint amontillado sherry*
*salt and pepper*

**1.** Heat the oil in a heavy-bottomed frying pan until smoking. Brown all the giblets including the liver, unless you have a stuffing recipe calling for its use. Transfer these to a pan and cover with the cold stock. Bring to the boil and simmer for an hour. Strain and cool.

*Roast Norfolk turkey with home-made sausages and stuffing;*
*sherried turkey gravy; pear and lemon sauce;*
*beetroot and orange purée; fennel served without a sauce*

**2.** Remove the cooked turkey to a warm platter. Decant all but 3–4 tablespoons of the remaining buttery fats and pan juices, leaving the browned vegetables and any residues which may have adhered to the tin. Stir in the small amount of tomato purée and scatter over the flour. Over a low heat, work everything together with a wooden spatula, letting it take on more colour (about 5–6 minutes).

**3.** Pour in the sherry and 1½ pints of giblet stock. Bring the contents of the tin to the boil, working away with the spatula. Allow to boil at a good roll for a couple of minutes, then season as needed. Strain into a smaller pan and continue simmering for a further 5–10 minutes when the sauce will be bright and a rich chestnut brown colour. Skim off any fat (this will rise to the surface if you take the pan away from the heat for a minute).

# PEAR, CELERY AND PARSLEY STUFFING

*2 oz butter*
*1 small onion, chopped*
*½ head of celery, washed and finely sliced*
*2 pears (ripe, but not too ripe)*
*juice of ½ large lemon*
*6 oz coarse white breadcrumbs*
*2 oz grated suet*
*1 teaspoon grated lemon rind*
*1 level teaspoon salt*
*freshly milled black pepper*
*3 heaped tablespoons chopped parsley*
*1 egg, beaten*

**1.** Melt the butter in a heavy-bottomed pan. Soften the onion in this until it turns a pale golden colour. Add the celery and soften, stirring to prevent over-browning. Cool.

**2.** Peel and core the pears. Cut them into small dice (or roughly, but adequately, chop them) and toss the pieces in the lemon juice.

**3.** Combine all the ingredients in a bowl and bind with beaten egg. Stuff into the turkey neck, wrap the skin over and secure with tooth picks. Makes enough for 2 small or 1 large bird.

# BACON AND HERB STUFFING

*4 oz well-flavoured bacon*
*2 oz butter*
*1 medium-sized onion, sliced*
*8 oz fresh white breadcrumbs*
*4 oz shredded suet*
*1 tablespoon mixed fresh lemon thyme and basil (or 2 teaspoons mixed dried herbs)*
*1 tablespoon freshly chopped parsley*
*salt and freshly ground black pepper*
*1 egg, beaten*

Cut the bacon into strips and fry these in the butter until golden brown. Add the sliced onions and fry until they are transparent. Mix with the breadcrumbs, suet, herbs and the butter in which you have been frying the bacon and onions. Season well and bind with the beaten egg. Makes enough for 2 small or 1 large bird.

# SIMPLE SAUSAGEMEAT AND GINGER STUFFING

*1 lb pork sausagemeat*
*1 clove garlic, crushed*
*1 level teaspoon black pepper*
*1 rounded teaspoon ground ginger*
*1 tablespoon chopped stem ginger*
*1 egg, beaten*

Mix all the ingredients together and fill into the neck of the turkey.

# HOME-MADE SAUSAGES

I like my sausages chunky in texture, so I put all the ingredients once only through the coarse blade of a mincer (a food processor does not give the right texture for the British banger!).

½ lb leg of pork or boned shoulder
½ lb pie veal
½ lb gammon (smoked or plain)
½ lb pork back fat
1 level tablespoon rubbed sage
1 level teaspoon milled black pepper
1 level teaspoon salt
½ lb Cox's apples, grated
2 oz crushed Bath Oliver biscuits
dripping or oil for frying

1. Mix all the ingredients, plus ⅛ pint cold water, together. Put once through a mincer.
2. Flour a work surface and, using a wetted tablespoon, scoop even amounts of the mixture on to this.
3. Dredge again with flour and roll into 3 × 1½ inch shapes.
4. Fry in lightly smoking bacon dripping or oil. Makes about 12.

## TOMATO MADEIRA SAUCE

Make the modest amount of sauce in a large 6 pint pan. It's easier and the result is better. It can be made two days in advance.

1 oz butter or olive oil for frying
1 medium (3 oz) onion, chopped
1 medium (3 oz) carrot cut into small dice
1 oz mushrooms cut into dice
1 heaped dessertspoon tomato purée
1 heaped teaspoon (a good ½ oz) flour
1 level teaspoon mild paprika
¼ pint red wine
¼ pint dry madeira
1 pint strong chicken stock (made from capon bones) or use 1½ stock cubes
½ lb fresh tomatoes, skinned, seeded and roughly chopped
salt if needed

1. Melt the butter, letting it take on an almond flavour and golden colour.
2. Add the onion and carrot, lower heat and brown, stirring regularly.
3. Add the mushrooms and mix in the purée letting it take on a little colour – but it must not burn. Sprinkle over the flour, stir in well and allow to colour for a minute, stirring all the time.
4. Turn the mixture on to a dinner plate, turn up the heat and pour in the red wine. Work all the residues from the bottom of the pan into the wine.
5. Add the madeira, stock, tomatoes, and the fried vegetable mixture. Bring everything to the boil. Reduce the heat, simmer the sauce for 30 minutes, when you will have approximately 1 pint of sauce. Strain into a clean pan through a fine-meshed strainer. Leave to cool. Refrigerate until needed.
6. To serve: bring the sauce to the boil. Add a small glass of dry or medium dry madeira, strain again into a sauceboat and serve. The sauce can be further enriched by whisking in 1 oz of fridge-hard French or Dutch butter cut into cubes immediately after reheating but before pouring into the bowl. Once the butter is whisked in, the sauce should not be boiled. Serves 6.

## STUFFED BONED CAPON

The capon can be prepared a day in advance. See photograph on page 236.

6–7 lb capon

HAM AND BRAZIL NUT STUFFING:
1 lb piece of gammon, soaked overnight in cold water if too salty
1 oz butter
1 small onion, finely chopped
4 oz fresh white breadcrumbs
4 oz brazil nuts, roughly chopped
1 teaspoon tomato purée
1 teaspoon finely grated orange zest
1 egg, beaten
½ teaspoon ground mace

1. To make the stuffing: cut gammon into small pieces and fry in 1 oz butter for 2–3 minutes only. Turn the ham but let it take on a little colour. Remove the ham pieces with a slotted spoon. Soften onion in the pan juices until transparent.

2. Put the ham and onion through the fine blade of a mincer. Mix with the rest of the ingredients and bind with the egg. No salt will be needed.

3. Form the stuffing into an oval shape. Turn the boned capon skin-side down on to a work surface. Spread it out whichever way it wants to go.

4. Place the stuffing on top of the breast meat. Then wrap, fold and tuck the leg and wing meat (and skin) round this, arriving at a nice shape.

5. Thread a bodkin with fine string or linen thread and approach the next step as if you were darning a badly torn and worn quilted dressing gown, darning, tucking and holding the seams together to hold in any stuffing or flesh. Sew and bind up.

6. Spread soft butter over the surface, seasoning with salt and pepper and ½ teaspoon of dried ground mace.

7. Stand the capon on a rack in a roasting tin. Cover the breast with 3 or 4 layers of butter muslin soaked in a little melted butter or a piece of buttered foil. Roast at Gas Mark 6 (200°C, 400°F) for 2 hours, lowering the temperature to Gas Mark 4 (180°C, 350°F) after an hour. Serve cut into handsome ½ inch thick slices, and pour a ladle of Tomato Madeira Sauce (see page 243) round each slice of meat.

## PEAR AND LEMON SAUCE

This is a savoury sauce, delicious with turkey, roast pork or ham.

*6 pears, peeled, cored and chopped*
*juice of 1 large lemon*
*1 teaspoon grated lemon rind*
*1 tablespoon caster sugar*
*1 level teaspoon milled pepper*
*1 oz unsalted butter*

Put all the ingredients, plus ½ teacup water, into a lidded non-stick pan. Simmer over a low heat until quite soft, tossing or stirring from time to time (takes about 20 minutes). Blend or mash to a fine purée. Serves 8.

## BRANDY/LEMON BUTTER

This can safely be made two or three weeks in advance, and should by no means be restricted to use on Christmas pudding, as it goes well with many other puddings, pies and sweets.

*4 oz unsalted butter*
*4 oz caster sugar*
*1 teaspoon finely grated lemon zest*
*1 teaspoon lemon juice*
*4 tablespoons brandy*

1. Cut the butter into 1 inch cubes and put into a basin with the sugar and lemon zest. Beat until creamy, add 1 tablespoon boiling water and continue to beat until all the sugar has dissolved.

2. Add the lemon juice and brandy and beat well in. Put into lidded wax cartons and store in the refrigerator, or form into a roll, wrap in foil and freeze. Serve the roll cut into discs.

## RUM/ORANGE BUTTER

*4 oz unsalted butter*
*4 oz soft brown sugar*
*1 tablespoon orange juice*
*1 teaspoon grated orange zest*
*¼ teaspoon cinnamon*
*4 tablespoons Jamaica rum*

Follow the method as for Brandy/Lemon Butter, using hot orange juice instead of water.

## THE SMITH CHRISTMAS PUDDING

My Christmas pudding is coarse-textured, nutty, fruity, sticky, dark and oozing with liqueurs – it's *not* a spicy pudding, and a little goes a long way. Remember that, like good wine, puddings improve with keeping, which is an excellent reason for making this pudding well in advance.

The recipe, designed round the size of packs of dried fruits available on today's market, can be halved or even quartered, but I recommend you make two large puddings, one to mature for Easter, a special birthday or for next year, remembering also to make a couple of smaller puddings in large breakfast cups for giving to single uncles, aunts and the like. The following quantities will make two 4 lb puddings.

*12 oz cold, hard, unsalted butter*
*6 eggs*
*juice and zest of 2 lemons and 2 oranges*
*1 pint sweet brown ale or barley wine*
*6 tablespoons Benedictine (2 miniature bottles)*
*½ lb white flour*
*½ lb fresh white breadcrumbs*
*½ lb ground almonds*
*¾ lb sultanas*
*¾ lb stoned raisins (muscatels)*
*¾ lb whole glacé cherries*
*2 oz chopped angelica*
*4 oz crystallized or dried apricots*
*4 oz whole sweet almonds, blanched*
*4 oz crystallized chestnuts*
*1 lb Barbados sugar*

1. Grate the butter. Beat the eggs. Grate the orange and lemon zest and squeeze the juice and add to the beer and Benedictine.

2. Combine all the dry ingredients. Mix well with the liquids. Put into buttered basins, cover with foil and steam for 5 hours for the first steaming, and then 3 hours on the day of eating.

# CHRISTMAS TANGERINE SOUFFLÉ

Tangerines to me have a flavour evocative of Christmas. This cold soufflé, or mousse, can be made in a large crystal bowl, or – as in the picture (page 246) – in a soufflé dish prepared with a collar.

If you mould it in this way, do not remove the paper collar until half an hour before serving as the soufflé is very light-textured and may well collapse – which in no way impairs its quality: in fact it is an indication of its lightness.

*7–10 tangerines*
*juice of 2 lemons*
*10 eggs, separated*
*4 oz caster sugar*
*1 dessertspoon gelatine crystals*
*½ teaspoon cochineal or edible red food dye*
*½ pint half-whipped cream*

1. Lightly grate the zest from five of the tangerines. Squeeze the juice from all of them, plus the juice of the lemons, so that you end up with ¾ pint juice in all.

2. Separate the eggs. Put the yolks into a round-bottomed bowl together with the sugar, juice and rind. Arrange the bowl over a pan of boiling water. Make sure the water is in contact with the bottom of the bowl. Whisk the mixture gently until it is thick and the whisk leaves a distinct trail. During the whisking, sprinkle the gelatine into the mixture and whisk in well. There is no need to dissolve the gelatine in water.

3. Now stand the bowl in a sink of cold water, stirring from time to time to ensure even cooling. Add the cochineal to the cream and half whip it until the whisk again leaves a distinct trail. Beat the egg whites until they stand up in peaks.

4. When the mousse mixture is cool but not setting, quickly fold in the cream and finally the stiffly beaten egg whites. I always add the first third of the whites and work them well into the mixture to slacken it so that I can work swiftly and lightly with the remainder.

5. Prepare a 2½ pint dish with a paper collar. Fill with the mousse mixture. It is better to let the soufflé set in a cool pantry; alternatively, cover it and put it in the bottom of your refrigerator.

6. Serve with double cream or dress it up with swirls and stars of whipped cream, but *don't* use tinned mandarin segments: these make the cream run and interfere with the flavour of this light mousse. Serves 8–10.

# PLAIN CHRISTMAS CAKE

*8 oz sultanas*
*12 oz seedless raisins*
*4 oz cut mixed peel*
*4 oz glacé cherries, roughly chopped*
*4 oz unsalted butter*
*4 oz lard*
*8 oz caster sugar*
*4 large eggs, beaten*
*8 oz plain white flour, sieved*
*2 oz split or whole almonds, blanched*

1. Wash and dry the fruits if necessary. Roughly chop the raisins after washing. Beat the fats and sugar until light and fluffy. Beat in the eggs a little at a time adding a spoonful of flour if they start to 'split'. Beat the mixture well until fluffy. Fold in the flour, without beating. Fold in fruits.

2. Line two 2 lb tins with buttered paper. Two-thirds fill with the mixture. Top with almonds. Bake at Gas Mark 4 (180°C, 350°F) for one hour, then lower the temperature to Gas Mark 3 (170°C, 325°F) for a further 1–1½ hours.

# CANDIED PEARS

*8 small pears peeled and left whole,*
*about 1 lb when peeled and cored*
*3 larger pears, peeled, cored and*
*quartered*
*lemon juice*
*½ pint of the juice the pears have been*
*cooked in*
*1½ lb caster sugar*
*a little red food colour*

1. Turn the prepared pears in lemon juice. Arrange in one layer in a pan (lay whole ones on their sides). Cover with boiling water. Simmer until *just* tender. Do not over-cook them. Arrange in a shallow glass or ceramic dish, which just contains them in one layer. Now the lengthy process begins.

2. Place the juice and 6 oz of the sugar into a pan, bring to the boil, stirring with a metal spoon until all the sugar has dissolved. Add a few drops of colour. Pour this hot weakish syrup over the fruit. Leave to soak for 24 hours, turning them carefully two or three times.

3. On day two, drain the syrup off the fruits, add a further 2 oz of the sugar, bring to the boil and pour over the fruits again. Leave for another 24 hours, turning them occasionally. You now have to repeat this exact process for *five* days.

4. On day six, add the remaining 6 oz of sugar to the syrup, bring to the boil, and adjust the colouring if necessary. This time, leave them for two days.

5. To finish off the pears: have ready a small pan of boiling water and a wire tray with some caster sugar in a dredger.

6. Dip each piece quickly into the boiling water and dredge or roll in the sugar. Store in a cool dry place, each piece wrapped loosely in wax paper.

# MARZIPAN STRAWBERRIES

Cooked marzipan will keep for up to 6 weeks if stored in a cool place, wrapped in wax paper or plastic film. It is also easier to mould than regular almond paste, which cracks and oils if handled too much. The following will make 1 lb of marzipan, yielding 2–3 dozen strawberries.

*8 oz caster sugar*
*tip of a teaspoon cream of tartar*
*(dissolved in a little water)*
*8 oz ground almonds (no lumps)*
*small teaspoon rose water (triple*
*strength) or lemon juice*
*red and green food colouring*

1. Bring the sugar and 4 fl oz water to the boil. Add cream of tartar. Continue boiling to 116°C, 240°F (measured on an all-purpose food thermometer). Remove from heat.

2. Stir in the ground almonds and flower water and enough *drops* of colour to give a

*Christmas*
*tangerine soufflé*

pretty strawberry pink. If you want to make different colourings then add the colouring at the kneading stage, having divided the paste into appropriate batches.

3. When cool, turn the paste on to a work surface dusted with icing sugar, and knead until smooth. Leave for a day or two to mature, wrapped in wax paper and in an airtight container in the refrigerator.

4. Form into cylinders 1 inch in diameter. Cut into pieces and form into strawberry shapes. Leave to 'set'.

5. Make marzipan leaves using green colour in a little of the original marzipan, or clip plastic leaves off some suitable cheap plastic flowers. Artificial leaves can be purchased for this purpose. To arrive at a more realistic strawberry, meticulously mottle the surface of the formed 'fruits' using a small paint brush and red food colour.

# BEJEWELLED CHRISTMAS CHARLOTTE

*2 packets langues de chats or boudoir biscuits*
*1 egg white, beaten*
*8 oz unsalted butter, softened*
*5 oz icing sugar, sieved*
*1 measure rum, Amaretto or other liqueur*
*5 egg yolks*
*2 oz glacé cherries, roughly chopped*
*2 oz glacé pineapple, roughly chopped*
*5 oz walnuts, pulverized in a blender or processor*
*2 oz walnuts, roughly crushed*
*2 oz toasted hazelnuts, roughly crushed*

GARNISH:
*½ pint double cream, whipped with 1 oz icing sugar and one good measure Amaretto di Saronno or other liqueur crystallized rose petals, violets or other glacé fruits extra walnut halves*

1. Line a 6–7 inch charlotte mould, basin or loaf tin with langues de chats or boudoir biscuits, trimming off any excess biscuit tips. To help line the mould it is a good idea to touch one side of each biscuit lightly with beaten egg white.

2. Cream the butter and sugar until white. Beat in the liqueur and egg yolks and mix in the fruit and nuts. Spoon and press the mixture into the lined mould. Chill overnight.

3. Turn out and decorate with whipped cream and plenty of other fruits and nuts. This sweet is very rich and thin slices should be cut. (I often make mine in an oblong tin as it is easier to slice.) Cut with a knife dipped in hot water. Serves 6–8.

# ROYAL PYES

This Old English recipe gives a new look to the more familiar mince pie. See photograph on page 250.

PASTRY:
*8 oz plain flour*
*5 oz butter*
*2 oz sugar*
*1 egg yolk*
*3 tablespoons water*

FILLING:
*8 oz good mincemeat*
*¾ oz unsalted butter*
*2 egg yolks*
*zest and juice of 1 lemon*
*2 tablespoons rum or brandy*

TOPPING:
*2 egg whites*
*4 oz caster sugar*

1. Make up pastry in the usual way. Cream thoroughly butter, yolks, lemon zest and juice and rum: combine well with mincemeat. Line tart tins or pie plate with thinly rolled pastry. Three-quarters fill with the mincemeat mixture. Bake at Gas Mark 5 (190°C, 375°F) for 30 minutes.

2. Whisk the egg whites until they stand in peaks. Add the sugar a tablespoon at a time, and beat until the meringue is stiff.

3. Top tarts with meringue (using a piping bag). Bake for 45 minutes at Gas Mark 2 (150°C, 300°F), or until meringue is crisp. Serve hot or cold.

*Bejewelled Christmas charlotte*

# WALNUT AND RAISIN BUTTER

½ *lb best butter*
*juice of ½ lemon*
*pinch of salt*
*8–10 screws milled pepper*
*4 oz seedless muscatel raisins, chopped*
*4 oz walnuts, roughly crushed*

Beat butter, juice and seasonings until fluffy. Fold in raisins and walnuts. Pack into a container and chill.

# OATMEAL BISCUITS

Cheese with celery; cheese, as in Yorkshire, with Christmas cake; cheese with fruit, nuts and port – they all belong to the Christmas board.

Stilton or my favourite, Blue Cheshire, are at their best when served with home-made oatmeal biscuits, spread liberally with Walnut and Raisin Butter (see above) for a special treat. This is adapted from Jean Butterworth's recipe at White Moss House, Rydal Water.

½ *lb brown flour*
½ *teaspoon salt*
½ *teaspoon bicarbonate of soda*
*3 oz butter, cold and cut into cubes*
*3 oz lard, cold and cut into cubes*
½ *lb rolled oats*
*3 oz caster sugar*

**1.** Sieve the flour, salt and bicarbonate into a bowl. Rub in the cold fats. Toss in the oats.

Add the sugar and mix to a firmish dough with a little milk.

**2.** Roll out on a floured board to ⅛ inch thick. Cut into rounds and bake on a lightly buttered baking sheet at Gas Mark 6 (200°C, 400°F) until cooked (about 10 minutes). Makes about 24.

# CAFÉ BRÛLOT

As far as I am concerned, after-dinner coffee should be hot, black, and with *white* sugar. Brown changes the flavour totally. If you must play around, then go the whole hog – and why not, for you will pay dearly in restaurant, hotel or local pub for this delicious and aromatic way of serving coffee.

*1 tablespoon crushed coffee*
*beans (after-dinner type)*
*2 fl oz cognac or armagnac*
*6 sugar lumps*
*2 strips (2 inch) orange and lemon rind*
*2 cloves*
*2 inch stick cinnamon*
*2 inch piece vanilla pod*
*2 demi-tasses well-made hot black*
*coffee (after-dinner roast)*

**1.** In a small enamel or stainless steel pan, roast the crushed beans until the aroma rises. Remove pan from heat.

**2.** Add the rest of the ingredients except the coffee. Stir until sugar is dissolved: leave to infuse for 10 minutes. Reheat gently and ignite.

**3.** Extinguish the flames by pouring in hot coffee. Stir well. Leave to settle. Decant into demi-tasses, using a tea strainer. *No cream please.* Serves 2.

*Royal pyes*

# METRIC CONVERSION TABLES

## SOLID MEASURES

*British*          *Metric*
16 oz = 1 lb    1000 grammes (g) = 1 kilogramme (kilo)

*Approximate equivalents*

| BRITISH | METRIC | METRIC | BRITISH |
|---|---|---|---|
| 1 lb (16 oz) | 450 g | 1 kilo (1000 g) | 2 lb 3 oz |
| $\frac{1}{2}$ lb (8 oz) | 225 g | $\frac{1}{2}$ kilo ( 500 g) | 1 lb 2 oz |
| $\frac{1}{4}$ lb (4 oz) | 100 g | $\frac{1}{4}$ kilo ( 250 g) | 9 oz |
| 1 oz | 25 g | 100 g | 4 oz |

## LIQUID MEASURES

*British*

| | | |
|---|---|---|
| 1 quart = 2 pints | = 40 fl oz | |
| 1 pint = 4 gills | = 20 fl oz | |
| $\frac{1}{2}$ pint = 2 gills | | |
| or 1 cup | = 10 fl oz | |
| $\frac{1}{4}$ pint = 8 tablespoons | = 5 fl oz | |
| 1 tablespoon | = just over $\frac{1}{2}$ fl oz | |
| 1 dessertspoon | = $\frac{1}{3}$ fl oz | |
| 1 teaspoon | = $\frac{1}{8}$ fl oz | |

*Metric*

1 litre = 10 decilitres (dl) = 100 centilitres (cl) = 1000 millilitres (ml)

*Approximate equivalents*

| BRITISH | METRIC | METRIC | BRITISH |
|---|---|---|---|
| 1 quart | 1.1 litres | 1 litre | 35 fl oz |
| 1 pint | 6 dl | $\frac{1}{2}$ litre (5 dl) | 18 fl oz |
| $\frac{1}{2}$ pint | 3 dl | $\frac{1}{4}$ litre (2.5 dl) | 9 fl oz |
| $\frac{1}{4}$ pint (1 gill) | 1.5 dl | 1 dl | 4 fl oz |
| 1 tablespoon | 15 ml | | |
| 1 dessertspoon | 10 ml | | |
| 1 teaspoon | 5 ml | | |

*American*

| | | |
|---|---|---|
| 1 quart = 2 pints | = 32 fl oz | |
| 1 pint = 2 cups | = 16 fl oz | |
| 1 cup | = 8 fl oz | |
| 1 tablespoon | = $\frac{1}{3}$ fl oz | |
| 1 teaspoon | = $\frac{1}{6}$ fl oz | |

*Approximate equivalents*

| BRITISH | AMERICAN | AMERICAN | BRITISH |
|---|---|---|---|
| 1 quart | $2\frac{1}{2}$ pints | 1 quart | $1\frac{1}{2}$ pints + 3 tbs |
| 1 pint | $1\frac{1}{4}$ pints | | (32 fl oz) |
| $\frac{1}{2}$ pint | 10 fl oz ($1\frac{1}{4}$ cups) | 1 pint | $\frac{3}{4}$ pint + 2 tbs |
| $\frac{1}{4}$ pint (1 gill) | 5 fl oz | | (16 fl oz) |
| 1 tablespoon | $1\frac{1}{2}$ tablespoons | 1 cup | $\frac{1}{2}$ pint − 2 tbs |
| 1 dessertspoon | 1 tablespoon | | (8 fl oz) |
| 1 teaspoon | $\frac{1}{3}$ fl oz | | |

# INDEX